Great Games, Local Rules

Great Games, Local Rules

The New Great Power Contest in Central Asia

ALEXANDER COOLEY

OXFORD
UNIVERSITY PRESS

OXFORD
UNIVERSITY PRESS

Oxford University Press, Inc., publishes works that further
Oxford University's objective of excellence
in research, scholarship, and education.

Oxford   New York
Auckland   Cape Town   Dar es Salaam   Hong Kong   Karachi
Kuala Lumpur   Madrid   Melbourne   Mexico City   Nairobi
New Delhi   Shanghai   Taipei   Toronto

With offices in
Argentina   Austria   Brazil   Chile   Czech Republic   France   Greece
Guatemala   Hungary   Italy   Japan   Poland   Portugal   Singapore
South Korea   Switzerland   Thailand   Turkey   Ukraine   Vietnam

Copyright © 2012 by Oxford University Press

Published by Oxford University Press, Inc.
198 Madison Avenue, New York, New York 10016

www.oup.com

Oxford is a registered trademark of Oxford University Press

Library of Congress Cataloging-in-Publication Data
Cooley, Alexander, 1972–
Great games, local rules : the new great power contest in Central Asia / Alexander Cooley.
p.   cm.
Includes bibliographical references and index.
ISBN 978-0-19-992982-5
1. Asia, Central—Foreign relations—1991– 2. Geopolitics—Asia, Central.
3. Asia, Central—Strategic aspects. 4. Asia, Central—Foreign relations—United States.
5. United States—Foreign relations—Asia, Central. 6. Asia, Central—Foreign relations—Russia (Federation)
7. Russia (Federation)—Foreign relations—Asia, Central. 8. Asia, Central—Foreign relations—China.
9. China—Foreign relations—Asia, Central. I. Title.
JZ1711.5.C66   2012
327.58—dc23   2011044188

3 5 7 9 8 6 4 2

Printed in the United States of America
on acid-free paper

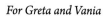

For Greta and Vania

TABLE OF CONTENTS

FIGURES AND TABLES

ACKNOWLEDGMENTS

Though this book is a recent endeavor, I have accumulated enormous debts from the individuals and organizations that have supported this project and its previous components. I am especially grateful to the Fellows Program of the Open Society Foundations (OSF) for giving me the opportunity, as one of its inaugural Global Fellows (thanks to Lenny Benardo, Bipasha Ray, and Steve Hubbell), to think through these issues, conduct research travel, and benefit from engaging with its world-class network. I am also grateful to the Central Eurasia Project of OSF, especially to Anthony Richter, who encouraged me to think about the policy implications of my work on military bases and Western security engagement in Central Asia. The OSF foundations in Kyrgyzstan, Tajikistan (thanks to Kumar Bekbolotov and Zuhra Halimova), and Brussels greatly facilitated my field research. Additional support was provided by Barnard College, including a generous gift by the Tow family, and Columbia University's Harriman Institute, including a Faculty Publication Grant, an educational exchange project with the Turkmen Ministry of Education, funds for my visit to the ODIHR office in Warsaw, and support through the 2010–2011 Core Project on Human Rights in the Post-Communist World, which I co-directed with Jack Snyder. I am also thankful to the members of the Columbia School of International and Public Affairs Capstone Project that I supervised in Spring 2011, who produced an excellent study on the political implications of China-Turkmen energy relations.

Different chapters and arguments developed in the book were presented at MIT, NYU, University of Toronto, Yale University, the American Academy of Arts and Sciences, the Association for the Study of Nationalities, the Center for Strategic and International Studies in Washington, D.C., a National Committee on American Foreign Policy roundtable at the Kennan Institute, and a joint Columbia-Harvard conference on "How Central is Central Asia?" Overseas, I received valuable feedback at the Shanghai Academy of Social Sciences, the 9th and 10th biannual SCO Academic Conferences in Shanghai (with thanks to Professor Pan Guang and Li Lifan), Columbia University's Global Center Beijing, the U.S. German Marshall Fund's Transatlantic Center in Brussels, the University of London's School of Oriental and African Studies, Carnegie Moscow, the American University of Central Asia, the OSCE Center in Dushanbe, as well as the PONARS Eurasia workshops held in Istanbul, Moscow, Tbilisi, and Bishkek.

I thank Ali Borochoff-Porte, Sasha Smyslova, and Nadia Bulkin for their research assistance and Sharone Tobias for her help in Beijing. I am especially grateful for the invaluable contribution of Matthew Schaaf, now of Freedom House, and his tremendous energy, dedication, and insights. He not only meticulously researched many of these tricky topics, but drafted the maps, charts, and Appendix 1 and copyedited portions of the manuscript. Dave McBride at Oxford University Press provided sage advice and good-natured encouragement from the project's beginning stages, while four external reviewers at OUP gave helpful feedback at various critical points. Nicole supported me through the completion of yet another book, which she too was initially surprised to hear about. She and Greta make research travel worth finishing.

Portions of "Russia and the Recent Evolution of the SCO" from *The Policy Worlds Meets Academia: Designing U.S. Policy Toward Russia*, edited by Timothy Colton, Timothy Frye, and Robert Legvold (2010), are reprinted by permission of the American Academy of Arts and Sciences. An essay entitled "Great Games, Local Rules" appeared in the Summer 2011 issue of the *Cairo Review*. As of January 2011, I have served on the Advisory Board of the Open Society Foundations' Central Eurasia Project, which funds the news site *Eurasianet*. Though I occasionally consult with their staff reporters and editorial office, I was not a source for any of the news stories that I cite. The book references leaked U.S. Embassy cables published by Wikileaks; though the manner in which these documents were obtained remains controversial, their scholarly value, now in the public domain, is undeniable.

Finally, my thinking has been greatly enriched and improved by colleagues who have given feedback on the project and individual chapters. I thank Edil Baisalov, Sam Charap, Ed Chow, Erica Downs, George Gavrilis, Jeff Goldstein, Cornelius Graubner, Sam Greene, Jacqui Hale, Scott Horton, Deniz Kandiyoti, Stephanie Kleine-Ahlbrandt, Andy Kuchins, Steve LeVine, Xiaobo Lu, Alexander Lukin, Erica Marat, Kim Marten, Neil Melvin, Lincoln Mitchell, Rebecca Nadin, Cathy Nepomnyashchy, Dan Nexon, Paul Quinn-Judge, Jenik Radon, Sean Roberts, Ed Schatz, Jason Sharman, Matt Siegel, Andrew Small, Jack Snyder, Andrei Tsygankov, David Trilling, Deirdre Tynan, Leslie Vinjamuri, Chris Walker, Cory Welt, Tom Wood, and Zhao Huasheng. All errors in fact and judgment are entirely my own.

Alexander Cooley
New York, October 2011

INTRODUCTION

This was not a book that I planned to write. Though a long-time observer of Central Asia, my previous work mostly looked at the region as "a case" when exploring topics such as comparative imperial legacies, the politics surrounding U.S. military bases or, in my joint work with Hendrik Spruyt, how countries divide, share, and transfer their sovereignty.

This project originally started as a more limited attempt to make analytical and practical sense of the Shanghai Cooperation Organization, a new regional organization comprising China, Russia, and the Central Asian states, which in the late 2000s appeared to be establishing itself as a rival to Western-led security and economic organizations in Central Asia. But the onset of the global financial crisis and the aftermath of the Russia-Georgia War underscored important differences in the agendas of its two biggest members, China and Russia, and the organization's development was halted.

Meanwhile, just a few months after my *Base Politics* book came out, the small country of Kyrgyzstan, in seeming collusion with Russia, announced that it would evict the U.S. military from its critical airbase at Manas, near the capital of Bishkek. U.S. officials launched a furious, and ultimately successful, behind-the-scenes efforts to reverse the decision, renegotiating an extended stay at an increased price. Just one year later, the regime of Kyrgyz President Kurmanbek Bakiyev, who had launched the U.S.-Russia bidding war, collapsed, prompting a domestic backlash against the United States and an investigation into the base-related service contracts and fuel deals that the U.S. military had reached with the previous regime. My testimony for a U.S. Congressional investigation into the fuel contracts at Manas rekindled my interest in the topic, but also emphasized that events in the region were moving with great speed.

Upon reflection, I realized that rather than understand specific developments in Central Asia as "cases" of certain political phenomena, the region's dynamic development, under the close engagement of the United States, Russia, and China, held important new lessons for the broader study of contemporary world politics. Central Asia had become a natural experiment for observing the dynamics of a multipolar world, including the decline of U.S. authority, the pushback against Western attempts to promote democratization and human rights, and the rise of China as an external donor and regional leader. Though each of the great powers has sought something different from Central Asia, the cumulative weight of their engagement empowered local governments and transformed the international norms, rules, and institutions that had previously governed the region. As such, I hope that this book's attempt to grapple with some of these issues will be of interest not only to students of Eurasia, but to those interested in the emerging questions of world order and governance in this increasingly "post-Western" world.

Great Games, Local Rules

The New Great Power
Contest in Central Asia

On April 6, 2010, the government of President Kurmanbek Bakiyev in the small Central Asian state of Kyrgyzstan collapsed, following a series of demonstrations that swept across the country's northern cities. Pundits and regional observers interpreted Bakiyev's ouster as an important victory for Russia in its ongoing geopolitical tussle with the United States for influence in Central Asia.[1] Just one year earlier, Bakiyev had brazenly double-crossed Moscow by promising to shut down a critical U.S. military base near Kyrgyzstan's capital, which stages nearly all U.S. troops entering and exiting Afghanistan, in exchange for Russian economic assistance during the financial crisis. Instead, the Kyrgyz ruler pocketed the first disbursal of Russian funds and then provoked the Kremlin's ire by renegotiating an extension for the U.S. presence at a higher rent.

Over the last decade, countless news stories have framed such episodes as skirmishes in a new "Great Game," a contest among the United States, Russia, and China for power and influence in Central Asia. The term, popularized by Rudyard Kipling's 1901 novel *Kim*, directly references the nineteenth-century competition between the Russian and British empires for control over Central Asia. In the original Great Game, British officials perceived the expanding Russian empire, which seemed to be insatiably annexing large swaths of the Caucasus and Central Asia, as a threat to India's northern entry points, access to the Indian Ocean, and even the prized British colony itself.[2] In response, London formulated a strategy to resist Russian influence, which included contesting frontier areas, wooing local rulers, and deploying a supposedly vast network of secret agents to gather intelligence.[3] It also prompted Britain's disastrous First Anglo-Afghan War in 1838, an attempt to turn Afghanistan into a friendly buffer state, which was brutally ended four years later when thousands of British and Indian troops were massacred in their retreat from Kabul.[4] British troops would return to Afghanistan with greater success in 1878 in response to the Russian imperial army's annexation of the Central Asian khanates of Kokand and Bukhara.

The original Great Game also informed the emergence of the modern study of so-called geopolitics. In his now famous 1904 article, British geographer Harold Mackinder observed that Russia occupied a position in the Eurasian heartland that served as "the pivot region of the world's politics," with its "potentialities in population, wheat, cotton, fuel, and metals so incalculably great."[5] Mackinder reasoned that if Russia, from this dominant geographical location, could expand its railway network over Eurasian territory and use these resources to build a maritime fleet, "the empire of the world would then be in sight."[6] Though the extent to which Mackinder's alarming analysis actually influenced British foreign policymakers is debated, his coining of the terms "heartland" and "pivot" crystallized perceptions of Central Asia's strategic importance.[7] Then and now, Central Asia has been viewed as an arena of high-stakes geopolitical sparring, while its location at the crossroads of multiple empires has subjected it to a rich array of pressures, influences, and cultures.[8]

The New Great Game: Looking Back or Leaning Forward?

These geopolitical concepts also have been revived in connection to the "New Great Game" underway in Central Asia, the area that today comprises the post-Soviet states of Kazakhstan, Kyrgyzstan, Tajikistan, Turkmenistan, and Uzbekistan.[9] In this latest iteration of the Game, the protagonists take orders from Moscow, Washington, and Beijing, rather than the nineteenth-century imperial capitals of Saint Petersburg and London, as the new players race in a winner-takes-all battle to secure vital strategic interests.[10] The scramble of Western oil companies in the 1990s to access Caspian oil riches has been frequently described in these terms, as has the post–9/11 geopolitical environment in which the United States established new military bases in the heart of Central Asia.[11] Russia and China, concerned about preserving their regional influence, have allegedly resisted and countered these Western economic and security forays.

On the sidelines, the international media carefully tallies scorecards as the pendulum swings back and forth among these outside powers. Just as Bakiyev's fall in 2010 was broadly interpreted as a victory for Russia, the 2005 collapse of his predecessor, President Askar Akayev, was popularly portrayed as a "Color Revolution" that the United States had supported.[12] Though vehemently denied by policymakers and often criticized by more nuanced regional observers, the "Great Game" metaphor is appealing precisely because it suggests that great powers still attempt to sway, coerce, persuade, and buy the loyalties of strategically vital governments, while blocking their rivals from doing the same. This is the stuff of geopolitics of the highest order.

But the Great Game metaphor also remains deeply blinding. The original Great Game featured expanding empires trying to conquer and wrest physical control of the region's territory from local rulers, warlords, and chieftains.[13] Today's regional suitors are nation-states, albeit powerful ones, that are attempting to influence other sovereign states in an increasingly multipolar and complex world. More important, the objects of today's competition are also established states;[14] they can be neither formally conquered nor dissolved by foreign powers, while their sovereignty affords them a wide range of international privileges and opportunities that their earlier counterparts lacked.[15]

Indeed, if we look more closely, rather than mirroring a previous era, the international politics of today's Central Asia is characterized by the emergence of distinctly novel, innovative, and even unique regional institutions and practices. After a decade of military operations in Afghanistan, U.S. diplomacy in Central Asia has been subordinated to the needs of the U.S. military, especially the powerful regional command CENTCOM, which has emerged as an influential and, at times, autonomous political and economic player. It is a region that has spawned the Chinese-led Shanghai Cooperation Organization (SCO), a seemingly dynamic regional organization that rejects Western hegemony and values, while claiming to promote a "new type of international relations."

The region has also experienced rapid normative change; the Central Asian governments' commitments to protecting political rights and human rights norms, first made when they entered the international community of states in the 1990s, have been shredded in the name of counterterrorism, while these same governments, with the backing of Moscow and Beijing, have effectively redefined human rights nongovernmental organizations (NGOs) and groups promoting democracy as agents of Western influence and regional security threats. Finally, we have seen international practices such as development financing and election monitoring, once exclusively controlled and administered by Western-controlled bodies, undermined by the emergence of new organizations and donors that have demanded fewer intrusive conditions than their Western counterparts. By constantly framing Central Asian politics in terms of timeless imperial competition, we have overlooked the important changes in world order and global governance that the region now visibly embodies.

The New Contest in Central Asia: Strategies, Games, and Rules

This book examines the dynamics of the interaction between the United States, Russia, and China as they attempted to exert influence in Central Asia from 2001 to 2011. It explores the different strategic interests of the great powers, identifies their tools of influence and assesses their impact on Central Asia's political institutions and practices.[16] I advance three main arguments, each of which departs from the classical Great Game framework.

The Strategies of the Big Three

First, I argue that the security goals and strategic purpose of the great powers in post-Soviet Central Asia have mostly differed, thereby allowing Washington, Moscow, and Beijing to simultaneously pursue their interests in the region.

In fact, U.S. and Chinese engagement with Central Asia has been primarily motivated not by a direct interest in the region's security, but by the pressing need to stabilize adjacent regions—Afghanistan, for the United States, and the western province of Xinjiang, for China. For the United States, Central Asia has provided military bases, transit routes for fuel and supplies, and border cooperation for Operation Enduring Freedom. With the region treated as part of the Afghanistan theater, security matters have displaced other issues from the U.S. diplomatic agenda. Though the Central Asian governments have issued public statements in support of the coalition campaign, in practice Washington has had to offer economic incentives to attain this security cooperation, including granting payments for the right to establish military bases and allowing these countries to profit from the transit of supplies to Afghanistan.

China's primary security goal in Xinjiang has been to clamp down on the activities of Uighur movements, viewed as threats to its territorial integrity, while it has upgraded the surrounding region's infrastructure to promote the regional economic development that it views as key to ensuring future political stability. China has implemented many of these policies through the SCO, a new regional organization founded in 2001 and headquartered in Beijing, thereby lending a multilateral face to these regional initiatives. At the same time, Beijing also has secured access to important sources of oil and gas in Central Asia, especially in Kazakhstan and Turkmenistan, and has rapidly completed the construction of new regional pipelines to transport this energy supply eastward.

As the former imperial power and after a decade of neglecting the region, Russia has sought to play a dominant or privileged role in Central Asia in the 2000s. Criticized by some Western commentators and politicians as exhibiting neo-imperial ambitions, Moscow's quest for renewed regional primacy is not dissimilar to other historical post-colonial powers, such as France in West Africa. Russia has tried to embed its relationships with the Central Asian states in new security and economic organizations, which it has modeled on the form, if not substance, of Western counterparts such as the North Atlantic Treaty Organization (NATO) and the European Union (EU). Nevertheless, the entry of the United States and China, both as strategic partners and competitors, has complicated Moscow's efforts. Many of Russia's Central Asian policies have been tactical reactions to U.S. and Chinese initiatives or reflections of the broader state of its relations with these great powers.

The Games: The Forms of Regional Interaction

Second, I argue that the interaction among the United States, Russia, and China in the region has intensified over the decade, but that zero-sum "competition" and the pursuit of relative gains has not been the exclusive nor even the dominant form of great power interaction.[17] All three powers have forged tactical partnerships with the other members of the "strategic triangle."[18] At times their agendas have generated some flash points, tensions, and direct responses, but for the most part they have coexisted in the region without nearly the level of conflict that Great Gamers perceive.

To be sure, some forms of classically competitive behavior have grabbed international headlines. For example, U.S. and Russian defense planners in 2009 did compete over the presence of the U.S.-run Manas air base in Kyrgyzstan, while Russian, Western, and Chinese energy firms have competed to develop Kazakhstan's oil fields and Turkmenistan's gas deposits (as most energy companies tend to do). But competition rarely operates in isolation and, in fact, is only one of several forms of regional interaction in the strategic triangle. We have also witnessed:

Cooperation: As some have noted but is frequently forgotten, the United States and Russia cooperated in important ways and at high levels following the events of 9/11. Russian and United States intelligence services bolstered their information sharing, while Russian President Putin initially agreed to allow U.S. forces to establish temporary military bases in Uzbekistan and Kyrgyzstan in support of its campaign in Afghanistan. Less well known is that even as U.S.-Russian relations deteriorated in 2008 and the Russian government encouraged the Kyrgyz government to expel the United States from Manas, an informal network of Russian-U.S. commercial and government partners ensured that U.S. forces at the base continued to receive a steady supply of the Russian jet fuel necessary for its operations. Since 2009, Russian cooperation has also been indispensable to the United States in establishing the Northern Distribution Network, the ground transport of supplies to Afghanistan from the north.

Enabling: Even when the external powers have not actively cooperated, they have frequently enabled each other's pursuit of their respective strategic goals. For example, the United States, China, and Russia all used the onset of the U.S.-led Global War on Terror (GWOT) to intensify their cooperation with Central Asian security services under the mantra of international counterterrorism, while they supported each other's branding of regional organizations as terrorists or extremists. Similarly, as part of its energetic efforts to counter Western influence in the mid-2000s, Russia participated in and strengthened the Chinese-led SCO, even though the group's activities would later grow to overlap and possibly compete with Russian-led organizations in the security and economic realms.

Emulation: Less appreciated is how the great powers emulated each other's tactics, organizational forms, and even public justifications. The Russian-led Collective Security Treaty Organization (CSTO) seemed to mimic NATO in its development, while the SCO has mirrored the institutional forms of the Organization for Security and Cooperation in Europe (OSCE).[19] In terms of "soft power," all three external actors opened cultural and language offices in Central Asia, mimicking Western programs and projects, sponsored new media outlets, and organized youth exchanges and educational programming to expose Central Asian students to their respective countries. By the end of the decade, all three powers had become regional donors, disbursing bilateral aid and assistance to the Central Asian states for a mix of humanitarian, political, and economic purposes.

Mimicking the form, but not content, of certain controversial Western international organizations and NGOs also proved a popular tactic for Russia and China, especially as regional anxiety grew about U.S. support for "democratic revolutions" and regime change. For example, in an attempt to counter the critical election-monitoring assessments of the OSCE's Office of Democratic Institutions and Human Rights (ODIHR), the Western-backed body that had been monitoring national elections in the region since the 1990s, both Russia and China established new "election monitoring" groups whose findings about the quality of Central Asian elections were far more upbeat than the ODIHR's.

Refraction: Finally, all three external powers found that their interactions in Central Asia forced them to reflect upon and even change their own domestic policies and/or broader foreign policy orientation. Both Russia and China feared that the Eurasian Color Revolutions of the mid-2000s might threaten their regimes at home, prompting both to pass new laws that curtailed the activities of external NGOs and the media. And in both the United States and Russia, cooperation with Central Asian security services, particularly over the secret transfer of terror suspects, prompted domestic debates over their commitments to long-standing international laws and human rights treaty obligations. In short, while the United States, Russia, and China all attempted to influence Central Asia, they also found themselves, often unexpectedly, changed by their engagement with Central Asia.

The Rules: Multiple Patrons and Local Imperatives

Third, I argue that the Central Asian states, even the weaker ones, are not passive pawns in the strategic maneuverings of the great powers, but important actors in their own right. Exclusively focusing on the objectives and interactions of the great powers neglects the considerable agency demonstrated by the Central Asian states in dealing with their geopolitical suitors. Central Asian governments have drawn up the "local rules" that guide many of these geopolitical interactions, learning to leverage this interest and even fuel perceptions of regional competition to guard their domestic political power and extract economic benefits.

In international relationships characterized by hierarchy or acute power symmetries, subordinate states typically cede some elements of their policymaking and sovereignty to a patron, while recognizing the stronger state's authority.[20] However, in settings where several patrons or great powers vie for influence, the authority and influence of any one state is potentially diminished. Organizational theorists refer to this phenomenon as the "multiple principals" problem, as the presence of several authority figures actually empowers subordinates to shirk their individual commitments to any one patron, weakening the overall control of these objectively more powerful actors.[21]

Consistent with this logic, the intensification of great power interaction over the course of the 2000s strengthened the position of Central Asian rulers in a number of ways. First, Central Asian elites directly played one external power off the other to extract increased benefits, assistance, and better contractual terms. The most skillful handler of these competing foreign powers has been Kazakhstan, which, under the helm of President Nursultan Nazarbayev, has gone to great lengths to present itself as the geopolitical crossroads of multiple identities and influences, invoking the often-quoted slogan that "happiness is multiple pipelines."[22] But, as we shall see, the other Central Asian states have also pursued multidirectional foreign policies.

Second, engagement by multiple patrons has allowed all of the Central Asian governments to pare down or even ignore those external demands that they deemed unpalatable or potentially damaging. In particular, the presence of Russia and China as alternative partners has empowered the Central Asian rulers to more forcefully resist Western attempts to promote democracy, economic reforms, and better governance. In response, over the course of the decade, Western powers and Western-led international organizations have scaled back their reform agendas. For example, in an attempt to placate the Central Asian governments and maintain a relevant presence in the region, the OSCE jettisoned the political conditionality clauses of its Central Asian police reform projects and focused exclusively on capacity-building.[23] Rather than reform the security services of these authoritarian states, these projects, quite unintentionally, actually strengthened them.

Finally, the Central Asian states have strategically and expediently used the norms and justifications provided by foreign powers to guard and support their own domestic political practices. Over the course of the decade, the Central Asian countries became experts in "norm localization," or the process by which local elites "borrowed foreign ideas about authority and legitimacy and fitted them into indigenous traditions and practices."[24] More cynically, the Central Asian elites have pushed the practice even further, framing much of their own suppression of all forms of political opposition as part of a wider set of international counterterrorism efforts. They have also "grafted" or associated new foreign norms with existing local practices, such as appropriating the Russian idea of "sovereign democracy" to oppose strict Western standards of democracy in the name of respecting local cultures and political traditions.

The Contours of the Arena

All of the Central Asian states have learned to play the great powers off one another for their local benefit. However, their exact tactics and demands have depended on their institutional structures, their capacity, and the natural resource endowments bequeathed to them as independent states.

For Kazakhstan and Turkmenistan, rich in oil and natural gas, engagement with the outside powers has been mostly focused in developing their energy sectors. In the Kazakh case, external competition among international investors, including U.S., Russian, and Chinese energy companies, began in the 1990s, but as the government gained greater technical expertise it was empowered to renegotiate old contracts on more favorable terms, invoking the interest of other companies to justify its tougher bargaining positions. Of the two, Kazakhstan has been more eager to build an international reputation and secure international approval for its policies.[25] In contrast, Turkmenistan's almost complete isolation under the presidency of Saparmurat Niyazov (1991–2006), justified by its foreign policy doctrine of "positive neutrality," turned the country into an international pariah, as the Turkmen ruler rejected almost all forms of foreign interaction as unwanted sovereign interference and meddling.[26]

With some natural resources, but also the largest population of the region (nearly 30 million), Uzbekistan competes with Kazakhstan for the mantra of the most important of the Central Asian states. Bordering Afghanistan, as well as every other Central Asian state, Uzbekistan's central geography and natural resource endowments have made it a self-proclaimed regional hegemon and an important strategic partner for all three foreign powers. Its tough president, Islam Karimov, has consistently asserted his independence from efforts to promote greater regional cooperation on economic and military issues and has regularly clashed with the West over his lack of political reforms and dismal human rights record.

By contrast, the resource-poor and increasingly weak states of Kyrgyzstan and Tajikistan have failed to attract the interest of major international investors.

During the 1990s, both small states depended on external funds from international financial organizations and aid providers, though in Tajikistan's case most of these funds targeted national reconstruction and reconciliation following a devastating civil war from 1992 to 1997.[27] Post–9/11, these governments strengthened their security engagement with foreign powers, by increasing military-to-military cooperation and by providing access to military bases. In the Kyrgyz case, this has meant hosting the Manas Transit Center, the vital staging facility for U.S. personnel going to Afghanistan, as well as a Russian-CSTO base nearby at Kant. Similarly, Tajikistan has hosted military facilities for Russia, France, and India, as well as the United States in the initial stages of the Afghanistan campaign. Thus, both the Kyrgyz and Tajik governments have commodified their very territory to extract economic and political benefits.

Moreover, both Kyrgyzstan and Tajikistan have pushed the frontiers of contemporary clientelism by invoking their weakness and the threat posed by Islamic militant movements in order to secure external military and economic assistance. This is not to say that these countries did not face some security challenges, including their infiltration by Islamic militants from Afghanistan and the surrounding region in 1999 and 2000.[28] Rather, as other commentators have observed of certain African states during the last decade,[29] Kyrgyz and Tajik elites have used their state weakness strategically, effectively dangling the prospect of their own collapse to maintain foreign engagement, especially in the face of growing international frustration with the poor state of their domestic governance.

Central Asia as a Window into the Multipolar World

In some ways, the onset of great power engagement in Central Asia recalls the dynamics of superpower rivalry and clientelism, as the Cold War provided ample opportunities for smaller client states to play the United States and Soviet Union off one another;[30] similarly, studies of alliances highlight the advantages that small states can accrue from balancing the interests of competing powers.[31] Elsewhere, I have explored how the governments of U.S. allies, including Turkey, Korea, Spain, the Philippines, and Italy, used the stationing of U.S. military forces to extract concessions from the United States in order to further their domestic political position. With the end of the Soviet Union and the rise of the United States as the unbridled superpower, this type of geopolitical maneuvering by client states appeared to have been rendered historically obsolete as Western power in the 1990s was unchallenged and Western conditions had seemingly regained their credibility.[32]

Two decades into the post–Cold War era, however, the United States now finds its power and influence increasingly challenged by the emergence of rising powers, new regional institutions, and alternative political values. Fareed Zakaria has referred to the current era of international politics as the "post-American world," arguing that the rise of new self-confident powers, such as China, India, and Brazil, is altering the power balance in international organizations;[33] Parag Khanna argues that the emergence of the United States, the European Union, and China as global superpowers in a shrinking world "heralds an age of competition more intense than any before."[34] Robert Pape and Stephen Walt warn that the unilateralism practiced by the United States has spawned new forms of "soft-balancing" against the superpower, including the denial of access for military bases in strategically important areas like Central Asia.[35] Other scholars now refer to the increasing connectivity among developing countries that bypasses Western influence as a burgeoning "world without the West."[36] And a number of studies now warn that China's global rise provides an alternative set of norms, practices, and institutions that will erode the West's global influence.[37]

The period under investigation in this book, 2001–2011, coincides with the rise of the so-called post-American world and serves as a potentially instructive laboratory for observing the emerging dynamics of a multipolar world. The findings, so far at least, of this natural experiment are decidedly mixed for Western policymakers. Though the United States has managed to lock in the necessary security cooperation of the Central Asian states for its Afghanistan operations, albeit after negotiating some political roadblocks along the way, it has achieved this cooperation mainly by offering economic incentives from the Pentagon's formidable war chest. At the same time, the United States has lost much of its "soft power" and its legitimacy as a global role model, while Russia and China have eroded U.S. influence by rolling out their own organizations, practices, and political justifications. To be sure, Moscow and Beijing face their own important challenges and constraints, but the unquestioned global dominance and reputation once enjoyed by the United States have diminished strikingly over just a few years.

Perhaps what is trickiest about the emerging multipolar order is that it requires policymakers and strategists to frame their goals in more pragmatic and expedient terms than in the past. One of the unfortunate, if understandable, legacies of the Cold War is that it has accustomed us to think of geopolitical influence as a purely zero-sum endeavor—the influence of one external power upon the politics of a target state necessarily entails a loss of influence for the other.

But the dynamics of a strategic triangle, and a multipolar world more broadly, are far less clear than those of the bipolar Cold War. A regional gain for China, such as the opening of a new pipeline that will transport Central Asian gas eastward, is not necessarily a loss for the United States and Russia, especially if it alleviates regional supply pressures and energy competition elsewhere. The opening of a new Russian military base in Kyrgyzstan or Tajikistan can hardly constitute a loss for the United States if it allows Moscow the prestige and political space that it needs to accept, if not wholeheartedly endorse, U.S. security cooperation with the Central Asian states. On the other hand, the rise of China as a regional donor, even if it finances much-needed upgrades to decaying regional infrastructure, may erode U.S. authority if it undercuts Washington's ability to leverage a future World Bank or IMF loan package to influence a Central Asian recipient. Questions of influence and authority cannot be divorced from specific regional goals and the greater global context; at times, they might even work at cross-purposes.

Plan of this Book

The next chapter delves further into the "local rules" that guide political life in Central Asia. It explores the Soviet origins of Central Asia's patrimonial political arrangements and their restructured role during the independence era. The chapter looks at the key role played by local elites in managing the demands made by outside powers, while simultaneously delivering benefits to their political clients.

Chapters 3 to 5 present the regional strategies and resulting dilemmas that each of the three great powers has faced over the last decade. Chapter 3 overviews the evolution of U.S. regional policy, recounting how its Central Asia strategy increasingly has become a function of supporting military operations in nearby Afghanistan. From establishing military bases and access agreements for OEF to concluding recent commercial agreements in order to expand the delivery of supplies via the Northern Distribution Network (NDN), U.S. policymakers have had to balance their security cooperation with a public commitment to promote political and economic reforms in the region. As the decade has worn on, Central Asian leaders have grown increasingly cynical and even dismissive of such demands, while the United States and its Western allies have become less vocal about the so-called values agenda in order to placate their regional partners.

Chapter 4 examines the strategic evolution and dilemmas of Russia, the region's former imperial power and, for some, continued privileged partner. The chapter analyzes Moscow's broad range of levers of influence, hard and soft, and traces its efforts to lock in its dominance by creating new regional organizations. At the same time, Moscow's regional policies and tactics have remained unstable and reactive, subject to Russia's self-image as a great power and its prevailing relations with the United States and China.

Chapter 5 recounts China's recent rise as a regional power in Central Asia. The chapter examines how the SCO has become China's preferred multilateral security forum to clamp down on Uighur separatism and nationalism. At the same time, Beijing has upgraded the regional infrastructure that connects Central Asia with the economic hubs, roads, and railway networks of its western province and has invested heavily in Central Asia's oil and gas sectors. Quietly, but effectively, Beijing's push into Central Asia already has dramatically reoriented the region toward the east.

Chapters 6 to 9 investigate how Central Asia's "local rules" have mediated these great power interactions and how the region's ruling elites have manipulated these foreign initiatives for their own narrow purposes. Chapter 6 explores in greater depth how cooperation between the Central Asian security services and their U.S., Russian, and Chinese counterparts on counterterrorism has eroded human rights norms, but also has generated novel forms of extralegal practices and procedures, such as the use of extraordinary renditions. The second half recounts how the Color Revolutions prompted the Central Asian states to brand foreign NGOs engaged in democracy promotion and human rights monitoring as security threats and, with Russian and Chinese support, effectively pushed back against the Western values agenda.

Chapter 7 focuses more narrowly on the issue of great power rivalry and regional political stability. It explores how even in the clearest-cut case of geopolitical competition between the United States and Russia—the bidding war over the Manas airbase in Kyrgyzstan during the tenure of President Kurmanbek Bakiyev (2005–2010)—the Kyrgyz premier and his local political allies actively fueled geopolitical competition for their private benefit. Bakiyev did so at the expense of promoting state-building and institutional stability, as the sudden collapse of his government in April 2010 was followed by ethnic rioting in the south on a level not seen since late Soviet times.

Chapter 8 examines the deteriorating levels of corruption in the region and shows how outside actors have contributed to some of these practices. The chapter includes overviews of alleged corruption scandals involving large U.S. and Chinese oil deals in Kazakhstan and the fuel deals for the Manas base in Kyrgyzstan. These cases demonstrate how these attempts to buy influence are embedded within broader transnational networks that linked local elites, private companies, external governments, and the offshore sector; these networks provide Central Asian rulers with private benefits, while allowing foreign governments and companies to maintain plausible deniability when allegations of corruption surface.

Chapter 9 examines the persistent lack of regional integration and explains how local rules, particularly the region's patrimonial structures and commercialization of borders, have checked outside attempts to promote greater cooperation and formal integration. It compares the difficulty of conducting formal cross-border transactions to the growing informal integration produced by the border shuttle trade and narcotics trafficking.

Finally, Chapter 10 evaluates the experiences of the "Big Three" and extends the general argument to other powers that have developed regional strategies to engage with Central Asia (the European Union and India). It then culls some of the lessons of Central Asia's new great power contest and applies them to other emerging multipolar regions (Africa, the Middle East, and Latin America). In these settings, as in Central Asia, we see the increasing politicization of the U.S. military presence, the rise of China as a public goods provider, and a regional backlash against Western democracy promotion efforts and calls for reforms. Applying these observations to the wake of the Arab Spring, the United States is likely to play a significantly less influential role in these new Middle East transitions than it did in the immediate post-Communist era.

Local Rules: How Central Asian Regimes Survive

Over the course of the 2000s, all of the Central Asian governments learned to effectively court different patrons, to reduce demands for political reforms by powerful Western states, and to justify their domestic actions by invoking the radically transformed geopolitical situation. They entrenched a set of domestic political and economic practices, or "local rules," that set the terms of external engagement and competition for influence. But what, exactly, are these local rules and where do they come from? Are these practices rooted in the region's distinct culture, ideology, or history? This chapter addresses these questions.

All of the Central Asian regimes have been aptly described as "patrimonial." In such polities, rulers maintain their positions of authority in return for distributing resources to a network of supportive political clients.[1] Political competition takes place informally and at the elite level, rather than through elections or the aggregation of interests via political parties. In the Central Asian cases, these informal institutions are based on regional and subregional identities, such as clans, and often operate in parallel to official state structures.[2]

The centrality of patronage politics is an enduring legacy of Soviet rule in the region, but two decades of independence have provided Central Asian elites with a new political context, opportunities, and resources with which to consolidate their authority. Over the course of their tenure, three important rules have come to characterize Central Asian regimes: the promotion of regime survival; the use of state resources for private gain; and the brokering between external actors and local constituencies. After reviewing the origins of Central Asia's patrimonial institutions in the Soviet era and the relatively quiet transition period of the 1990s, this chapter examines these rules in greater detail, setting the scene for our analysis of the interaction between external powers and their Central Asian counterparts.

Understanding the Legacies of Soviet Rule

Soviet Rule in Theory and Practice

Central Asia shares a long colonial history, first as a colony under the Russian Empire (1865–1918) and then, after the triumph of the Red Army during the interwar years, under Soviet rule.[3] The topic of how to understand Soviet rule is itself sensitive and emotionally fraught in the region, especially when Western scholars compare Soviet Central Asia to other cases of European colonialism.[4] A common refrain heard across the region is that the Soviets "brought education and electricity" and therefore cannot be compared to the exploitative colonial European powers.

In practice, a distinct mix of both imperial and state-building practices characterized Soviet rule in the region.[5] The center did follow some classical colonial patterns by designating the region as a primary commodity producer, especially in cotton and energy, underrepresenting it in Union-wide decision-making bodies, and mediating interactions among the individual Central Asian republics.[6] At the same time, Moscow introduced a number of new industries and economic sectors that were integrated into Union-wide structures and administrative organs. Simply applying the colonial "divide and rule" argument to Soviet Central Asia fails to capture just how much the Soviet regime actually wanted to modernize and transform the region.[7] The considerable resources poured into the region by Moscow "resulted in an unusual system of relationships which could hardly be found anywhere else and can hardly be [studied] in the framework and terminology applicable to other Third World countries."[8] Another key governing strategy employed by Moscow was to empower cadres of titular nationals from each of the republics. This gave rise to an interesting form of "Soviet affirmative action," in which the lead nationalities of each republic were preferred in important areas of political career development, economic planning, and higher education over minority nationalities and even Slavs.[9]

As a result, the Soviet system retained strong control over Central Asia in some areas (internal security, heavy industry), but deferred to the Central Asian cadres in others. In turn, this ensured the growth and institutionalization of informal patronage networks within the Soviet system, as republican cadres managed to graft themselves onto the formal hierarchical institutions of the Soviet state, such as the collective farm or the regional Communist Party.[10] The Soviet system of administrative regions and units reinforced the importance of these local cleavages.[11]

A so-called black market, or dual economy, existed throughout the Soviet Union, but it was particularly important in Central Asia, where agricultural producers regularly collaborated with local officials to falsify quotas and set up alternative networks of exchange for their products.[12] Central Asian party officials actively protected economic managers from oversight and central sanctioning, while local law enforcement, by all accounts, also played a critical role in allowing the functioning of black markets, private entrepreneurship, the embezzlement of state property, and the expansion of regional informal networks.

The late Brezhnev era also brought about a distinct political equilibrium in Soviet Central Asia, one in which officials in Moscow tolerated local patrimonialism in exchange for republican rulers guaranteeing political stability and ensuring unwavering allegiance to the center.[13] One of the greatest economic scandals of the period remains the so-called Uzbek Cotton Affair, perhaps the single most instructive episode of how corruption and patronage had become institutionalized among Soviet Central Asian cadres.[14] In 1986, Moscow investigators discovered that officials at every level in the Uzbek Soviet Socialist Republic had conspired to defraud central planners by creating a complex network of cotton plan falsification, systemic kickbacks, and bribes. The scheme had cost Moscow the equivalent of over $1 billion, as implicated officials protected themselves by commanding the loyalty of tens of thousands of workers and local law enforcement.

The patrimonial institutions of the Soviet era worked so effectively, subsidized by increasing fiscal transfers to the Central Asian republics from the center, that the centrifugal forces unleashed by Mikhail Gorbachev's twin policies of Glasnost and Perestroika did not mobilize any mass movements that advocated for independence. Contrary to the expectations of many Central Asian experts that the region's Muslim population might challenge the power and authority of the Soviet system, the region was the last to come to terms with the Soviet state's unraveling and to accept independence.[15] Also, unlike the Caucasus, the transition happened relatively peacefully, save for the ethnic violence that occurred between ethnic Uzbeks and ethnic Kyrgyz over local land transfers in May 1990 in the southern Kyrgyz city of Osh.[16]

Central Asia after Independence

1990s: Quiet Independence and the Transition Paradigm

With no mass social movements or civil societies clamoring for democratization, Central Asian republican elites simply assumed the reigns of power, this time as rulers of newly independent states; they transformed their former republican apparatuses into new ruling state bureaucracies and hegemonic political parties and established control over domestic security services. The biggest exception was Kyrgyzstan, where the old Communist party was disbanded following the ethnic tensions in Osh and replaced with a slate of reformers that, in turn, supported the rise and election of Askar Akayev, a former scientist who presented himself as the most liberalizing of the new Central Asian state elites.[17] Yet, for the most part, these Soviet patrimonial legacies and local party structures continued well into the independence period. The relative calm in the region was punctured by a brutal civil war that broke out in 1992 in Tajikistan between members of the Moscow-backed ruling clan and a coalition of Islamists, nationalists, and Pamir-speaking ethnic groups. Tellingly, analysts have explained the conflict as a result of the breakdown of Soviet-era patronage networks.[18]

Despite the endurance of these strong informal institutions, most foreign ministries and international organizations placed the Central Asian states in the category of post-Communist "transitioning countries." Given that the Soviet Union was in tatters and Communism had been discredited, international officials and policymakers simply assumed that the Central Asian states' only option was to transform into pluralistic polities with market economies, as debates at the time mostly revolved around the speed of reform and institutional design. The International Monetary Fund (IMF) and the World Bank became involved in advising all of the Central Asian governments, first over their exit from the Russian-based ruble zone, and then over designing and sequencing a set of market-friendly reforms.[19] Disengaging from the previously integrated Soviet economic system also created sharp losses in industrial output throughout the region, as enterprises struggled to cope as independent economic firms without the centrally coordinated system of supply and distribution.[20] The abandonment of the ruble in favor of new national currencies generated widespread macroeconomic chaos.[21]

The lack of robust great power interest encouraged a variety of smaller outside actors to view Central Asian as a *tabula rasa*, a space ripe for new conquering influences and ideas. Western-sponsored foundations and organizations used the window of transition to push for programs similar to those they had established in other post-Communist spheres. Civil society actors and international donors looked for partners to network with and promote exchanges, while the United States and European powers dutifully funded projects to work on the technical aspects of constructing new democratic institutions and introducing legal reforms. At the same time, a variety of religious groups—ranging from Turkish nationalists to Wahhabi ideologues to Christian evangelists—also perceived Central Asia as a blank slate to promote their religious and normative agendas.[22]

The Big Three in the 1990s

In terms of developing external relations, most of the Central Asian countries did not command the interest of the three great powers, with the exception of Kazakhstan, whose oil riches were already attracting Western, Russian, and even Chinese energy companies.[23] During the Yeltsin years, Russia remained relatively weak and focused on muddling through its domestic reforms and economic troubles, while China concentrated most of its diplomatic energies, from 1996 onward, on concluding border demarcation talks with the Central Asian states and Russia in a forum known as the Shanghai Five. This organization was the precursor to the Shanghai Cooperation Organization, the regional body inaugurated in 2001 that facilitated China's more robust regional engagement over the next decade. U.S. policymakers, inasmuch as they were interested in the post-Communist sphere, were mostly focused on issues that did not involve the Central Asian states, such as promoting NATO expansion. Washington did engage with Kazakhstan in an effort to secure opportunities for U.S. energy companies in the energy sector, especially the large Tengiz and Kashagan fields.[24] The United States also, with Russian cooperation, helped Kazakhstan to secure and give up the nuclear weapons it had inherited from the Soviet Union.

During this time, Russia remained the most powerful actor in the region, but more by default rather than choice. Most of these forms of engagement pragmatically addressed problematic Soviet-era legacies. For instance, Russia reached agreements to retain control over key Soviet-era defense assets, such as the Baikonur spaceport in Kazakhstan, while it also reached agreements with individual states to jointly manage Central Asia's external borders. Russia's military presence declined during the transition period, save for Moscow's almost reluctant intervention in Tajikistan's civil war (1992–1995). It would not be until Vladimir Putin's election to the Russian presidency that Moscow would develop a more robust plan for defining and pursuing its Central Asian security interests.

For its part, by the end of the 1990s, the Western-led international community was demonstrating a palpable fatigue at the seeming lack of progress on political and economic reforms. As the Central and Eastern European states were rapidly undergoing political, economic, and social reforms in anticipation of joining the European Union and NATO, Central Asia seemed distinctly stagnant, with entrenched rulers now fending off all major challenges to their state authority.[25]

2000s: New Decade, Paradigm Shift

The relative calm and indifference shown by the international community was shattered in the aftermath of the 9/11 attacks on the United States. Suddenly, Central Asia went from a backwater to the front line for operations against Al-Qaeda and the Taliban in Afghanistan in the new Global War on Terror. Within weeks, U.S. officials negotiated bilateral agreements for basing rights, flyover rights and refueling arrangements with the Central Asian states. Though U.S. officials regarded their new Central Asian presence as a by-product of the Afghan campaign, Russian and Chinese officials were more skeptical about

Washington's long-term plans, fearing U.S. military encirclement after the Taliban, Al-Qaeda, and its allies were routed from Afghanistan.

This renewed external interest proved a political boon for all of the Central Asian leaders, though some chose to publicize their membership in the U.S.-led coalition more loudly than others. The Central Asian elites not only profited from this renewed external engagement and competition, but actively encouraged it. If they were to be the site of new geopolitical interest, they would have an important say in establishing the ground rules and would profit from bargaining simultaneously with Washington, Moscow, and Beijing. Unlike the 1990s, when the Central Asian governments tended to couch their activities in terms of prevailing international norms and practices, the intensification of U.S., Russian, and Chinese engagement in the 2000s empowered local elites to tout their authority, reject unwanted demands as infringements on their sovereignty, and more aggressively leverage their geopolitical standing to serve their domestic agendas.

Rule #1: Regime Survival Is State Security: Conflating External and Internal Threats

First and foremost, all Central Asian governments have made regime survival their overwhelming political imperative, formulating domestic and foreign policies in order to maintain power, entrenching one-party patrimonial systems and eliminating threats to their authority.[26] Authorities clamped down on political opposition, drove political opponents into exile, and established control over the media. The Central Asian regimes channeled resources into building their security services in order to consolidate state authority, thereby subordinating the powerful Ministry of Internal Affairs to the office of the President.[27] The resulting conflation of internal and external threat under the broad rubric of "state security" is a hallmark of all the regimes of the region.

Varieties of Central Asian Authoritarianism

Each of these regimes practiced a different style of authoritarian politics. In Kazakhstan, President Nursultan Nazarbayev, who during the Soviet era had effectively worked himself up Kazakhstan's party ranks from an inauspicious beginning working at the Karaganda Metallurgical Works, has positioned the country as the crossroads between East and West and has overseen a remarkable economic boom that has lifted the country into the middle-income tier of post-Soviet states, well above its Central Asian neighbors. The development of Kazakhstan's vast oil reserves has been a key part of this state-building, but

Nazarbayev has also deliberately crafted an image of forging a tolerant multina-
tional state, simultaneously reassuring Russia about the plight of the large ethnic Russian population while appealing to his Western suitors by allowing the
entry of some non-governmental actors and nominal political opposition.[28] In
practice, the political system has shown little pluralism, but it has given the
appearance of relying on persuasion, as opposed to coercion and, at every
opportunity, has showcased Nazarbayev's domestic and international popu-
larity.[29] Securing the chairmanship of the 2010 Organization for Security and
Cooperation in Europe (OSCE) marked the zenith of Nazarbayev's attempts to
establish himself as a world leader; the same year, in a typically scripted fashion, he rejected public calls to extend his term by referendum to 2020, opting,
instead, for the "more democratic" option of moving up presidential elections
to April 2011, which he won with over 95 percent of the vote and an 89.9
percent turnout.

But two decades into his tenure, the political stability that has characterized
the Nazarbayev era has increasingly come into question. According to German
press reports, the Kazakh President underwent surgery in Germany for prostate
cancer in July 2011, fueling renewed questions about his succession plans.[30]
Then in December 2011 the outbreak of violent clashes in the western town of
Zhanaozen, the most serious of the country's brief independent history, between
local police and hundreds of disgruntled oil workers killed at least thirteen and
injured over one hundred, while video footage surfaced that showed Kazakh
police shooting indiscriminately into the crowd.[31]

In contrast to Nazarbayev's unchallenged tenure, its small mountainous
neighbor Kyrgyzstan has experienced the collapse of two successive presidents
in 2005 and 2010 during periods of popular protests and counter-mobilizations
by the country's political elites.[32] Initially, the country was presented as a site for
reform by former academic and self-styled liberalizer President Askar Akayev,
but it had devolved into a one-party kleptocracy before his ouster by street protests in the so-called Tulip Revolution of March 2005. Akayev's successor, the
brusque Kurmanbek Bakiyev, gave the appearance of restoring the reform
agenda for about a year, before he also embarked on a concerted campaign of
repression and plundering of state assets that was even worse than that of his
predecessor. He, too, was ousted following a series of popular protests in April
2010, ushering in yet another round of constitutional change and a switch to a
mixed parliamentary-presidential system in the volatile small Central Asian
country.

The other regimes were more ruthless in their authoritarian practices. In
Uzbekistan, Kazakhstan's regional rival and the traditional heart of Central Asian
power, control was assumed by President Islam Karimov, a hard-nosed Soviet-
trained economist from the ancient Silk Road city of Samarkand. From the time

of his election as president of the Uzbek Socialist Soviet Republic in 1990, Karimov has never wavered from eliminating all political opponents, from liberal opposition forces, to Uzbek nationalists to Islamic groups.[33] He is more feared than revered, with his regime defended by a brutal coercive apparatus, headed by the National Security Service (SNB) that monitors internal security and collects intelligence. According to the Moscow-based human rights organization Memorial, Uzbekistan has jailed 10,000 political prisoners, a number that exceeds political imprisonment in all of the other former Soviet states combined.[34] Unlike Nazarbayev's opening to the world, Karimov has kept the country's physical and economic borders tightly closed, with the state retaining tight control of all-important areas of economic activity such as mining, gas, and cotton. His daughter and possible successor, Gulnara Karimova, was described in 2005 by one U.S. embassy cable as the "most hated person" in Uzbekistan, forging a business empire over the last decade from her close political connections, while she spent time as Uzbek Ambassador to the United Nations in Geneva and Spain.[35]

In Turkmenistan, an expansive desert country that borders Afghanistan and Iran, its first president, Saparmurat Niyazov, matched Karimov's ruthlessness, but further pushed the bounds of political megalomania by fashioning a bizarre personality cult equal to that of Soviet Stalinism and Kim Jong-Il's North Korea. Niyazov proclaimed himself "Turkmenbashi," or "father of the Turkmen," and tried to remold Turkmen society in his image.[36] He saturated the country's public spaces with portraits of himself, including erecting a rotating gold statue, renamed months of the year after his relatives, closed down all links between his country and the outside world in the name of preserving sovereignty, and mandated that all schools and civil service positions spend most of their time studying the *Ruhnama*, his personal book of philosophical musings. Following Niyazov's death in late 2006, President Gurbanguly Berdymukhamedov has taken some steps to court international investment, but Turkmenistan's political space remains highly restricted, while its knowledge base and human capital have been decimated by 20 years of isolation and capricious social engineering.

Finally, Tajikistan emerged from a brutal civil war (1992–1997), which cost the lives of up to 100,000 and displaced over a million people, that pitted the ruling national government and its representative clans, backed by Moscow and Tashkent, against the United Tajik Opposition (UTO), a loose coalition of democratic intelligentsia leaders, ethnic Gamiris and Parmis, and Islamists.[37] Under a UN-brokered cease-fire of 1997, President Emomali Rahmon reached a power-sharing arrangement with the UTO and its largest faction, the Islamic Renaissance Party, promising 30 percent of parliamentary seats to the opposition. Since, Rahmon has been reelected in 1999 and, more controversially, in 2006, and has skillfully used externally sponsored state-building and reconciliation efforts to centralize and strengthen his rule, has extended his control over the country's former warlords, and has steadily co-opted and divided the opposition.[38] Like Nazarbayev, Rahmon has mastered the art of appealing to different international partners. Though his resource base is considerably less than that of oil-rich Kazakhstan, the large presence of international organizations, NGOs, and special diplomatic missions in the capital, Dushanbe, has legitimized Rahmon's rule, while he has evoked the scepter of the civil war and potential destabilization to justify his increasingly authoritarian tendencies.

The Post-9/11 Era: Antiterrorism and Color Revolutions

Notwithstanding these important variations in authoritarian regime types, the increased engagement with the United States, Russia, and China in the 2000s clearly strengthened the capacity and authority of these regimes.

In the wake of the 9/11 attacks, all three external powers intensified their security cooperation with the Central Asian states in the name of counterterrorism (see Chapter 6), while these local elites shrewdly adapted to the new security environment. President Islam Karimov presented the Global War on Terror (GWOT) and Uzbekistan's security cooperation with the United States as a vindication of the warnings he had expressed about the dangers posed by growing Islamic movements in the area.[39] He and the other Central Asian regimes took advantage of external concern about the potential for Islamic extremist spillover to upgrade the technological capacity of internal security forces. Increased cooperation with Russia through the Collective Security Treaty Organization (CSTO) and with China via the Shanghai Cooperation Organization has further aided this effort.

Second, and more controversially, this conflation of internal and external security drove Central Asian regimes to reclassify other external actors engaged in democracy promotion and human rights advocacy as enemies of the state. In the wake of the Color Revolutions, as democratization became conflated with enacting regime change, Central Asian rulers identified external NGOs and democracy monitors as actual security threats, not just political nuisances. They responded by clamping down on the activities of Western democracy-promoting NGOs, human rights movements, and international media outlets and correspondents, which all faced increasing restrictions or outright evictions.

Of the three external actors, the United States had the most difficulty in adapting to the local rule of "regime survival." On the one hand, U.S. security officials provided significant security and economic assistance to these regimes and helped them to crush local Islamic groups, including the Islamic Movement of Uzbekistan (IMU). On the other hand, U.S. officials continued, at least officially, to support democratic goals in their assistance programming and diplomatic consultations, sending a distinctly "mixed message" to Central Asian governments.[40] These two different elements of U.S. policy would clash head-on in May 2005, following the Uzbek government's brutal crackdown on demonstrators in the eastern city of Andijan; Uzbek officials, and their backers, claimed to have killed 180 demonstrators, most of them terrorists, whereas human rights organizations and political dissidents claim that Uzbek security services killed over 700 civilians, who were, for the most part, in the city's central square protesting peacefully. The United States unsuccessfully struggled for a coherent response, trying to balance Western condemnations and calls for an international investigation with maintaining U.S.-Uzbek security cooperation (see Chapter 3). In contrast, Russia and China held no such reservations. They strongly backed the actions of the Uzbek government and led the regional pushback against the threat posed by Western political interference.

Rule #2: State Resources and Private Economic Gain

Central Asia's second operating rule is that state resources are used for private gain, especially for the ruling elite. The Central Asian states can be aptly described as "predatory"; state positions and administrative resources are used as a way of accumulating individual power and amassing personal fortunes. In a political evolution that strikingly resembles Robert Bates's account of the trajectory of post-colonial African states, Central Asian presidents have used state resources and administrative appointments to cement political clientelism and to entrench one-party rule, ensuring that "private benefits" have displaced "public goods as the coin of the realm."[41]

The roots of rent-seeking and state predation lie not in some distinct notion of "Central Asian culture," as is sometimes described, but rather in the types of patrimonial institutions and parallel networks of economic distribution that were consolidated during Soviet times. As long as these republican cadres maintained their loyalty to Moscow, they were granted great leeway to implement policies that bolstered their own patronage networks within their republics.[42]

The New Marketizing Context

Throughout Central Asian state agencies and administrative bodies, corruption has entrenched itself as a standard form of political reward and exchange. Many commentators have correctly faulted initial Western proposals to radically transform former planned economies into markets, accusing Western reformers of paying inadequate attention to these countries' institutional context and the ways in which insiders and elites would manipulate the process.[43] But in the

Central Asian states, analysts also failed to appreciate that the planned economy had operated very differently in practice than on paper, allowing for the development of various networks of unsanctioned entrepreneurship, informal distributive networks, and criminal activity. In both the old planned context and the new marketizing context, securing control of state institutions and administrative positions has been critical for leveraging them for personal gain. Market reforms provided additional opportunities for graft and enrichment, as valuable assets across the region were privatized at a fraction of their market value to connected insiders and their supporters.[44]

Again, the specific forms of personal rent-seeking have varied across the region, depending upon a particular country's economic resources and development profile. The energy-rich states have been the most obvious arenas for reported collusion between international investors and domestic elites. The most notorious of these, as Chapter 8 details, has been the so-called Giffen affair in Kazakhstan, where an American consultant was accused of violating the U.S. Foreign Corrupt Practices Act by arranging hundreds of millions of dollars in bribes from U.S. energy companies to Kazakhstan's ruling elite. More recently, Chinese energy companies have also been at the center of several alleged corruption scandals as they have increasingly focused on controlling Kazakhstan's oil production. Turkmenistan's energy transactions remain opaque, as Turkmen deliveries of gas to Russia's network via Ukraine have been structured by murky intermediary trading companies, while potential foreign investors report that the country's energy sector officials at all levels routinely demand bribes for "pay-to-play" meetings and kickbacks.

In the non-oil-rich economies, predatory elites have found new and creative ways to squeeze their own impoverished populations. In Kyrgyzstan during the Bakiyev era (2005–2010), the newly privatized Kyrgyz electricity sector illegally exported its production to Kazakhstan, even while parts of the country endured blackouts, kept raising prices on domestic consumers, and embezzled new funds supposedly earmarked for new plant construction.[45] In Tajikistan, Tajik citizens were pressured to fund President Rahmon's attempt to build the massive Rogun hydroelectric dam by volunteering portions of their salary in exchange for shares in the still uncertain project.

And for all these states, the increase in international security engagement has also offered new economic opportunities to secure funding and private goods. The opening of the U.S. military's so-called Northern Distribution Network to transport goods and materials for the campaign in Afghanistan via Central Asia has established a new web of contracting and commercial ties that are now benefiting connected elites within these transit countries. In the case of Kyrgyzstan, the U.S. logistical base at Manas base became a source of rents and private economic benefits for two ruling regimes and connected Kyrgyz insiders.

New Offshore Instruments and Patrimonialism

One final point worth bearing in mind is the new international financial context and the rise of the global offshore sector that has coincided with Central Asia's independence. Commentators tend to view the Central Asian states, with the exception of Kazakhstan, as economically underdeveloped and relatively isolated from the global economy. Yet elites in all of the states have increasingly forged sophisticated links to the offshore financial sector.[46] For example, Tajikistan's largest industrial producer, the Tajik Aluminum Company (TALCO), is registered in the British Virgin Islands. After many years of not disclosing its finances and accusation of widespread bribery, the IMF finally conducted TALCO's first international audit in 2009, but the results were kept confidential.[47] In Uzbekistan, the Zeromax company, which amassed an empire from energy to soft-drink bottling, was widely believed to be controlled by the president's daughter Gulnara Karimova, but was registered in Switzerland.[48] And the mysterious Mina Corp, one of the private companies that was awarded the huge fuel contracts at the Manas base in Kyrgyzstan, is registered in Gibraltar, with no previous company history or available corporate profile.[49] Clearly, Central Asian elites have deftly learned how to use the instruments of globalization to structure and conceal their economic activities.

Of course, these leaders' vast personal fortunes are also safely stashed in a network of offshore bank accounts. Perhaps the most brazen example of personal predation and fortune accumulation occurred under President Niyazov in Turkmenistan. According to an investigation by the anti-corruption and environmental NGO Global Witness, revenues from the state's sale of natural gas flowed directly into Niyazov's personal bank account in Deutsche Bank in Frankfurt, bypassing the national budget and even the state-controlled gas companies.[50] Niyazov's bank account is estimated to contain more than $2 billion in diverted funds. In sum, while external engagement did not cause Central Asia's pernicious governance problems, outside actors have fueled and helped to reinforce these private economic pursuits.

Rule #3: Elites as Brokers and Gatekeepers

The third main rule of political life in Central Asia is that Central Asian elites have perfected the art of serving as intermediaries between their local constituencies and external patrons and suitors. What sociologists refer to as "multivocal signaling" or, in common parlance, "talking out of both sides of their mouth," is a critical practice for leveraging international engagement for domestic political and economic gain.[51] Appealing to a broad range of constituents and patrons is especially critical in a patrimonial political system, in which a ruler's legitimacy rests on being able to steadily funnel resources to key political clients.[52]

This elite brokering and gatekeeping did not emerge during Central Asia's independence. These practices are also Soviet patrimonial legacies, as republican elites perfected the art of fulfilling the interests of their immediate clients, while assuring Soviet authorities of their loyalty, ideological commitment, and compliance with dictates emanating from the center.[53] Moreover, the dependence of Central Asian government budgets on Moscow's fiscal transfers—which in 1990 ranged from 23 percent of the Kazakh budget to 47 percent of the Tajik—gave them significant experience in managing the redistribution of external financial transfers.[54]

These brokering practices have carried over nearly intact to the post-independence era across a variety of issue areas. Since independence, Central Asian elites, particularly of the aid-dependent states, have shown great skill in communicating to international donors the sincerity of their desires for reform, but, in turn, have managed to effectively use foreign aid disbursements not to establish functioning markets, but rather as sources of patronage for preserving their rule.[55] Kyrgyzstan's self-branding as the "Switzerland of Central Asia" garnered significant engagement from the donor community until, toward the end of the decade, it became clear that Kyrgyzstan's promised reforms were permanently stalled. Perhaps the most remarkable example of such "dual practices" was uncovered in 2009 in Tajikistan, when an international accounting audit revealed that between 1996 and 2008 the former chairman of the Tajik Central Bank had diverted over $850 million in IMF credits to a local agricultural bank that lined the pockets of his family members and political clients.[56]

Since 9/11, Central Asian elites have actively supported the U.S.-led campaign in Afghanistan, while beneath the surface they secured a variety of side deals for their cooperation. For the United States, these Central Asian partners offered access to military bases and infrastructure as part of a larger coalition of countries committed to stabilizing Afghanistan. However, for Central Asian rulers, the quid pro quo obtained from the United States in exchange for cooperation was used for local benefit and regime survival. In the Uzbek case, this has involved securing hundreds of millions of dollars in security assistance and basing rental payments from both the United States and Germany, its main European security partner. In Tajikistan, the post–9/11 geopolitical landscape and the great powers' jockeying for military access allowed political elites there to secure debt write-offs from Russia, increase military-to-military assistance from the United States, and secure commitments from France to upgrade the facilities at the nation's main airport in Dushanbe. And in the Kyrgyz case, awarding a series of murky, no-bid contracts to politically connected local companies to supply fuel to the Manas base appears to have been a key component of the unofficial quid pro quo given to the ruling regimes of presidents Akayev and Bakiyev to support U.S. operations.

Conclusion

The Central Asian states all practice a version of patrimonial politics. Though they vary in their degree of authoritarianism, natural resource endowments, and engagement with the international community, all follow a similar set of local imperatives: they conflate internal and external security threats to further their regime survival, they use state office for private gain; and they act as brokers between their political clients and the international community. These local rules all have their roots in the institutions, practices, and legacies of Soviet times, but have been revived and recrafted since independence.

These local rules operated in both the 1990s and the 2000s. The critical difference between the two decades is that during the first decade of independence, these legacies and local rules were camouflaged, as the Central Asian states were assumed to be in transition and publicly affirmed their commitments to international institutions and practices. In the 2000s, by contrast, the entry of the United States, Russia, and China as external actors with geopolitical agendas emboldened Central Asian elites to more aggressively assert their authority and consolidate their power base. Their rule became more authoritarian, corruption became more brazen, and all of these governments learned how to play their external suitors off one another more effectively.

This analysis should not excuse or justify the individual policies or choices made by these outside powers. Local rules are not immutable and are themselves reproduced when outside governments, companies, and militaries defer to them. However, as we shall see in the U.S. case, the multiple-principals problem diminished U.S. credibility in demanding political reforms, as the Central Asian governments leveraged the availability of alternative partners to pare down these external demands. Over the course of the decade, Washington, like Moscow and Beijing, learned to play by local rules.

|| 3 ||

Washington's Central Asian
Detour to Afghanistan

The events of 9/11 almost instantly transformed U.S. interest in Central Asia. What had been a remote and low-priority area in the 1990s, the site of some educational exchanges and U.S. Agency for International Development (USAID) technical assistance projects, became the strategic frontline for U.S. military operations in Afghanistan. U.S. policymakers initially did not plan for a permanent military presence in the region, nor did they anticipate many of the local political complications that would later arise.

But inertia took over. As weeks turned into months, what was meant to be a temporary military presence, especially in Uzbekistan and Kyrgyzstan, acquired the appearance of permanency. Ad hoc political and economic agreements with Central Asian governments for securing basing rights became more contentious, even as U.S. planners sought to connect Central Asia with Afghanistan through new political, economic, and security initiatives. These developments alarmed Moscow and Beijing, which believed that the United States was intent on exerting broad influence in the region well beyond the scope of its mission in Afghanistan.

The fundamental policy tension that emerged for the United States was balancing the growing inconsistency between engaging these authoritarian regimes on security issues, while calling for them to accelerate domestic reforms and uphold human rights. During this period, the Bush administration had adopted a "freedom agenda," under which the United States would aggressively promote democratization in Iraq and the greater Middle East, even, if need be, via externally sponsored regime change. This caused great concern among the Central Asian governments, especially as the Color Revolutions swept old regimes out of office in Georgia (2003) and Ukraine (2004) and replaced them with pro-Western leaders.

When in March 2005 Kyrgyz President Askar Akayev was toppled in the so-called Tulip Revolution, regional concern about U.S. policies and motives reached fever pitch. That summer, the Uzbek government evicted U.S. forces from the Karshi-Khanabad base, demonstrating that external demands for democratization would not be tolerated, even at the expense of Afghanistan-related security cooperation. Following the eviction, Central Asian elites would deliberately frame the values and security issues in opposition to each other. When they reestablished security cooperation in 2008 to open the northern supply network, U.S. planners stopped pressing Central Asian regimes on political matters and focused on security and economic ties.

The Eagle Has Landed: Establishing the Presence

U.S.-Uzbek military cooperation began well in advance of the events of 9/11.[1] In 1999 and 2000, U.S. Special Forces helped to train and equip Uzbek counterparts, while in 2000 Tashkent also granted permission to the CIA to secretly launch Predator drone flights into Afghanistan from its airfields.[2] The Uzbek government was the most eager of all the Central Asian states to pursue security cooperation, as it had been battling with the Islamic Movement of Uzbekistan (IMU), a militant Islamic group that had forged ties to Al-Qaeda during the rise of the Taliban.[3] During the summers of 1999 and 2000, IMU fighters had descended from mountain camps to conduct raids and kidnappings in the eastern Ferghana Valley, skirmishing with Uzbek and Kyrgyz security services. The group also claimed responsibility for a bombing attack in Tashkent in February 1999. Active support for the United States would elevate Uzbekistan's regional prestige, help to wipe out the IMU, and seemingly vindicate Uzbek President Karimov's tough domestic policies by placing his campaign within a broader international coalition against terrorism.

According to U.S. Secretary of Defense Donald Rumsfeld's minutes of his first meeting with the Uzbek president in October 2001, the United States initially had sought permission to use Uzbek territory for major combat operations against the Taliban; however, Karimov refused to allow U.S. air strikes from Uzbek territory.[4] Instead, Karimov insisted that the two sides concentrate on intelligence sharing, restricting U.S. use of Uzbek territory to "forces for search and rescue operations," understood as Special Forces operations. These would be the first steps in developing a long-term relationship. Commenting on Russia's potential concerns, Karimov mentioned that, though President Putin publicly supported the policy of Central Asian states' granting military access rights to the United States for operations in Afghanistan, the Kremlin privately wanted to mediate U.S.–Central Asian cooperation in the hope of gaining concessions on issues such as its war in Chechnya and U.S. plans for National Missile Defense.[5]

The resulting agreement granted the U.S. military the use of the old Soviet air base near the southern towns of Karshi and Khanabad, just 90 miles from the

Afghan border. In addition to establishing Camp Stronghold Freedom at Karshi-Khanabad, or K2 for short, the United States was granted permission to transit Uzbek airspace and was afforded access to some auxiliary airfields, though these other arrangements were not made public.[6] In December 2001, K2 was operating as a logistical hub, officially for humanitarian purposes, from which supplies were trucked into Mazar-e-Sharif, Afghanistan. By summer 2002, the base hosted 1,000–1,300 U.S. troops and hundreds more contractors.[7] In addition, the United States successfully concluded transit and refueling arrangements with Turkmenistan, Kazakhstan, and Tajikistan.[8]

But with restrictions on its activities at K2, U.S. officials continued to search for additional regional facilities that could serve as staging grounds. A suitable site was quickly identified in Kyrgyzstan at the civilian airport of Manas, just outside the capital, Bishkek. The airport's runway had just been repaved by a Japanese consortium and was deemed durable enough to handle heavy cargo planes and refueling aircraft. A deal for its use was signed with the Kyrgyz government in December 2001. In just a few months, the United States had gone from having a few covert forces in the region to signing high-profile basing deals with two Central Asian countries, and related logistical support agreements with the rest. The region's strategic map of the region had been redrawn (see Figure 3.1)

Partnership Promises and Quid Pro Quo

In public, the Central Asian states cooperated with the United States as committed partners in the international coalition for the OEF (Operation Enduring Freedom) campaign, but behind the scenes each demanded quid pro quo for granting basing rights. The nature of these bargains reflected these Central Asian leaders' particular domestic political challenges. At the time, few U.S. officials or outside observers concerned themselves with how these agreements might impact these host states or how these security partnerships might entangle the United States in their domestic affairs;[9] but in both Uzbekistan and Kyrgyzstan, acrimonious disagreements over the terms of these deals would emerge in the future.

Uzbekistan and K2: Strengthening Karimov's Grip on Power

The basing deal provided Karimov with a number of security and political benefits. U.S officials agreed to target the IMU in their operations, and the two sides agreed to share intelligence about regional militant networks. The security partnership was also a major domestic political victory for Karimov, as it granted credibility and international legitimacy to the Uzbek president's public fight

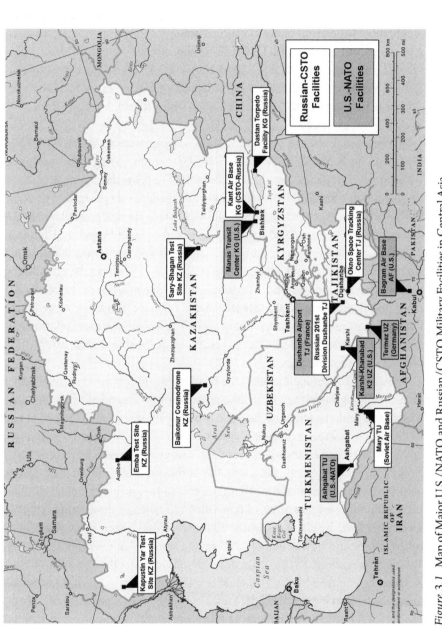

Figure 3.1 Map of Major U.S./NATO and Russian/CSTO Military Facilities in Central Asia

against the IMU. In 2002, the United States provided $120 million in military hardware and surveillance equipment to the Uzbek army and $82 million to Uzbek security services, and agreed to pay $15 million in annual rent to lease the K2 field. Much of this equipment was highly advanced surveillance technology, sought more for reasons of organizational prestige and use in a domestic setting than for its use on the battlefield.[10] To round out the "unofficial" base rights package, that same year the U.S. Export-Import bank granted the Uzbek government $55 million in credits. Overall, U.S. military aid and economic assistance to Uzbekistan topped $300 million in 2002, a nearly fourfold increase from 2001 levels.[11]

The new U.S.-Uzbek security partnership was formalized in March 2002 when Presidents Bush and Karimov signed a Declaration on Strategic Partnership in Washington. The Uzbek government committed to providing basing access and overflight rights for OEF-led operations, while the U.S. side pledged to preserve the "security and territorial integrity" of Uzbekistan. Though downplayed at the time, the Uzbek regime also agreed to undertake domestic political reforms, committing to "ensuring respect for human rights and freedoms . . . enhancing the role of democratic and political institutions in the life of society; establishing a genuine multiparty system . . . ensuring the independence of the media . . . [and] improving the judicial and legal system."[12] Some U.S. officials viewed these Uzbek commitments as sincere, though others reasoned that these reform commitments provided political cover to justify the deepening of security cooperation between the countries.

Soon after the formalization of the relationship, it became clear that, rather than upholding his pledge to democratize, Karimov intended to use his new partnership with the United States to consolidate his stranglehold on power and to conduct a sweeping campaign against political dissent. Already in January 2002, Karimov had extended his presidential term by decree to December 2007, a move that was met with silence by U.S authorities. Later in the year, Uzbek security services escalated their domestic crackdown, arresting hundreds of alleged militants on accusations of fomenting terrorism. A devastating report in December 2002 by UN investigator Theo Van Boven documented widespread mistreatment and torture in the Uzbek prison system.[13] In the summer of 2004, Washington rescinded $18 million in promised aid under the Freedom Support Act, due to a finding by the U.S. Congress that Uzbekistan was not in compliance with human rights standards; a few weeks later, the Department of Defense (DOD) offered a supplemental package worth $21 million, suggesting increasing schisms across the U.S. government on the direction of Uzbekistan policy.[14]

Around this time, U.S.-Uzbek security cooperation expanded in more controversial ways. The CIA and the U.S. military transferred prisoners and suspected terrorists to the Uzbek security services, where they were interrogated and tortured at so-called "black site" facilities (for more details, see Chapter 6). Former British Ambassador to Uzbekistan Craig Murray, a controversial and outspoken critic of the Karimov regime, also alleges that Uzbek intelligence and security services exaggerated and even fabricated reports about militant activity in order to maintain U.S. security engagement.[15] Murray's embarrassing protests revealed the extent to which the United States and its allies were operating according to Tashkent's "local rules," including receiving intelligence that was routinely gathered by the use of torture; but his outspoken actions also threatened to disrupt the long-standing signals intelligence–sharing agreements between the United States and the United Kingdom. Murray was reprimanded and then removed from his post in October 2004, but a steady stream of stories questioning the scope and purpose of U.S.-Uzbek security cooperation continued to appear in the Western media.[16]

Kyrgyzstan and Manas: Economic Incentives and Base Contracts

The Manas air base, popularly known as Ganci-Manas, also became a critical facility for the OEF campaign. By May 2002, the base hosted 2,000 troops from nine coalition countries and was being used to conduct refueling operations, staging flights, and cargo transit.

For President Askar Akayev, previously an academic and self-proclaimed reformer, the OEF campaign also came at an auspicious political moment. Throughout the 1990s, Akayev had initiated some liberalizing reforms in an effort to brand Kyrgyzstan the "Switzerland" of the region, but international donor fatigue had set in after years of stalled progress, mounting governance problems, and allegations of nepotism.[17] Unlike his Uzbek counterpart, Akayev was not as enthusiastic about developing a bona fide security partnership with the United States, in part because of the Kyrgyzstan's close ties to Russia and its large Russian minority. However, promises of potential economic gains and benefits seemed to persuade the Kyrgyz president, and, with Moscow's approval, he signed the initial basing deal and Status of Forces Agreement with the United States in December 2001.

Given Kyrgyzstan's poor, aid-dependent economy, with a GDP of barely $2 billion, any type of substantial foreign military presence would provide a badly needed economic boost. In its early years (2001–2005), the base also represented the United States' largest economic investment in Kyrgyzstan, contributing an estimated $40 million annually to the Kyrgyz economy, in the form of service and construction contracts, and directly employing about 500 Kyrgyz nationals.[18] By 2009, the annual economic impact had exceeded $100 million dollars, with over 700 Kyrgyz nationals employed.[19]

However, from early on, most of these economic benefits would flow not to the Kyrgyz general budget, but, in accordance with "local rules" of patronage and rent-seeking, to the Kyrgyz president, his family, and his inner circle. At just $2 million a year, the initial formal rent paid by the United States to the Kyrgyz authorities for the lease of Manas was relatively low. However, one of the more curious aspects of the initial Manas accord was its mandate that U.S. and coalition aircraft pay civil aviation fees (set by the International Civil Aviation Organization) for military takeoffs and landings. Given that the bulk flights were being conducted by heavy cargo and refueling planes, these sums could reach $7,000 per takeoff and landing, or several hundred thousands of dollars a day.[20] These fees were transferred to the Manas Airport Authority, a technically public entity with close ties to the ruling family. Kyrgyz and U.S. officials justified the fee structure on the grounds that Manas was a civil aviation entity. Tellingly, however, former U.S. Ambassador to Kyrgyzstan John O'Keefe has observed that while the original fee structure could have been avoided, it was implemented in order to generate the necessary economic incentive to ensure Kyrgyz cooperation with OEF.[21] The United States also paid an assortment of ad hoc parking and maintenance fees.[22]

But by far the most lucrative, as well as secretive, economic aspect of the U.S. basing presence involved the contracts for fuel procurement, which are valued over the last decade at nearly $2 billion (see Figure 8.1, Chapter 8). Following the collapse of the Akayev regime in 2005, U.S. and Kyrgyz investigations learned that the base's main fuel subcontractors were controlled by President Akayev's immediate family and had earned tens of millions of dollars in profits. Chapter 8 explores in greater detail the mysterious offshore companies, local contractors, and behind-the-scenes collusion and graft that characterized fuel procurement practices at the base over the last decade. The Manas fuel contracts also became the subject of a U.S. Congressional investigation in 2010, and now represent one of the most intriguing episodes of U.S. engagement with Central Asia's "local rules."[23]

Unlike K2 and the U.S.-Uzbek security relationship, which were drawing significant attention from the Western media and nongovernmental organizations (NGOs), operations at the base at Manas went relatively unnoticed for the first three years. Some Russian-language media would run occasional negative stories about the base, alleging smuggling or other illicit activities, but for the most part U.S. and Kyrgyz authorities succeeded in keeping Manas under the radar. Domestically, few Kyrgyz politicians questioned the purpose of the base or criticized its underlying legal and contractual arrangements. This "depoliticization" would dramatically change following the tumultuous political events in the spring of 2005.

The Honeymoon Sours: Geopolitical Rivalry and Eviction from K2

The events of 2005 in Central Asia, especially the collapse of President Akayev's regime in March 2005 in the so-called Tulip Revolution, proved a decisive point for the United States in the region. In Georgia in 2003 and then in Ukraine 2004, opposition leaders, who in both cases were more pro-Western than the entrenched incumbents, had used the political opportunity presented by a national election to accuse the government of rigging the vote. Taking advantage of transnational networks of support, international observation missions that declared the polls flawed, and international media attention, they quickly mobilized a groundswell of mass protests to topple these regimes.

Perceptions of U.S. Bids for Regime Change and a "Greater Central Asia"

Across Central Asia, conspiracy theories abound that an alliance made up of the U.S. government, U.S. intelligence services, and pro-democracy NGOs, such as the network of foundations affiliated with George Soros and the National Democratic Institute, had conspired in an effort to bring about these regime changes.[24] The enthusiasm with which Washington greeted these regime changes certainly reinforced this perception, but the actual causes and external dynamics of these political changes were more subtle. As Valerie Bunce and Sharon Wolchik have shown, transnational networks of NGOs, youth groups, and media personnel actively learned from one another and diffused their lessons and techniques.[25] Kyrgyz protestors emulated aspects of the Georgian and Ukrainian electoral revolutions, just as Ukrainians and Georgians had learned from their predecessors in Serbia in 2000.[26] But the Kyrgyz case was more the case of a brittle regime collapsing than a planned attempt at an overthrow.[27] The new interim President Bakiyev did not advocate for the same pro-Western shift that his counterparts in Georgia and Ukraine had. Nevertheless, the classification of the Akayev regime's collapse in March 2005 as the "Tulip Revolution" reinforced the view that his ouster had the full support of the U.S. government. Statements by deposed President Akayev to that effect reinforced this impression, as did some misguided public comments by USAID staffers and contractors who were eager to claim that their civil society and media programming had demonstrable impact.[28]

The regional characterization of the Color Revolutions as part of a broader U.S.-led geopolitical effort was compounded by the public rise of the so-called Greater Central Asian Project (GCAP), set forth in a series of publications by Johns Hopkins Professor Frederick Starr.[29] In a series of papers published in 2005, Starr argued that the United States had a unique opportunity to develop a new regional organization that would promote economic and commercial links between Afghanistan and the rest of Central Asia, deliver U.S. aid and economic assistance, and quickly establish itself as a major regional institution. In order to secure the cooperation of Central Asian governments with the GCAP, Starr advocated that the traditional U.S. demands for political reforms within the Central Asian states be dropped. Though Starr acknowledged that Russia and China might view the GCAP as a competitor to their own regional initiatives, he argued that its overall positive impact on regional development might eventually win them over. Not surprisingly, Russian and Chinese officials were not convinced, as they interpreted the GCAP as an initiative designed to undermine Russian and Chinese regional influence.

Russian and Chinese fears over U.S. plans and regional aspirations appeared to be vindicated when, in early 2006, the U.S. State Department announced that it was re-assigning the administration of its Central Asian diplomatic missions from the Eurasian bureau, which included Russia and the other post-Soviet states, to the South Asia Bureau.[30] Secretary of State Condoleezza Rice had planned to create the new Bureau for South and Central Asia in 2005 as part of her "transformational diplomacy" initiative.[31] Officially, the bureaucratic restructuring was meant to "foster increased cooperation among the countries of Central Asia and South Asia as they work towards our shared goals of security, prosperity, stability, and freedom" and "to build on the Central Asian states' natural partnership with Afghanistan."[32] The latter reference to the region's supposed "natural partnership" with Afghanistan was particularly alarming to Moscow and Beijing, as it signaled that U.S. officials intended to extend U.S. Afghanistan-based influence northward. The bureaucratic change was followed by several high-profile U.S.-led conferences that focused on strengthening economic links between Afghanistan and Central Asia, including in the electricity and power-generating sector.[33]

Andijan and Security Realignment

On the evening of May 12, 2005, in the southern Uzbek city of Andijan, an armed group stormed a prison and staged a break, attempting to free 23 businessmen who had just been convicted of belonging to Akramiya, an illegal Islamic movement. According to the Uzbek government account, this armed group took several policemen hostage and the proceeded to storm government buildings in the city. A few hours later, during the morning of May 13, a crowd once again amassed in the city's Babur Square, as it had done during the businessmen's trial, but in far greater numbers, reaching the thousands; speakers at the gathering called for political and economic reforms, including an end to corruption. After a day of tension and occasional gunfire, Uzbek security services and police opened fire on the protesters in the early evening. The Uzbek government claims that it killed 187 people, all of them terrorist or insurgents, while human rights organizations estimate that 800 were killed, most of them innocent civilians caught in waves of indiscriminate fire.[34] Calls by international human rights groups for an international investigation have been resolutely rejected by Tashkent.

The Andijan events proved fateful for the U.S. basing presence in Uzbekistan. U.S. reaction was mixed, with DOD supporting the Uzbek government's general position that its crackdown was justified and had targeted terrorists. As more details emerged of the scale of the shooting, most branches of the U.S. government lined up against the Pentagon. At a U.S. government meeting on Andijan, Rice reportedly asserted that "human rights trumps security," while Rumsfeld claims to have been the only one pushing for easing up on Tashkent.[35] Soon, the State Department supported the call from human rights organizations that demanded an international investigation. Around the same time, a bipartisan group of U.S. senators, led by Senator John McCain, launched an investigation into Andijan, especially the issue of whether U.S. military hardware was used in the crackdown; later in May, the group visited Tashkent, where it met with Uzbek human rights groups and gave a critical press conference on the state of human rights in the country.[36] McCain also led a Senate group that initially blocked the Uzbek government's reimbursement request for $23 million that it claimed it was owed for its services after the eviction from K2.

U.S. criticism of Uzbekistan contrasted with the strong support shown to the Uzbek government by Beijing and Moscow. At the SCO Astana Summit of 2005, regional leaders denounced foreign meddling in internal affairs and issued a now famous communiqué stating that foreign military bases in the region had served their primary purpose and should be placed on a timetable for removal. In June and July of 2005, it seemed clear that the U.S.-Uzbek security relationship had neared its breaking point. Uzbek authorities demanded that the United States start paying a significant rent for K2 and imposed a number of restrictions on U.S. activities and flights, citing environmental concerns.[37] The last straw for Tashkent appears to have been the U.S. announcement of support for a UN proposal to relocate refugees from Andijan who had been living in southern Kyrgyzstan to Romania, rather than turn them over to Uzbek security services for interrogation. On July 29, a messenger from the Uzbek Ministry of Foreign Affairs delivered notice to the U.S. Embassy that it was activating the termination clause of the K2 agreement and that U.S. forces had 180 days to leave the facility.

The aftermath of the K2 eviction appeared to support perceptions that the geopolitical pendulum in the region had realigned from Washington to Russia (and, to a lesser extent, Beijing).[38] In November 2005, Uzbekistan joined the Russian-led Collective Security Treaty Organization, with President Karimov proclaiming at the signing ceremony that Russia had always been Uzbekistan's natural security partner. Soon after, Kyrgyz officials seized on the fact that Manas remained the only official U.S. base left in the region and demanded a hundred-fold increase in rent (see Chapter 7). In a memo to National Security Advisor Stephen Hadley in early 2006, Rumsfeld lamented, "We are getting run out of Central Asia by the Russians. They are doing a considerably better job at bullying those countries [than] the US is doing to counter their bullying."[39]

But the rift in U.S.-Uzbek relations was temporary, reflecting the immediate threat to regime survival that Karimov felt in the wake of Andijan and the Color Revolutions, rather than a fundamental realignment toward Moscow. Just a few years later, U.S.-Uzbek military cooperation would flourish in a different form. The more lasting impact of the K2 eviction was to caution U.S. officials to not push Central Asian regimes too hard on democracy and human rights issues, especially when important security cooperation and basing rights were at stake.

The Proconsuls on the Ground: CENTCOM's Autonomy

The K2 eviction placed the U.S. on the defensive and resulted in the transfer of some operations to other venues, including Manas in Kyrgyzstan. However, after K2 basing rights were curtailed, U.S.-Uzbek security cooperation, and U.S.-Central Asian cooperation more broadly, continued in a more low-key fashion. For example, according to a 2006 Protocol, Uzbekistan granted permission to the U.S. Department of Defense to conduct flights by authorized civilian aircraft over Uzbek airspace, raising the possibility that contractors may have carried on security-related activities after the U.S. military's official departure from K2.[40]

Much of this U.S. security assistance came not from the State Department or even official congressional appropriations, but from discretionary pots of money distributed by Central Command (CENTCOM), the regional command operating in the area. According to an investigative survey of these discretionary funds, in 2006 CENTCOM drew upon at least 19 separate programs to channel its assistance and cooperation with the Central Asian militaries.[41] Most of these categories are not designated as assistance by the Department of Defense, but rather as part of the operating budget of CENTCOM and therefore discretionary to the needs and decisions of CENTCOM commanders.

The categories for these so-called "walking around" moneys include funds for the Support of Coalition Forces in Combined Operations (Coalition Readiness Support), the Combatant Command Initiative Fund (CIF), the Combined Operations and Exercises, Joint Combined Exchange Training, and the National Guard State Partnership program. Also included under the CENTCOM budget is a $1.5 billion pot (in FY 2006) for "Reimbursement to Countries for United States Expenses," designed to reimburse countries for logistical and military support for U.S. military operations, including the fees paid for the Manas Transit Center. The report also notes, echoing an earlier assessment by a *Washington Post* reporter who traveled in the region, that CENTCOM commanders freely can move money from these accounts to fund regional exercises, training conferences, and other collaborative events with target country militaries.[42]

To put these figures in context, in 2007 the total amount of unreported or "uncounted" DOD military aid to the Central Asian states exceeded official State Department security assistance by nearly three to one. Further, in FY 2007, the U.S. government spent at least six times as much on supporting the Central Asian militaries as it did on regional democratization (see Table 3.1).[43]

These spending patterns also suggest that U.S. regional command carries considerable influence and regional decision-making power as an autonomous actor. At times, tensions between the State Department and DOD personnel have been acute. An Inspector General report of the U.S. Embassy in Bishkek notes the strained relations between U.S. embassy staff and the personnel at the Manas base in Kyrgyzstan.[44] The sheer imbalance in numbers—over 1,000 troops at Manas versus a couple of dozen at the Embassy—would naturally tilt the diplomatic balance from State to DOD, but Kyrgyz officials and press members also note that base personnel tend to deal directly with their Kyrgyz counterparts over matters such as base-related contracting, public relations, and charitable programs, often excluding the Embassy from these communications.[45]

The issue is not one of direct bureaucratic competition; rather, each of these entities reports to a different chain of command. Military personnel, including basing commanders, report directly to the regional command at CENTCOM, which treats the Central Asian states as part of their Afghanistan theater of operations. At the same time, such autonomous behavior and ground-level activity has had the unintended consequence of undercutting the claim that the United States is not interested in pursuing influence or playing the "Great Game." While the U.S. president and his close advisors might regularly proclaim that the United States is not interested in competing with Russia for regional influence, CENTCOM'S military-to-military cooperation continues relatively unconstrained, well beyond the purposes of keeping Afghanistan's logistics and supply chains running. For example, commanders at Manas revealed that in 2010 they had participated in 40 military-to-military contacts with their Kyrgyz counterparts.[46]

In this light, one of the most important lessons learned by U.S. defense commanders is to avoid close scrutiny of U.S. military activities by not referring to facilities as "bases." Yet, a look at recent activities and proposed construction suggests that the regional command continues to invest in "base-like" projects and installations, particularly the establishment of a number of anti-terrorism

Table 3.1 U.S. Assistance to Central Asia, FY2007, Including Security Estimates and Official Government and Democracy Totals ($millions)

	Central Asia Regional	Kazakhstan	Kyrgyzstan	Tajikistan	Turkmenistan	Uzbekistan	Total
Security and Police Aid	10.96	60.67	38.30	23.19	5.86	0.85	144.81
Department of State (DOS) and USAID	7.36	8.69	6.05	11.74	1.82	0.80	41.76
Department of Defense (unofficial estimates)	3.60	51.98	32.25	11.45	4.04	0.05	103.05
Official U.S. Government Aid	7.59	165.59	54.41	46.72	19.84	35.21	329.36
Democracy Assistance (DOS and USAID)	0.65	5.70	5.36	3.68	3.38	5.2	23.97

Note: DOD figures include funds allocated for CENTCOM CIF, counternarcotics, counterterrorism, CTFP, counter-proliferation, officer education, officer exercises, Section 1206, Section 1208, Warsaw Initiative Fund, CENTCOM JCET Training and EDA. Not all data were available for all categories, so estimates are probably lower than actual totals.

Source: Calculated based on Lumpe 2010, Tables 6–9.

"training centers." In October 2009, U.S. and Kyrgyz officials opened a $9 million training center in Tokmok for elite Kyrgyz Special Forces that, according to U.S. Ambassador to Kyrgyzstan Tatiana Gfoeller, had received "extensive training from U.S. forces."[47] In early 2010 U.S. officials announced that they would construct a major anti-terrorism center in Batken, Kyrgyzstan, that, after the fall of the Bakiyev regime, was reslated for the southern city of Osh. In 2009, a solicitation from the U.S. Army Corps of Engineers describes a proposed $5–10 million National Training Center for Karatog, Tajikistan, to include "construction of a garrison compound and training ranges."[48] Other facilities in what appears to be a "mini-construction boom" for the Pentagon include building new border-crossing checkpoints in Turkmenistan, a second project in Kyrgyzstan, and an earmark for a $5 million project in Kazakhstan.[49]

Finally, a series of leaked U.S. Embassy cables reveal that U.S. and Turkmen officials reached a "divert agreement" in 2006, which Ashgabat has insisted ever since on keeping strictly informal, to permit the United States emergency use of the Mary Northeast Military air base (Mary 2).[50] Some Russian and Turkmen dissident news sites even have alleged that the U.S. military is regularly using the Mary 2 airfield as an actual supporting base for Afghanistan operations, though there is no direct evidence of this in other sources.[51] Regardless of the exact status and use of Mary 2, a survey of the region reveals a web of "low-profile" and informal arrangements that have extended U.S. military cooperation with the Central Asian states into several areas well beyond formal basing arrangements.

A New Silk Road Strategy: Establishing the Northern Distribution Network

Origins and Branches

U.S. military engagement with the Central Asian states would pick up again in 2008 as a result of events in distant Pakistan. Throughout 2008, a series of Taliban and insurgent attacks on U.S. supply lines transiting to Afghanistan highlighted the vulnerability of the U.S. southern supply effort. In December 2008 alone, militants attacked logistics terminals in Peshawar, overrunning security personnel, and destroyed or looted 250–300 trucks bound for Afghanistan.[52]

The opening of the so-called "northern option" had been considered for some time, but was now made a priority. U.S. defense planners concluded a series of negotiations with Central Asian governments to facilitate the opening of the new "Northern Distribution Network" (NDN), to bring supplies and materials to U.S. and NATO forces in Afghanistan from northern routes. Contracting for NDN transit is undertaken on a commercial basis with private entities, though for many of the Central Asian states, these logistical companies retain significant ties to certain government actors and ruling regimes. Original NDN agreements allowed only the transit of non-lethal supplies and materials and only one-way transport (no return legs from Afghanistan).[53]

The NDN routes span thousands of miles across Eurasian landmass (see Figure 3.2). The first route originates in the Baltic ports of Riga (Latvia), Tallinn (Estonia) and Klaipėda (Lithuania), where cargo is off-loaded onto the old Soviet rail network, then transits Russia and Kazakhstan, before entering Uzbekistan, where it terminates at the Termez crossing on the Afghanistan border. A second main spur, known as "NDN South," originates on the Black Sea Georgian port of Poti, transits across Georgia and Azerbaijan by train, before it is off-loaded onto ferries bound for Aktau, Kazakhstan. From there, trucks take the shipments across Kazakhstan and into Uzbekistan once more. A third variant route, known as the KKT route, relies on trucks to traverse Kazakhstan, Kyrgyzstan, and Tajikistan, before crossing into northern Afghanistan, though according to TRANSCOM officials, poor road conditions in Tajikistan seem to

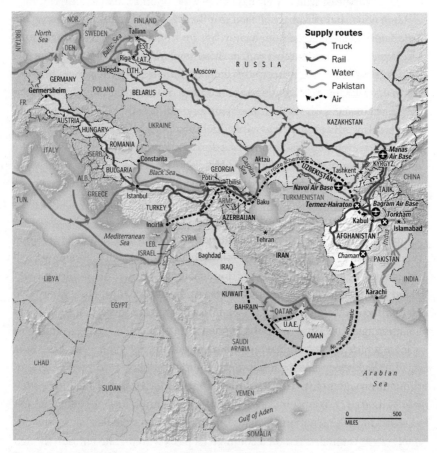

Figure 3.2. The Northern Distribution Network Source: Gene Thorp/Washington Post

be reorienting the final leg back into Uzbekistan.[54] Southern Uzbekistan, then, has become a critical transit hub, with U.S. officials stating in summer 2011 that five out of six NDN shipments traverse Uzbekistan.[55]

Since 2009, when agreements with Uzbekistan and Kazakhstan were finally concluded, the increase in NDN traffic has been spectacular. At the end of 2009, just 10 percent of cargos for U.S. and ISAF forces in Afghanistan were moving through NDN. By the end of 2010, the NDN accounted for 30 percent of cargos; the United States was shipping 1,000 containers a week, with 98 percent of these shipments passing through Uzbekistan.[56] By the end of 2011, U.S. officials hope that the NDN percentage will have increased to 75 percent, a shift that seemed all the more important as U.S.-Pakistan relations deteriorated following the U.S. killing of Osama Bin Laden in his Pakistani hideout in April 2011.[57] To complement these efforts, the Defense Logistics Agency (DLA), in cooperation with cargo companies, also created a virtual storefront in Uzbekistan to encourage Uzbek vendors in the border town of Termez to supply additional construction materials to U.S. forces in Afghanistan.[58]

In addition to the NDN routes traversing Uzbekistan, in 2008 and 2009 the U.S. military tried to secure new routes through Turkmenistan, without much success, and much to the frustration of U.S. defense officials and logisticians. However, other areas of logistical cooperation between Washington and Ashgabat have been kept quiet, so as to not violate Turkmenistan's public stance of neutrality. Since 2002, Turkmenistan has been providing air flight rights and blanket clearances for 1,600 flights a year; indeed, U.S. officials in 2009 pressed Turkmen officials to increase this number.[59] The United States also maintains a small team to conduct refueling services at Ashgabat airport, though the refueling operation has been subject to holdup over payment disputes.[60] Most intriguingly, according to U.S. logistical publications, Turkmenistan also is a transit corridor for shipping aviation fuel, refined in Azerbaijan and Turkmenistan, to Afghanistan.[61] According to a leaked U.S. Embassy cable from 2009, the arrangements surrounding these deliveries are "not discussed in deference to Turkmen desires to maintain some plausible deniability."[62] Further, the cable states that the arrangement has not even been mentioned in NDN discussions in order to "keep the Turkmen Government from rethinking the support it already tacitly provides."

The NDN also has established a new air hub in Uzbekistan to replace the former logistical and staging role played by K2, though the new facility is shrouded by various layers of commercial partners and third-party contracts. In May 2009, President Karimov announced that the newly renovated international cargo airport in the city of Navoi was being used for the transit of non-lethal goods to NATO forces in Afghanistan.[63] But, rather than deal directly with the U.S. military, Uzbekistan opted to deal with the South Korean state-operated

Hanjin Group, the parent company of Korean Airlines. According to an Uzbek–South Korean agreement, Korean contractors will upgrade the airport's facilities and Korean Airlines will operate the cargo center at Navoi for five years (effective January 1, 2009), renewable for another five.[64] Tellingly, in 2008, Korean Airlines had responded to a market survey by U.S. Transportation Command (TRANSCOM) by sketching out the potential role of Navoi as a potential logistics hub, stating that the airport could provide "an integrated commercial-based solution to meet U.S. forces' transportation requirements to Afghanistan."[65] A series of U.S. Embassy cables confirm that the use of Navoi has been part of overall U.S.-Uzbek NDN planning from the outset;[66] however, U.S. officials, as of 2010, had not been able to obtain permission to conduct direct staging flights from Navoi to Afghanistan and have been limited to ground transport to move supplies from the new air hub.[67] According to a report by a former U.S. Marine working as a commercial contractor, by summer 2009 Korean-based companies were operating 24/7 via Navoi to transport material and equipment by truck from the airport to U.S. forces in Kandahar.[68] Uzbek reports indicate that total freight traffic through Navoi airport in 2009 totaled 674 flights with 18,500 tons of cargo, triple the amount from 2008, though they did not provide details of cargo destination.[69]

Revitalizing the Silk Road?

The establishment of the NDN has also led some analysts and policymakers to predict that these military transiting agreements could have beneficial spillover effects by increasing trade and commercial traffic across Eurasia. Kuchins and colleagues have suggested that planners could use NDN "both to increase throughput capacity and to create more competitive market conditions that promote greater cost-efficiency and produce positive spillover in the surrounding region."[70] Frederick Starr, the intellectual founder of the earlier "Greater Central Asia Partnership" proposal, renewed his earlier claims that the trade and transit links established by NDN in Central Asia could serve as a unique opportunity to fundamentally transform the region's political geography. Starr elaborates:

> The reopening all these age-old transit routes across Afghanistan is the single greatest achievement of U.S. foreign policy in the new millennium. It was unintended, unrecognized, and, by most Americans, unacknowledged, even though they paid for it with the lives of loved ones and with hard-earned tax money. Nonetheless, this development offers the most promising solution to the U.S.' present strategic dilemma and the key to possible success in Afghanistan and the region.[71]

U.S. government officials and policy planners plan to strengthen North-South ties between the Central Asian states and Afghanistan, especially in the areas of electricity transmission, railways, and highways. For example, the new railway link from Termez to Mazar-e-Sharif (funded by the Asian Development Bank, the U.S., and Japan) is likely to spur future trade and transit between the countries, given that the only existing border crossing remains the backed-up Termez "Friendship" bridge.[72] At a New York Ministerial conference in September 2011, jointly hosted by the United States and Germany, proposals were discussed for expanding these North-South market linkages into a "New Silk Road."[73] But as Chapter 9 will show, there is little empirical evidence to back the claim that the NDN, or any other regional transport proposal, has improved more general import/export times across the region (see Figures 9.1 and 9.2). Maintaining the limited goals of NDN has proven to be challenging in and of itself, given the deteriorating state of the region's railroads, growing bottlenecks at the Uzbek-Afghan border, and the seemingly constant demand for informal payments.

Corruption on the New Silk Route

In practice, it is difficult to separate the commercial arrangements on which NDN has been created from the corruption and graft that pervade the political economy of the Central Asian countries and the logistical companies that they control. U.S. defense officials intentionally amended routine contracting procedures so that they could procure more supplies locally, thereby offering incentives to Central Asian governments to offer logistical cooperation with the Afghanistan campaign. The authorizations stipulated that preference in supply acquisition be shown for products or services from "Central Asia, Pakistan, or the South Caucasus" and that competition for these suppliers be limited.[74] The same memorandum justified the change in procedure as necessary to "encourage states of Central Asia to cooperate in expanding supply routes through their territory in support of operations in Afghanistan" and to "help develop more robust and enduring routes of supply to Afghanistan."

In response to an August 2009 Defense Support Agency Center (DESC) query for Uzbek procurement evaluations, several contracting companies testified to the corruption and informal barriers that plague NDN transit.[75] The Afghan Management Group (AMG) noted that the payment of "informal fees" to Uzbek authorities may be required to keep business moving, and observed that with the "payment of informal fees [rail transport from Bukhara, Uzbekistan, to Hairaton] can be reduced to 7 to 18 days" from the 35 days without the "speed-up" charge. Another contractor, Agility, stated, "government taxes and leases will always present challenges"; however, Uzbek government and commercial officials signal that they are willing to work with U.S. officials to "find suitable business arrangements." And the Uzbek Ministry of Foreign Affairs revealed that Navoi's profitability increased tenfold in 2009 compared to 2008 (pre-NDN agreement).[76]

One of the largest Uzbek commercial contractors, FMN Logistics, was a former self-described contracting arm of Zeromax, the giant Uzbek conglomerate reportedly connected with Gulnara Karimova, President Karimov's daughter.[77] FMN representatives now deny any connection between FMN and Zeromax or Karimova, though the U.S. Embassy in Tashkent in leaked cables also connected these entities.[78]

An even more secretive set of arrangements has characterized U.S.-Turkmen logistical cooperation. From the very beginning of refueling operations in 2002, the negotiations with the Turkmen government and civil aviation authorities were "problematical"; according to U.S. officials, "Turkmenistan's billing of the United States has not always reflected the arrangements agreed to."[79] According to an investigative report by Eurasianet's Deirdre Tynan, U.S. officials actually lost track of payments to the Turkmen government from 2002 to 2008 for air base access, navigation fees, and refueling operations.[80] The same report stated that, according to a 2009 Air Force Notice to Air Men, payments sent to Turkmenistan should be sent to a Deutsche Bank corresponding account, the same one that had been used by Turkmen strongman Niyazov, according to German press reports, to "park" about $3 billion in state revenue.

The increase in U.S. forces in Afghanistan in 2010 under the United States' surge strategy also increased the importance of NDN and all of the Central Asian logistical partnerships cultivated by the U.S. military.[81] But growing dependency on the network also appears to be empowering Central Asian elites to drive harder bargains and ratchet up political and economic demands. Politically, the Uzbek government has been using its critical role in the NDN to push back against criticism of its human rights record. In a leaked cable from March 2009, U.S. Ambassador Richard Norland described how President Karimov gave him a "tongue-lashing" when broaching the topic of human rights and then implicitly threatened to suspend cooperation on NDN transit.[82] Economically, the Uzbek government twice increased transit fees for goods bound for Afghanistan in 2010, while in February 2011 Tashkent announced a "significant" hike in NDN tariffs.[83]

On September 22, 2011, the U.S. Senate Committee on Appropriations approved a waiver to lift restrictions, in place since 2004, on providing U.S. military assistance to Uzbekistan. The DOD and diplomats engaged in NDN negotiations had long sought for the waiver, which appeared to be yet another concession made to Tashkent to obtain its cooperation on security matters. Tellingly, the Senate made the waiver contingent on the DOD providing reports on how Pentagon funds were being spent on NDN contracts, though these reports will be classified.[84] The Senate report on the foreign aid bill included the statement, "The committee is concerned with reports of pervasive corruption [in] Uzbekistan and therefore expects to be informed of public and private entities that receive support, directly or indirectly, from United States Government funds used to pay the costs of Northern Distribution Network supply routes through that country."

The rent seeking, hard bargaining, and allegations of corruption that have accompanied NDN expansion have created some inescapable paradoxes about U.S. policy in Central Asia that conflict with the U.S. mission in neighboring Afghanistan. On the one hand, most U.S. planners acknowledge that the greatest obstacle to building an effective and legitimate state in Afghanistan is the problem of corruption that continues to erode the legitimacy of the Karzai government and its political allies. At the same time, behind the scenes in neighboring Central Asia, the deals established by the NDN seem to be doling out private economic benefits and lucrative contracts to the Central Asian regimes to maintain their cooperation. Just as the United States has had to juggle its strategic interests and values agenda with respect to Central Asia's promotion of democracy and human rights, it seems that maintaining U.S. operations in Afghanistan necessitates tolerating and actively contributing to Central Asia's corruption and governance problems.

Conclusion

U.S. policy toward Central Asia in the 2000s became a function of supporting its war effort in neighboring Afghanistan. Shortly after 9/11, the United States established military bases and signed security cooperation agreements with all of the Central Asian states that agreed to logistical support, flyover rights, and security cooperation. In the earlier part of the decade, U.S. planners also engaged with the Central Asian states on issues relating to democracy, governance, and the rule of law. But, by the summer of 2005, the onset of the Color Revolutions, the collapse of the Akayev regime in Kyrgyzstan, and events in Andijan had escalated regional fears that the U.S. democratization agenda threatened regime stability. U.S. democracy NGOs, it seems, were as threatening to these regimes as anything coming out Afghanistan.

The eviction from K2 was both a turning point and a learning moment for U.S. officials. Uzbekistan terminated an important aspect of security cooperation for domestic political purposes, and U.S. planners learned that pushing Central Asian governments too hard for domestic political reforms might threaten key U.S. security relationships. This perceived trade-off is one that Central Asian rulers have eagerly framed and cultivated. These lessons later were applied to the design and operation of the NDN, as U.S. defense planners decided to secure the cooperation of Central Asian elites for opening a new series of supply routes by providing them with economic incentives, such as logistical contracts and transit fees. U.S. authorities also refrained from publicly criticizing the region's governance and political practices, which, as we shall see, steadily deteriorated over the decade. Rather than challenge local rules, as some officials had sought in the aftermath of Andijan, U.S. policymakers learned to play by them.

4

Moscow's Quest for a Privileged Role

Russian policy in Central Asia over the 2000s is often characterized as "resurgent." In certain Western circles, some even refer to it as neo-imperial and consistent with Moscow's revisionist attempt to push back against the Western-led international order.[1] Perhaps the main challenge in analyzing Russian policy toward Central Asia is that it lacks a single overriding strategic goal. Whereas Washington and Beijing have instrumentalized their engagement with the Central Asians states in pursuit of stabilizing an adjacent region, Moscow has pursued a basket of different objectives, including cooperating on counterterrorism, gaining access to Central Asian energy sources, promoting political stability, building a common economic space, and protecting the rights of Russian citizens abroad.

Above all, Moscow has sought regional primacy in Central Asia as a marker of the great power status that it considers central to its foreign policy identity.[2] Following the Russian-Georgian war, President Medvedev emphasized that Russia sought to maintain a position of "privileged influence" in Central Asia and other parts of the post-Soviet space.[3] Unlike opening a pipeline or securing a contested territory, however, concepts like privilege, status, and prestige are social rankings, not material facts, and can only be judged in relation to other actors.[4] Accordingly, Russia's actual policies in Central Asia have been a function of its prevailing relationship with other great powers, especially the United States, and its broader efforts to assert its place within a multipolar world.[5] For a brief period following the beginning of America's Global War on Terror (GWOT), Moscow viewed partnering with the United States in Central Asia as a means of enhancing its international status and regional position. However, as U.S.-Russian relations deteriorated, Russia increasingly came to view its relations with the United States in the region as competitive and zero-sum.

Russia's lack of strategic coherence in Central Asia coexists with, or perhaps even derives from, the fact that, of all the great powers, it easily possesses the most extensive array of regional ties. Interconnections inherited from the Soviet period, both in terms of physical infrastructure (pipelines, electricity grid, railways, and integrated defense networks) and human capital (education, technical training, common use of Russian, and ethnic Russians living abroad), have served as powerful post-imperial bonds. Russian armed forces, intelligence services, and internal security services all cooperate extensively with their Central Asian counterparts and even train them, while economic links have been reforged in the areas of energy and industry; most recently, millions of Central Asians migrants have entered Russia in search of work, and the remittances that they send back to Central Asia are a vital source of hard currency. Finally, Russia also has a number of "humanitarian" or "soft power" levers in the area, which include regional media and broadcasting, and educational scholarships, funding for pro-Russian institutions, cultural and language programming.[6]

Critically, Russia's intensive reengagement with the region took place beginning in 1999–2000, not following its formal disengagement in 1992. With renewed interest in pursuing its great power status and more centralized leadership in the Kremlin under President Vladimir Putin, Russian planners embarked on a new campaign for regional influence. In this pursuit, Moscow's main instruments have been neither "Soviet" nor "neo-imperial," but distinct attempts to emulate other successful contemporary regional organizations. Ironically, these new organizations, most notably the Collective Security Treaty Organization (CSTO) and EurAsEC/Customs Union, were modeled on rival Western bodies, but in substance have been fashioned to promote Russian leadership in Eurasia. Despite championing these new bodies, Moscow has proven less successful when it has sought to monopolize relations with the Central Asian states, while it has struggled to disentangle itself from intraregional rivalries and has proven incapable of checking the regional rise of China.

Relations with the West: From Enabler to Competitor

Russia in the 1990s and Putin's Rise

During the 1990s, Russia's relations with the West focused more on the contours and directions of its state-building, and economic and political reform in Russia, rather than questions of foreign policy and international partnership. Russia's brief flirtation with joining the West, under Foreign Minister Andrey Kozyrev, quickly gave way to Yevgeny Primakov's attempt to reassert Russian sovereignty and great power standing by focusing attention on the post-Soviet region. Though the Primakov and Putin policies shared much in common, Russia's weakened position in the 1990s, especially its poor economy, seriously hampered these aspirations.[7]

President Vladimir Putin's election in 1999 intensified Russia's foreign policy ties both with the West and with the post-Soviet states. Putin immediately set about consolidating the institutions of the Russian state and gave priority to reviving the economic basis of Russian power, especially reasserting government control over the energy sector.[8] Under Putin, Russian foreign policy aimed to solidify great power status, cultivate partnerships with other great powers, and maintain a system of pragmatic relations with the West. The National Security Concept of 2000 referred to Russia as one of the "influential centers of a multipolar world," despite "its own temporary difficulties," and identified Russia's weakening influence in the world, the weakening of CIS integration processes and the eastward expansion of NATO as among the most fundamental threats to Russia in the international sphere.[9]

9/11 and the Window of Active US-Russian Cooperation

It is often forgotten now, but in the aftermath of the September 11, 2001, attacks, President Putin was the first world leader to speak to President Bush. After offering him his condolences, Putin reassured the American president that, "there is no doubt that such inhuman actions cannot be left unpunished. The whole international community must rally in the fight against terrorism."[10] On September 12 in Moscow, a statement by the Russian president declared that "the event that occurred in the U.S. today goes beyond national borders. It is a brazen challenge to the whole humanity, at least to civilized humanity."[11] Putin also spoke of the need to pool the efforts of the international community in the struggle against terrorism, what he characterized as the "plague of the 21st century."

Beyond such strong public statements, the Russian president offered a broad set of practical measures to assist with the U.S. effort in Afghanistan and Central Asia. The two countries increased their intelligence sharing, and Russia provided fly-over rights and support for the anti-Taliban Northern Alliance, with which its intelligence services retained strong links. And, in a move that simply would have been unthinkable before 9/11, Putin agreed to let the United States establish military bases on Central Asian territory, with the understanding that they would be temporary.

Though some have dismissed this gesture as simply accepting a *fait accompli*, it is important to remember that Putin's leadership was decisive, as the Russian General Staff was extremely cautious about intelligence sharing and allowing U.S. troops into the former Soviet region.[12] When asked at a meeting with Bush in Crawford, Texas, in November 2001 about the potential for U.S. bases to lead to a "struggle for power and influence," Putin responded firmly: "I am more concerned with the presence of the terrorists' training camps in northern Afghanistan, who send guerrillas to the Caucasus."[13] In this early phase, Putin clearly believed that the U.S. campaign would facilitate a number of Russian foreign policy goals. U.S. forces could eradicate the growing Taliban threat that Russian officials viewed as potentially networking with Chechen and Central Asian militant groups. The U.S. campaign also allowed the Kremlin to frame its campaign in Chechnya as part of a larger international campaign against terrorism.

But there was also an important geopolitical benefit to Russia: the U.S. campaign could enable Russia to demonstrate its regional importance as a leading power and U.S. partner. Either implicitly or explicitly, Russian officials envisioned a grand bargain; in exchange for its regional assistance, Washington would consult with and recognize Moscow as the mediator for U.S. relations with the Central Asian states. At that point Russian public opinion was strongly supportive of Russian-U.S. cooperation in Central Asia, with a large survey conducted in April 2002 finding that 74 percent of respondents believed that a U.S.-Russian alliance in the struggle against international terrorism was a good thing, despite indications that they also believed that the relationship was one-sided and that the United States had imposed its agenda.[14] Interestingly enough, the same survey found that only 17 percent of respondents believed that U.S. bases in Central Asia were intended for the purpose of fighting the war in Afghanistan.[15]

Bilateral Relations Deteriorate

But the cooperative relationship in Central Asia would soon deteriorate, following a number of policy disagreements in U.S.-Russian relations. In 2002 the United States withdrew from the Anti-Ballistic Missile Treaty, despite vocal Russian objections, and pushed ahead with plans to deploy a missile defense system in Eastern Europe. At the Prague Summit in 2002, NATO made the decision to admit seven new members, including the Baltic States, which became the first actual post-Soviet states to join the Western security alliance. And within the region itself, rather than dealing with Moscow as an interlocutor, Washington forged bilateral relations and direct security cooperation with each of the Central Asian countries individually.

Washington's march to its 2003 war in Iraq diminished the importance of Afghanistan, in which Russia viewed itself as a critical player, and showcased Washington's unyielding unilateralism. In opposing U.S. plans for regime change, Russia vocally sided with France and Germany in the United Nations Security Council. U.S. officials presented Russian objections primarily as economic, emphasizing Iraq's Russian debt, but to Moscow the bypassing of the Security Council signaled that U.S. officials were unwilling to accept any multilateral checks or international legal constraints on their actions.[16]

Regime Change Close to Home: The Role of the Color Revolutions

In addition to these questions of international security, the wave of so-called "Color Revolutions" across Eurasia brought the Bush administration's "freedom agenda" and support for democratic regime change right to Moscow's doorstep.[17] In 2003, long-time Georgian President Eduard Shevardnadze was dislodged after a faulty parliamentary election by a coalition of pro-Western young

Georgian leaders, headed by the soon-to-be President Mikheil Saakashvili.[18] One year later, in the Orange Revolution, Washington not only denounced the initial election results in Ukraine that were won by pro-Kremlin candidate Viktor Yanukovych, but seemingly played a critical role in overturning the result in favor of pro-Western Viktor Yushchenko, by funding pro-democracy nongovernmental organizations (NGOs), technical election assistance, youth groups, and friendly media.[19] In response to what it perceived to be clear Western interference in Ukraine's domestic politics, Moscow formulated a number of responses and countermeasures and introduced new legislation limiting the activities of NGOs (see Chapter 6). Whereas the United States had projected an image of promoting regime change across the region, Russia quickly positioned itself as the role of the backer of the political status quo.

This perceived U.S. unilateralism and aggressive promotion of pro-Western regime change sealed the fate of U.S.-Russian cooperation and provoked a new regional assertiveness from Moscow. Russian elite opinion and public sentiment about relations with the United States quickly deteriorated from one of cautious partnership to outright competition. Central Asia now became a central area of concern, with the presence of U.S. military bases in Kyrgyzstan and Uzbekistan taking on renewed importance. In a fascinating research exercise, Jason Lyall of Yale University has analyzed the evolution of Russian elite public speeches on U.S.-Russian relations from 2001 to 2004, revealing how initial proclamations about a common civilizational struggle against barbarism gave way to declarations of a competitive U.S.-Russian "security dilemma" in Central Asia.[20] From this perspective, Uzbekistan's eviction of the United States in 2005 marked a critical victory in this regional competition and would encourage Russian policymakers to pressure Kyrgyzstan to do the same (see Chapter 7). In sum, U.S.-Russian bilateral relations provide a critical context for understanding how Russia designed its engagement policies with Central Asia.

Crafting the Institutions of Influence: Anti-Terrorism, Security, and the CSTO

Having abandoned the ineffectual and costly Commonwealth of Independent States (CIS) in 2001, the Kremlin set its sights on both centralizing the management of security policy and establishing primacy in the post-Soviet region. Putin immediately increased the number of direct meetings between himself and the Central Asian heads of states, creating a new office in the Kremlin to oversee the management of inter-elite contacts, and soon introduced a new architecture for managing Russian-Central Asian security issues.[21]

The issue of "international terrorism" presented a unique opportunity for reestablishing close ties with the Central Asian states.[22] Not only had Russia launched its new military campaign in Chechnya under the banner of fighting terrorism, but the 1999 incursions of the Islamic Movement of Uzbekistan (IMU) into Batken, Kyrgyzstan, and the Taliban's gains in Afghanistan were causing grave concern throughout the region. In 2000, Putin used the terrorism issue as a platform to try to reengage with Uzbekistan, which had been drifting away from Moscow's orbit. At a CIS Defense Ministers meeting in May 2001, Russian Defense Minister Sergei Ivanov proposed that counterterrorism could provide the impetus for drawing up a single defense policy for the eleven CIS members;[23] earlier, Moscow had proposed establishing a permanent joint military force for anti-terrorism operations, as well as a new Anti-Terrorism Center. The Central Asian states were reluctant to commit to these plans, but terrorism would soon become the defining regional and geopolitical issue.

The Emergence of the CSTO

The Collective Security Treaty Organization (CSTO, or *ODKB*) has been Moscow's primary forum for engaging the Central Asian states on security issues. Founded in May 2002 (though its charter was ratified in September 2003), the security group comprises Russia, Armenia, Belarus, Kazakhstan, Kyrgyzstan, and Tajikistan, with Uzbekistan joining in 2006, following its fallout with the United States over K2. At his press conference announcing the CSTO's formation, Putin described the organization as an adaptation to the changing geopolitical environment.[24] The organization adopted a unified command and rotating presidency, and pledged to integrate member military forces.[25] As part of the founding agreement, Russia allowed CSTO member states to purchase military hardware at the same price as the Russian military, while Russia agreed to foot the bill for the organization's costs.

Initially, the structure of the CSTO provided Russian planners with a potential tool for re-creating security dependencies with the Central Asian states, but also a forum for channeling potential engagement with NATO. From its inception, Russian planners and policymakers at various points have argued that the two organizations could cooperate in Afghanistan, adopt a common framework for assessing threats to regional security, share classified information, and hold regular consultations.[26] For their part, U.S. and NATO officials consistently have refused to engage with the organization, in Central Asia or elsewhere, viewing any engagement with the Russian-led bloc as undermining their bilateral relations with individual Central Asian countries, as well as the existing NATO-Russia forum.[27]

During its first year in 2003, the CSTO displayed a somewhat schizophrenic attitude on whether to view the West as a regional partner or a competitor, mirroring Russia's inconsistent policy on the matter at the same time. For example, in May 2003, the CSTO's Secretary General Nikolai Bordyuzha, a former secretary of the Russian National Security Council and the country's Border Guard, dismissed concerns that the CSTO would clash with NATO, indicating that the two organizations could cooperate because they faced "common tasks and problems."[28] But in an interview during the same month, Bordyuzha argued that the U.S. military presence in Central Asia was generating a competitive security dilemma when he mused "I do not quite understand the [American] rationale of creating and upgrading bases in the immediate proximity of the borders of the Collective Security Treaty or Russia. . . . So, naturally, a state (and this is theory) must respond to any strengthening of military groups on any side by similarly adequate efforts to ensure preemptively its security."[29] Later, the organization's public declarations would openly criticize U.S. policies, such as its support for NATO expansion, its plans to deploy a missile defense system in East Europe, and its support for the Georgian position during the August 2008 war.[30]

Without ever explicitly declaring itself as a balancer against NATO, the CSTO seems to have evolved in direct reaction to the Western alliance. The competitive spur over anti-terrorism following 9/11 was particularly important to Moscow. Russian commentators increasingly viewed U.S. counterterrorism activities in Central Asia as a cover for establishing a regional sphere of influence, claiming that such cooperation eroded the use of Russian as a lingua franca, exposed Central Asian officers to Western ideas in training programs, and threatened to impose NATO standards for interoperability and weapons systems.[31] In the CSTO's first years, the organization focused on conducting high-profile anti-terrorism exercises in Kyrgyzstan and Tajikistan, while strongly backing domestic crackdowns by Central Asian governments, especially Uzbekistan, made in the name of anti-terrorism.

Moscow would later focus on developing the organization's Collective Rapid Reaction Force (CRRF), an integrated group of 15,000 troops made up of 10,000 Russian troops, 3,000–4,000 Kazakhstani troops, and one battalion from each of the organization's other members. In the wake of the Russia-Georgia War, Russian President Medvedev clarified that the CRRF would be "just as good as comparable NATO forces," with a sufficient number of units that would be "well trained and equipped."[32] He continued that it was tasked with anti-terrorism and counter-narcotics trafficking activities, but that it could also counter regional aggression from an outside power.[33] Uzbekistan has refused to formally join the CRRF, as Tashkent harbored reservations about integrating militaries, the potential for the organization to interfere in domestic disputes, and Russian plans to build a CSTO base in southern Kyrgyzstan, near the Uzbek border.[34] Indeed, just a year later the organization's credibility was severely eroded by the ethnic violence that erupted in southern Kyrgyzstan, as Moscow refused to intervene, despite interim President Roza Otunbayeva's appeals for Russian and CSTO peacekeepers.[35] Just a few weeks earlier, the organization had denounced the change of government in Kyrgyzstan as "extra-constitutional"; Belarus's outspoken President Alexander Lukashenko, who granted asylum to deposed Kyrgyz President Kurmanbek Bakiyev, lambasted the organization for failing to act to preserve the Kyrgyz regime. In the wake of these criticisms and perceived inaction, CSTO officials clarified at an informal summit in Astana in August 2011 that they would be empowered in the future to intervene in domestic matters in order to "restore constitutional system" of a member state.[36]

Moscow also used the organization to provide the legal framework to establish new Russian military bases in the region.[37] In 2003, Russia and Kyrgyzstan concluded an agreement to open a Russian air base, under CSTO auspices, on the site of an old Soviet airforce training center at Kant, just 30 kilometers from Manas. In 2004, Moscow and Dushanbe concluded a series of agreements that formalized the presence of the Russian 201st Motorized Division in Tajikistan, in exchange for Moscow writing off Tajik debt and promising to invest in hydropower projects;[38] in 2011 both sides announced that the agreement would be extended for another 49 years, though the terms of the "base payment" or other quid pro quo involved remained unclear. And after President Bakiyev backtracked in June 2009 on his promise to close the Manas base (see Chapter 7), Moscow demanded that it open a second base in the southern city of Osh, an apparent compensation for the geopolitical sleight.

In all of these cases, the actual functional purpose of these facilities is either unclear or extremely vague. For example, Russian forces at Kant are officially assigned to provide air support for counterterrorism operations and to "control the Central Asian airspace," which presumably does not include the dozens of U.S. military aircraft that conduct daily operations within a few miles.[39] Tellingly, at the December 2011 CSTO summit, the organization adopted a preliminary agreement prohibiting member states from allowing the stationing of non-CSTO military troops and bases without mutual consent, effectively giving Moscow a veto over future regional basing deals.[40] Moscow's seeming fixation with bases in Central Asia derives from the fact that they are perceived as critical symbols of Russia's regional prestige, status, and enduring political presence in the region.[41]

Ultimately, the endurance and deepening of the CSTO is less a result of its success as an alliance or security group, but more a reflection of the fact that it provides different distinct benefits to Russia and its Central Asian members. For Russia, it has allowed Moscow to fashion the image of heading a NATO-style alliance and has legally allowed it to reestablish a military presence in the region.

But Russia has been unsuccessful in using the group to actually engage the West or monopolize security relations with the Central Asian states. The organization also has failed to back Moscow's requests on some key issues, such as its request to recognize the independence of the breakaway territories of Abkhazia and South Ossetia following the August 2008 Russia-Georgia War.

The Central Asian states view the CSTO primarily as a political forum that placates Moscow's self-image and regional ambitions; the organization also offers selective benefits to the Central Asian militaries and security services (i.e., discount military equipment, training, integration), given that Russia foots almost the entire bill. More cynically, the organization also serves as a useful tool for promoting regime survival; its credibility was thus undermined, for some of its members, by its inability to prevent the collapse of two governments in Kyrgyzstan.[42] But, as the previous chapter demonstrated, while participating in the CSTO's deepening structures, most of the Central Asian states also have maintained, if not strengthened, their bilateral relations with the United States. Intensifying security cooperation with the great powers has not been mutually exclusive.

Crafting the Institutions of Influence: Economics, People, and Energy

As with security policy, the Kremlin sought to both centralize its Central Asian policy-making and institutionalize its regional interactions. Beginning in the early 2000s, the Russian government actively sought to advance the interests of major Russian energy players in the region, especially Gazprom and Unified Energy System (UES), as well as to coordinate the finance sector with government policy.[43] From a decade of isolated economic contact, the 2000s saw the blossoming of economic ties between Russia and Central Asia, mostly in energy-related areas. Over the decade, Russian trade with Central Asia has skyrocketed, starting from a baseline of under $2 billion annually to reach $27 billion in 2008, just before the onset of the financial crisis (see Figure 4.1)

The Rise of EurAsEC, the Customs Union, and the Eurasian Union

The CSTO's economic counterpart is the Eurasian Economic Community (EurAsEC), comprising Russia, Belarus, Kazakhstan, Kyrgyzstan, and Tajikistan. The group was founded in Astana in October 2000 as a successor to the ineffective Central Asian Economic Cooperation Organization (1998) and the Commonwealth of Independent State's Customs Union of Russia, Belarus, and Kazakhstan (1996). EurAsEC's goal is to promote a common economic space

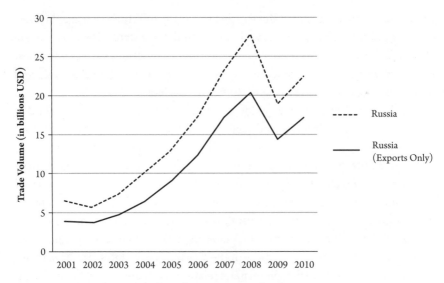

Figure 4.1 Central Asian Trade with Russia, Annual, 2001–2010 Source: International
Monetary Fund (IMF), Direction of Trade Statistics (DOTS), 2001–2010

that includes a regional trade regime, common customs procedures, and unified
tariffs and non-tariff barriers. Moving beyond the purview of its predecessors,
EurAsEC has sought to establish a supranational system of governing rules and
regulatory bodies, including an Interstate Council, Secretariat, Parliamentary
Assembly, Integration Commission, and Community Court. In 2008, the organization formed the EurAsEC Customs Union Commission (CUC), modeled
loosely on the European Commission in Brussels, to coordinate the move to a
system of common duties and customs procedures (the "Customs Union"),
which went into effect in 2010 for Russia, Belarus, and Kazakhstan.[44]

Just as the CSTO has modeled itself on NATO, the Customs Union is mimicking aspects of the European Union. On January 1, 2012, the group introduced
the single economic space, covering trade and investment and labor, In the
future, the economic body aspires to promote the integration of energy and
transportation policy, social and legal policies, and even adopt, in an EU-like
fashion, a unified currency.[45] Russian policymakers and analysts now speak of
the organization as potentially becoming one of several competing global trade
blocs, such as the EU or ASEAN, giving Russia the leadership of a common economic zone to complement its security area. In his first foreign policy speech
after announcing that he would once again run for the Russian presidency in
2012, Vladimir Putin declared his interest in fashioning a new "Eurasian Union,"
similar to the EU, that would deal with other regions from a position of strength.[46]

Like the CSTO, the EurAsEC is also competing, though perhaps less obviously, with a Western-backed organization—the World Trade Organization.

Keith Darden has argued that EurAsEC and its post-Soviet predecessors were driven initially by the logic of reintegrating a regional economic space as an alternative to states' joining the world economic institutions that promote free trade and more liberal-based market exchange.[47] All regional economic zones protect domestic producers and offer them dedicated markets, but the high external tariff rate of the Russian-led group, for Darden, makes it antithetical to the goals of WTO membership.[48] With Russia's admission into the WTO finally concluded in December 2011, it remains unclear how Moscow will reconcile its new WTO obligations, such as its commitments to liberalize its market and end subsidies to favored industries, with its politically driven Customs Union agenda.

Like the CSTO, the EurAsEC has evolved in fits and starts, often in reaction to external events. For the first part of the decade, it appeared as if the organization would become just the latest in a long list of failed regional attempts to reintegrate the post-Soviet economic region. Though the organization has fostered Russian-Central Asian trade, its impact on intra-Central Asian economic activity was less pronounced. As with the CSTO, Uzbekistan's membership in the economic organization has been volatile—after joining in 2006 as part of its pro-Russia shift, Tashkent withdrew again in November 2008, as Uzbek officials refused to commit to adopt the group's stricter border and customs practices. But the organization's plans to create the Customs Union received new impetus during the 2008 world financial crisis, as Moscow feared the possible loss of regional economic influence to the EU and China and their growing relations with the post-Soviet states.[49]

The Birth of the Customs Union

The implementation of the Customs Union's common duties policy in July 2010 among the Russia-Belarus-Kazakhstan troika marked an important stage in the organization's development. In 2008, Russian-Kazakh trade reached a record $20 billion in total volume, with most of it concentrated in border regions, making the bilateral trading relationship Kazakhstan's most important and Russia's third most important.[50] Proponents argue that the Customs Union will cement these ties, expanding both markets and more efficient vertically integrated production, with Sergei Glaziyev, the head of the CUC (and former outspoken critic of IMF policies in Russia) optimistically forecasting GDP gains of 15–17 percent in member countries by 2015.[51] Russian officials and analysts appear especially upbeat about the opportunities for Russian firms to relocate their production to Kazakhstan to take advantage of lower-cost labor, much like U.S. firms moved operations to Mexico after the passage of NAFTA.[52] At a meeting with the Kazakh president in July 2010, President Medvedev observed: "We've now neared a very high level of integration. . . . Looking forward, there's cooperation on the common economic space, and in the future . . . a common market and, I think, ultimately the creation of the foundations for a shared currency zone."[53]

Not all Kazakh officials or commentators have welcomed the Customs Union. Liberalizers viewed the move as locking Kazakhstan into Russia's embrace and potentially delaying its accession into the WTO, while some consumer groups complained of the higher Russian tariffs, especially on imported cars, that the country adopted as a result of the deal.[54] On a political level, critics have accused the CUC, which is officially a supranational body, of imposing a legal framework that favors Russian businesses and regulators, without adequate input from Kazakh associations.[55] Moreover, the haste with which Moscow has implemented various measures has left many technical and regulatory issues yet to be worked out.[56]

For Kyrgyzstan and Tajikistan, members of EurAsEC but initially excluded from the Customs Union, their relative economic weakness provides two incentives for joining the Customs Union. First, the Customs Union provides an updated vehicle to secure cheap, subsided Russian energy. Since independence, Russia has used energy as a tool of influence, but found less space to do so as the post-Soviet countries entered trade agreements with outside partners and organizations.[57] By establishing a common space for tax-free Russian energy transfers, the Customs Union resurrects Moscow's ability to use energy as a foreign policy tool. Second, access to the EurAsEC anti-crisis fund, currently envisioned as a pool of $10 billion, three-quarters of which has been promised by Russia, could potentially provide a more readily accessible and cheaper borrowing source for the cash-strapped Central Asian countries than the International Monetary Fund or international capital markets. Also, the conditions and monitoring mechanisms of the EurAsEC fund appear underdeveloped and far less stringent than those of other international donors.

The Kyrgyz case is especially significant, as it has been a member of the WTO since 1998, and, through its growing low-cost trade with China, has become a reexporting hub for Chinese products to the rest of the region.[58] Kyrgyz officials such as former President Otunbayeva and current President Almazbek Atambayev have enthusiastically championed Kyrgyzstan's entry, while others have warned that Kyrgyzstan's entry into the Russian-led economic group will sacrifice its thriving reexport business and hurt middle class consumers, all for access to cheaper Russian energy.[59] When in April 2010, as part of its move to the exclusive Customs Union troika, Russia started taxing energy exports to Kyrgyzstan, it spiked fuel costs 15 percent overnight, which precipitated the popular demonstrations that triggered the collapse of President Bakiyev's regime. Though the WTO accommodates several regional free trade blocks, including the EU, WTO rules about admitting members affiliated with non-WTO regional free trade agreements are unclear.[60]

The Ties That Bind: Migration and Remittances

For Tajikistan, Kyrgyzstan, and increasingly much of Uzbekistan, the most important economic relationship with Russia is not in industry, but in people. Over the course of the decade, millions of Central Asian workers have sought to take advantage of Russia's and, increasingly, Kazakhstan's economic boom by finding seasonal work in service sectors and construction.[61] In 2008, prior to the financial crisis, the remittances provided by these migrants, according to the World Bank, provided the equivalent of 49 percent of Tajikistan's GDP, 27 percent in Kyrgyzstan, and 13 percent in Uzbekistan.[62] Between 2006 and 2008 alone, the total value of remittances had more than doubled in these three countries. These inflows provided lifelines to millions of families, helped to finance these countries' trade deficits, and stocked central banks with some reserves of international currency. At the same time, the mass flight of working age men, which, in Tajikistan, the International Labor Organization (ILO) estimates at 18 percent of the total population, has emptied areas of Tajikistan and Kyrgyzstan; some maintain that this has also kept them out of Central Asian politics and kept the lid on social mobilization.[63]

Though it is commonly stated that the city of Moscow could not function without the cheap labor provided by Central Asian migrants, their working conditions are often atrocious and their legal status is fraught. Migrants suffer from widespread discrimination and make easy targets for corrupt security officials, transportation workers, and border guards to shake down.[64] Lured by promises of high wages, migrants are often tricked into taking lower paid jobs or are denied wages altogether, while they are often sold counterfeit documents by predatory middlemen. Aside from the support provided by a few overstretched NGOs and volunteer organizations, they have little, if any, legal recourse after suffering abuses.

Every year, the Russian government allots a quota of permits for guest workers that falls well short of labor demand and the number of migrants in the country; in 2010, in response to the financial crisis, the number of visa-free permits (for which Central Asian migrants qualify) was halved from 2.75 million to 1.33 million.[65] The millions who cannot acquire paperwork remain trapped in the country and are particularly vulnerable to exploitation, such as harassment and the non-payment of wages.

The presence of large amounts of undocumented workers also affords Moscow an important lever when dealing with the Central Asian governments on other issues. For example, in 2004, when Dushanbe demanded that Russia pay rent for stationing its forces and military installations, Russian negotiators reportedly threatened to send back hundreds of thousands of Tajiks who were working without documents in Russia.[66] In November 2011, following the jailing of a Russian pilot and his Estonian colleague by Tajik authorities on charges of illegal entry and smuggling, officials in Moscow rounded up over 300 Tajik migrants and began deporting them, forcing the Tajik government to overturn the verdict and free the airmen.[67] With migrants commonly outstaying their visas or not having the proper paperwork, Russia's use of Central Asian migrants as a political weapon has proven credible.

Energy Relations: Pipeline Politics and Breaking the Gazprom Monopoly

Of all its economic interests, Moscow's energy relationships with the Central Asian states have attracted the most scrutiny. Under Putin, higher world oil prices became critical to the growth of the Russian economy and served as the foundation of the Kremlin's new power base.[68] Securing access to Central Asia's energy supplies for Russian companies became the major economic interest in Moscow's emerging regional strategy, as Moscow sought entry into the mega-deals in Kazakhstan and Azerbaijan that it initially had been excluded from in the 1990s by Western companies.

In Kazakhstan, a country deeply intertwined with the Soviet-era transit infra-structure, Russian companies such as Lukoil jostled for the acquisition of new fields, while Russia tried to block the expansion of new pipelines that it could not control.[69] Russian planners were ultimately unsuccessful in their bids to pre-vent the construction of the Baku-Tbilisi-Ceyhan pipeline, opened in 2006, which was the first major oil pipeline constructed in the post-Soviet era to com-pletely bypass Russian territory; and after years of holding up the expansion of the Caspian Pipeline Consortium (CPC), meant to ship oil from the large Ten-giz project, Moscow acquiesced to expand the pipeline in 2008 after it had secured a greater stake.[70] For its part, following a typical pattern of resource na-tionalism, the Kazakh government has leveraged effectively growing external interest, especially from China, and used it to renegotiate contracts signed with the West in the early 1990s.[71] By the end of the decade, albeit with some reluc-tance, Moscow had acquiesced to Kazakhstan's policy of courting various inter-national investors and pursing different export routes, including the 1,380 mile pipeline Kazakhstan-China oil pipeline, completed in 2009, that spans Kazakh-stan to bring oil from the Caspian to the city of Alashankou on the Kazakh-Chinese border.[72]

The more controversial, and ultimately geopolitical, energy battles have been waged in the realm of natural gas, where Gazprom has become the dominant po-litical and economic actor, fusing Russian government power and strategy with a near monopoly over Soviet-era assets.[73] Unlike oil, natural gas functions not as a global market, but as a spot-to-spot transfer through fixed pipelines. Upon the collapse of the Soviet Union, Turkmenistan and Uzbekistan had ample supplies of gas, but were hemmed in by the old Central Asia–Center Soviet pipeline network, which exported Central Asian gas into Russia, via Ukraine. During the 1990s, Turkmenistan was forced to supply most of its gas to cash-strapped CIS customers, which paid low prices and often relied on barter trade. Without alternative partners, save for a 10 billion cubic meters (bcm) pipeline to Iran built in 1998, Turkmen authorities had no choice but to accept these unfavorable terms.

Under Putin, the Kremlin sought to take advantage of its pipeline geography and reorient Central Asian gas production for the benefit of supplying Gazprom. This included a Russian proposal in 2000 to form a new regional gas alliance or cartel among the Central Asian producers and Russia. Though this agreement was never formalized, over the course of the decade the Central Asian producers, especially Turkmenistan, became "top-off" suppliers to Gazprom. Russia used its monopoly power to reexport Turkmen gas, which it was buying at a low price, reselling it to its hard currency–paying European customers. Russian exports of natural gas to the critical European market rose from 129 bcm in 2002 to 184 bcm in 2008, even though Russia's overall net export volume remained relatively constant, at about 195 bcm.[74] However, Russia's actual domestic production at the time actually declined, meaning that Gazprom increasingly relied on gas purchases from Turkmenistan, Uzbekistan, and Kazakhstan to make up for its supply gap (see Figure 4.2). In an attempt to lock in Turkmen gas in 2007, Gazprom finally offered European prices to Ashgabat and spent $11.7 billion buying Central Asian gas, a massive increase in expenditure from the roughly $1 billion it had spent in 2005.[75] As the financial crisis took its toll and both prices and demand for gas plummeted, Russia in 2008–2009 was actually losing money on its resale of Central Asian gas.

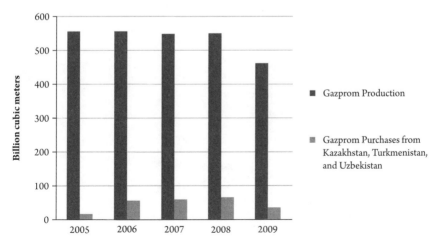

Figure 4.2 Gazprom Production and Central Asian Purchases, 2005–2009 Source: Gazprom, "Gas Purchases" and "Gas and Oil Production," http://www.gazprom.com

This peculiar and one-sided relationship also explains why, in the gas issue, Russia aggressively opposed the construction of new pipelines that could allow the Central Asian states to bypass the Russian-controlled network. For example, the construction of a Transcaspian pipeline (such as the Nabucco pipeline) would give Turkmenistan an alternate market for its production, undercutting Russia's pricing leverage. Eventually, as the next chapter shows, this is exactly what happened, though the Russian transit monopoly was broken not by the West, but by China, with the completion of a new pipeline to bring Turkmen gas eastward.

Financial Crisis, Diminishing Resources, and Russian Credibility

The onset of the global financial crisis has also eroded Russia's standing as the dominant economic player in Central Asia. As Figure 4.3 shows, until 2008 both Russian foreign direct investment and total trade with Central Asia had skyrocketed from a very low starting point in 2000. The Russian economy was one of the most severely affected by the crisis, as the collapse in energy and commodity prices blew a hole in the Russian budget. Russian GDP contracted by 8 percent and the Russian stock market tumbled by 70 percent. Moscow burned through over $100 billion of its accumulated hard currency reserves as many Russian firms and banks faced mounting external debts.[76]

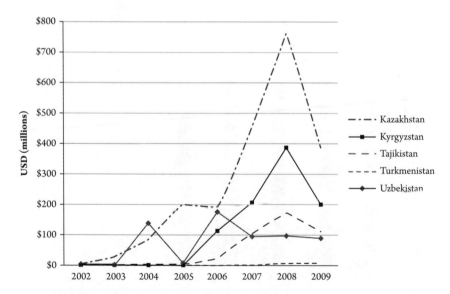

Figure 4.3 Russian Investment in Central Asia, Annual, 2002–2009 Source: Federal State Statistics Service of the Russian Federation, Russian Statistical Yearbook, 2002–2009

The crisis devastated large portions of Russia's economic activity in Central Asia. As Figure 4.3 shows, from 2008 to 2009, Russian investment in Central Asia dropped in every country, with the largest falls in Kazakhstan (-48 percent), Kyrgyzstan (-48 percent) and Tajikistan (-35 percent). Total trade also plummeted across the region, except with Turkmenistan.

Despite its own economic difficulties, Moscow still tried to play the role of a stabilizing regional hegemon by dispensing emergency loans to Belarus and Kyrgyzstan, for which it demanded political quid pro quos. In the Kyrgyz case, in February 2009, President Medvedev and President Bakiyev announced that the Russian Federation would provide a $2 billion emergency relief package to Kyrgyzstan, while the Kyrgyz president announced that he was closing the Manas base (see Chapter 7). Just a few weeks later, Bakiyev pocketed the first disbursements of the relief package, before renegotiating the stay of U.S. troops at Manas and extracting a higher rent (see Chapter 7). Russia subsequently canceled the promised foreign direct investment payment. Far from using the crisis as an opportunity to consolidate regional influence, Russia was exposed as greatly weakened in its ability to deal with even the most dependent of its post-Soviet allies.

The crisis also halted several Russian commitments to invest in large-scale energy and infrastructure projects in the region. In the spring of 2009, Tajik President Imomali Rahmon demanded that Russia finally deliver on promises it had made in 2004, as part of a bilateral basing and security accord, to provide $2 billion worth of investments in Tajik hydroelectric projects and infrastructure. Rahmon was particularly upset that the Russian company Rusal had not followed through to invest in the massive Rogun hydroelectric plant and that the Kremlin has not provided assistance for the project due to the objections of Uzbekistan, which strenuously opposes the construction plan.[77]

But nowhere was Russia's influence and credibility more diminished during the financial crisis than in its relations with Turkmenistan. When, in 2007, Russia and Turkmenistan concluded a new deal to buy and transport Turkmenistani gas, Moscow seemed to have locked the Central Asian country into its distribution network for the foreseeable future. The contract was of the "take or pay" variety, standard for long-term natural gas deals, which mandates that customers pay for agreed-upon gas shipments even if they do not receive them. Under the terms of the deal, Gazprom had agreed to purchase 70–80 bcm of gas in 2009 at European prices of $300 dollars per one thousand cubic meters.

But, as a result of the financial crisis, energy prices and global energy demand plummeted, including European demand. In spring 2009, Gazprom found itself importing a surplus of unwanted gas on which it was losing money. On April 9, 2009, an explosion ruptured the main Turkmen-Russian gas pipeline, which the Turkmen side claims was caused by Russia suddenly reducing the volume of

Turkmen gas.[78] Whether Russia deliberately intended to cause the explosion is still unclear, but Turkmenistan's gas trade with Russia was abruptly halted, and relations were plunged into crisis as Ashgabat incurred a loss of an estimated $1 billion worth of monthly revenues. A U.S. Embassy cable from the time describes Turkmen President Berdymukhamedov as "indignant," with the premiere colorfully characterizing the relationship with Gazprom as, "They robbed us for many years! They were buying our gas for forty dollars and reselling it for three hundred."[79] The sides struggled to reach new terms, doing so only in December 2009 when Turkmenistan agreed to sell 10–12 bcm to Russia in 2010, but with the inauguration of the Central Asia–China pipeline in December 2009, Ashgabat had secured a new major partner for its exports.

The Problems of Exercising Privilege: Russia's Structural Dilemmas

But setting aside the role of the West and the financial crisis, Moscow still faces three important structural impediments to its attempts to secure regional primacy: the multiple-principals problem, the difficulties of pursuing a "unite and rule" policy, and the rise of China as a regional power.

"Don't Lock Me In": Multivectorism in Pipelines and Security

Despite its efforts to craft a new set of regional institutions, Russia still faces the enduring multiple-principals problem that will undermine any attempt to act as the exclusive patron of the Central Asian states. All of the Central Asian states are committed to pursuing some variant of a multidirectional foreign policy. In terms of energy politics, this has led producers like Turkmenistan and Kazakhstan to vigorously pursue multiple partners and pipeline options, both for diversification and to increase their leverage when dealing with Moscow. But the same logic applies in the area of security; even though the Central Asian states may sign up to join regional organizations or other institutional arrangements controlled by Moscow, they will always seek alternative partners as a strategic hedge and to provide some protection from and leverage with Moscow.

Despite Russian efforts to formally institutionalize greater military integration through the CSTO and to conclude further bilateral deals, all of the Central Asian states continue to actively play Russia off other regional powers and security partners in order to secure their own position and to extract benefits. Thus, within a three-year span between 2008 and 2011, we saw Tajikistan actively approach Washington and NATO with offers to cooperate on flyover rights and possible basing access, and Kyrgyzstan, under Bakiyev, initiate a bidding war over the

Manas base after he had promised Moscow that he would close the base. Even Uzbekistan, heavily touted by Russian commentators in 2005 and 2006 as a successful case of pro-Moscow realignment, tacked heavily back into the Western camp. By 2011 Uzbekistan had become the hub of U.S.-led logistics and resupply efforts for Afghanistan and continued to provide basing rights at the Termez airfield for German and authorized NATO forces. By the end of the decade, all of the Central Asian militaries were cooperating in some form with the United States, despite the deepening of security ties via the CSTO (and SCO).

"Unite and Rule" versus "Divide and Rule"

Moscow's regional political moves also run the risk of involving Russia in local conflicts and disputes, forcing it to juggle its backing of various parties in its bid to preserve primacy. For example, in the politically thorny issue of regional water management, Russia must carefully toe the line between reassuring the region's most significant power and water consumer, Uzbekistan, and safeguarding its own hydroelectric investments in the upstream producers of Kyrgyzstan and Tajikistan. The dam-construction issue is particularly sensitive for Uzbekistan, which fears that it could lose access to the water resources it requires for its large-scale irrigation and cotton cultivation. Uzbekistan is particularly incensed at Tajikistan's plans to construct the Rogun dam project and has been preventing trains carrying materials for Rogun construction from entering Tajikistan via the Uzbek border.[80]

On a visit to Uzbekistan in January 2009, President Medvedev publicly stated that Russian investments in major hydroelectric power stations in neighboring Kyrgyzstan and Tajikistan would only go ahead once the interests of all states in the region on the water issue had been adequately addressed.[81] The Russian president's remarks were greeted with alarm in Bishkek and Dushanbe, as they seemed to signal a shift away from Russia's previous position of unequivocally supporting the construction of hydroelectric power projects in these upstream countries. Just a few months, in the fall of 2008, before Uzbekistan had withdrawn from EurAsEC in protest over a deal reached by Kazakhstan, Kyrgyzstan, and Tajikistan to provide reciprocal supplies of coal, oil, and water. To be sure, Russia sees itself as playing a constructive role and even brokering a future regional solution to the water management dispute. In practice, however, tensions over the water issue are escalating, as the upstream and downstream countries now view the issue in stark zero-sum terms and there are no signs that the parties would accept Russian arbitration (or that of any other third party).

Similarly, Russia has consistently faced a political backlash from Uzbekistan whenever it has proposed to establish a second military base in southern Kyrgyzstan or to expand the operational role of the CSTO. For example, in the wake of the Manas "bidding war" of 2009, Moscow did not consult with Tashkent before securing a pledge from Kyrgyzstan to open a second base. Uzbekistan complained that it had not been consulted on the decision and warned that it could not accept a foreign military presence in southern Kyrgyzstan, especially a force that might potentially intervene in any regional resource disputes.[82]

Moscow's "unite and rule" problem could potentially be overcome if Russia adopted a more traditional patron-client relationship of "divide-and-rule" with selected states in the region, backing their local agendas in exchange for monopolizing their security or foreign policy.[83] In Central Asia, this would probably mean siding with Tajikistan and Kyrgyzstan in its water disputes against Uzbekistan, and placing military facilities in these countries that Tashkent would view as threatening. Such a move would push Uzbekistan further into the Western orbit, but, as some Russian security analysts now advocate, Tashkent's exclusion would yield greater policy consensus in CSTO decision making.[84]

Beijing Rising, West Receding?

Finally, Russia's quest for primacy in Central Asia now faces its most significant geopolitical challenge since independence. However, this competition comes not from the West, with which Russia has been so preoccupied, but from the East. For much of the decade, Russia has pursued a strategic partnership with China in what has aptly been described as an "axis of convenience."[85] Moscow's most robust support for the Shanghai Cooperation Organization came in the mid-2000s, when it was aggressively trying to check Western influence in Central Asia. Around 2005, Moscow and Beijing could jointly protest the "unilateralism" of the United States, question the long-term presence of U.S. bases in the region, and call for the "democratization of international relations."

Despite much alarm over the new potential Russia-China strategic partnership, Beijing has shown little appetite for becoming a global revisionist power and has gone about achieving its strategic goals in Central Asia with remarkable focus. After 2005, the height of counter-Western cooperation in response to the Color Revolutions, Russia and China have diverged on important policy questions, such as Moscow's recognition of the independence of Georgian breakaway territories of Abkhazia and South Ossetia. Since 2006, Moscow also has halted the sales of new generations of aircraft and weapons systems to Beijing, apparently out of concern that prized hardware, such as the Sukhoi Su 27, were being reverse-engineered.[86] Earlier in the decade, Russia had accounted for up to 90 percent of Chinese arms imports.

Relations between the Russian-led CSTO and the Chinese-led SCO remain uncertain and potentially competitive. Though the organizations are said to coordinate at the Secretariat level, they have not reached a clear division of labor, nor have they followed through on earlier announcements to implement joint programs.[87] The higher global profile and prestige of the SCO as a regional security organization clearly frustrate Russian policymakers, who argue that the CSTO is more advanced in its institutional functions and operational capacity than the Beijing-based organization. Russia continues to insist that the West should engage with the CSTO as the region's most relevant security organization, something that the West consistently has refused to do, either in Central Asia or over Afghanistan. With such differences in their international prestige, the organizations risk getting drawn into "covert and dangerous competition," at least from Moscow's perspective.[88]

Moreover, the sheer relative economic potential revealed by China's rise is causing alarm in Russia. While the financial crisis forced Russia to retrench from its regional economic commitments, it empowered China to expand its Central Asian activities and conclude similar loans for equity shares in the Turkmen and Kazakh energy sectors that it has used elsewhere in the world. For the first time since independence, China's total trade volume in 2008 with Central Asia passed Russia's (see Chapter 5, Figure 5.1); factoring in the border shuttle trade, this number is probably significantly higher. Beijing is also offering aid and investment packages to all of the Central Asian states and seems intent to open a host of new regional road and railway transit corridors that bypass Russia altogether. Some analysts even interpret Moscow's plans for the Eurasian Union as an attempt to balance against this accelerating Chinese regional activity.[89]

Yet, bound by their SCO membership and the rhetoric of strategic partnership, Russian officials have rarely voiced concerns about China's ascendancy in public. As Stephen Kotkin of Princeton University has suggested, by acquiescing to China's rise in Central Asia in its attempt to balance against Western influence, Russia has sanctioned China's newly elevated regional role and now even risks becoming Beijing's "junior partner."[90] Consistent with Kotkin's observation, it has become a standard script for Chinese officials, from Beijing to Dushanbe, to preface their comments about Central Asia by underscoring that the region remains "Russia's special zone of influence." But rhetorical flourishes aside, in practice Beijing rarely has made any compromises to its security or economic agenda to curry favor with Moscow.

Conclusion: Influence to What End?

Russia's Central Asian resurgence is neither an attempt to resurrect Soviet ties, nor is it a typical post-colonial engagement with a former periphery, such as France's role in post-colonial West Africa. Rather, Moscow has channeled its many instruments of leverage into forging a new set of regional institutions, the

CSTO and the Customs Union, which will provide it the legal framework to reassert its regional primacy. These regional organizations both emulate and compete with more established Western counterparts, such as NATO and the EU.

Russia's policies toward Central Asia have reflected a variety of goals, but have been motivated by its desire to establish a position of regional privilege or dominant influence. Accordingly, Russia's broader bilateral relations with the great powers, especially the United States and, increasingly, China, have been important drivers in the formulation of Moscow's Central Asian policies and tactical shifts. Periods of bilateral cooperation with the United States have translated into better regional relations, whereas the deterioration of U.S.-Russian relations from 2003 to 2008 was also reflected in perceptions of more intensified geopolitical competition in Central Asia.

The "reset" of Russia-U.S. relations initiated by the Obama administration in 2009 appears to have dampened some of this more competitive rhetoric and geopolitical maneuvering in the region. Though U.S.-Russian relations have not returned to the closeness, or the single-issue focus on terrorism that followed 9/11, they have improved, as Moscow has agreed to support the operations of the Manas airbase, has opened new air corridors, and has expanded its participation in the NDN. On April 13, 2011, at a Russian Duma hearing on Central Asia, Russian Deputy Foreign Minister Grigory Karasin declared that "Russia does not claim an exclusive role in Central Asia and it is open for cooperation," adding that "Russia cooperates with the West in that region, minding mutual interests."[91] Such a statement would have been unthinkable in 2005 or 2006, at the height of Russia's regional security dilemma.

But Russia's hand has also been forced. The rise of China's economic power, NATO's increasing cooperation with the Central Asian countries, and the impact of the global financial crisis would not prove themselves insurmountable obstacles if Moscow wanted to impose "undisputed" hegemony in the region. Some liberal Russian analysts talk of the need to abandon its fixation on Central Asia altogether, viewing Moscow's interest in the region as antithetical to a modernization agenda and more contemporary foreign policy sensibility. However, this is unlikely to materialize, precisely because Russian officials believe that by maintaining regional primacy, Moscow will be afforded its coveted "Great Power" status and a seat in future international decision making in other issues and areas.

Despite Moscow's formidable array of hard and soft power instruments in the region, its own future success in Central Asia will depend on designing a new strategy that is more realistic, refined, and forward-looking. Ultimately, Moscow will have to give up the aspiration that it can automatically represent the Central Asian countries in the international arena and must formulate a positive agenda for the region, one that is not constantly reacting to Western or Chinese initiatives.

If Moscow chooses to promote and deepen institutions like the CSTO and Customs Union, but allows Central Asian states to also foster other external partnerships, Russia will surely be publicly acknowledged as the dominant regional player for many more years to come. This may well satisfy Moscow's desire to maintain prestige and status. On the other hand, if Moscow, in an open-ended quest for regional dominance, seeks to use its new institutions to lock-in Central Asian states into a new "Eurasian Union" or otherwise press them to exclusively align themselves on economic, energy, or security matters, it risks suffering more embarrassing public rebuffs, which will only further erode its own regional prestige and credibility.

|| 5 ||

The SCO and Beijing's Great Leap Westward

Russia's strongest competitor for regional influence lies not to its west, but to its east. China's increasing sway in Central Asia is nothing short of remarkable, though it is less frequently commented on than the U.S.-Russia regional "Great Game" dynamics. Like the United States, China has engaged with Central Asia with the primary aim of stabilizing an adjacent region—China's own Western province of Xinjiang. Beijing has sought to clamp down on the activities of Uighur groups, enlist regional cooperation for its security agenda, and promote economic links as a means of spurring regional economic development.

From this strategic starting point, China's engagement with Central Asia swiftly has expanded and deepened, with Beijing proving itself the most nuanced and skilled of the great three powers in its regional diplomacy; over the course of a decade, Beijing successfully transformed an area that it considered at the start of the 2000s to comprise weakly governed states, lingering border disputes, economic underdevelopment, and uncontrolled transnational threats into a region of strategic partnership.[1] At the same time, Beijing has tailored its engagement to each of the Central Asian countries. Thus, in Kyrgyzstan, the only fellow WTO member in Central Asia, China has established a major trade and reexport hub to the rest of the region, while in Tajikistan, Beijing has focused on upgrading electricity transmission and distribution and improving direct road links. In Kazakhstan and Turkmenistan, the region's most important hydrocarbon producers, China has carefully and deliberately cultivated partnerships and has built major new pipelines that will provide oil and gas to the Chinese market for many decades.

As in other parts of the developing world, China has sought to convince the Central Asian states that it seeks "win-win solutions," a "harmonious region of peace and prosperity," and non-interference in their domestic affairs, while it has tirelessly sought to reassure Russia that it harbors no regional hegemonic ambitions and continues to recognize Moscow's claim to be the region's privileged power. But upon closer examination, China has also countered both Washington and Moscow when its interests did not align on important security and economic matters.[2]

China's main vehicle for achieving these regional goals has been a new regional multilateral organization that it has founded and promoted. The Shanghai Cooperation Organization (SCO) emerged in 2001 as the successor to the Shanghai Five, a forum that had facilitated negotiations among Russia, the Central Asian states, and China over delimiting disputed Sino-Soviet borders. Over its first decade, the SCO was composed of six members—China, Russia, Kazakhstan, Kyrgyzstan, Tajikistan, and Uzbekistan—but Beijing's agenda, resources, and diplomatic energy have been the driving force behind its evolution. Originally established as a forum for fostering security cooperation with its Central Asian neighbors on Xinjiang-related issues, the organization has also launched a number of non-security initiatives in the areas of economic cooperation, development and project financing, education, and youth development. As we will see, however, these have proven less successful, both because of other member states' concerns with China's relative economic power and because "local rules" have checked many of Beijing's more ambitious economic plans.

China's use of the SCO as its primary instrument of regional influence and engagement offers important insights into the broader question of China's growing role in world affairs. Over the last few years, scholars have debated whether China is challenging the contemporary Western-led global order or is "playing by the rules" established by the West.[3] The SCO is an important case for this debate, perhaps even a forward-looking indicator, as it is not an existing international body, but rather was founded by Beijing to promote its security and economic interests in an adjacent region. It is one of China's most ambitious contributions to global governance, embodying a "new international relations" that rejects U.S. unilateralism and, according to its official mission statement, promotes cooperation based on principles of sovereign non-interference and cultural diversity.[4] Accordingly, the success of the SCO, how the organization is treated by its other member countries, and how it interacts with other multilateral organizations and external actors operating in the region are also important indicators of the current scope and depth of China's growing global power and influence.

China's Emerging View of Central Asia and the SCO

Stabilizing Its West: Xinjiang and the Role of Central Asia

Initially, China's engagement with Central Asia was primarily driven by an internal concern: securing its territorial integrity and stabilizing its Xinjiang Uighur Autonomous Region, which borders Kazakhstan, Kyrgyzstan, and Tajikistan.

The multiethnic region, home to the Uighurs but also to 55 other recognized ethnicities (including all the major Central Asian groups), remains China's largest administrative division with an unsettled history.[5] During the interwar years, the territory rebelled from the Republic of China and bounced between regional powers; the short-lived independent Islamic state known as the East Turkestan Republic was mostly absorbed by China in 1934, while the northern area became a de facto Soviet satellite from 1945–1949 as the Second East Turkestan Republic, before it too was brought under Chinese Communist control. Since, Beijing has ruled Xinjiang as an integral part of China, though its ethnic diversity, Islamic establishment, and comparatively low level of development have greatly complicated central attempts to maintain control. The region was the site of regular violent clashes during the Cultural Revolution and a renewed campaign of ethnic and religious violence in the 1990s.

In its efforts to develop and assimilate the region and its inhabitants, Beijing promotes the official doctrine of the "three inseparable ties," stressing that, "the Han Chinese cannot live without the minority groups, that the minority groups cannot live without the Han Chinese, and [that] no one minority group can live without the other minority groups."[6] Much like the Soviet Union's policy of modernization and nationalities, Chinese policy toward the Uighurs has assumed that promoting rapid development and contacts with the center will eventually change local ethnic and cultural identifications. Yet, despite state building, massive economic subsidies and investment, educational "affirmative action" and new bilingual policies, population transfers and careful monitoring of regional administrators, much of the region's population has resisted assimilation Beijing's efforts.[7] Most notably, the influx of Han, who in the 2000 census had reached 40 percent of region's population, has exacerbated ethnic tensions, as the Han have assumed prominent political and economic roles and now dominate large cities such as Urumqi, while Beijing's drive to develop Xinjiang's considerable natural resources (minerals, oil, gas and water) have also been viewed as exploitative by Uighur nationalists.

For its part, Beijing has never hesitated to use force in the area, targeting a number of Uighur organizations with either nationalist or actual separatist platforms. In 1998, Chinese authorities initiated the "strike hard" campaign, which sought to clamp down decisively on the activities of Uighur movements and their supporters. According to the Chinese government's figures, over the 1990s "East Turkestan Terrorist Forces"—which include the East Turkestan Islamic Movement (ETIM), the East Turkestan Liberation Organization (ETLO), and the Uighur Liberation Organization (ULO), among others—instigated over 200 "bombings and assassinations" that killed 164 people and wounded 440 people.[8] Some Western scholars remain skeptical as to whether Uighur organizations such as the ETIM or the ETLO actually demonstrated the kind of coordinated campaign and threatening capacity attributed to them by Beijing, especially given that violent incidents within Xinjiang appeared to have tapered off after 1997.[9] But a series of political assassinations involving Uighurs in Kyrgyzstan in 1999 and 2000, some inter-communal and others targeting Chinese officials, elevated regional awareness of the issue and pushed Chinese officials to demand better security cooperation and the formalization of these ties.[10] The Chinese domestic security imperative of combating the "three evils"—terrorism, separatism, and extremism—would be directly transplanted into the founding language of the SCO Charter as its guiding principle of security cooperation.

In the economic sphere, developing Xinjiang is viewed as the key to fostering stability and countering the power of separatist appeals. Beijing's so-called Great Western Development Project (2000), or the "Go West" campaign, was designed to promote the impoverished province's modernization, industrialization, and economic development in a bid to reduce socioeconomic disparities between West and East.[11] As a bordering region, Central Asia has become a crucial component of this strategic economic planning. With the necessary economic development, infrastructure upgrades, and legal environment (especially reducing corruption), the region could potentially provide a critical economic partner for Xinjiang and, over the long run, a direct portal for the Western province to the outside world. Tellingly, according to World Bank researchers, about one-third of China's growing trade with Central Asia is actively managed by the large state-run Xinjiang Production and Construction Corps, while barter and unofficial cross-border shuttle trade account for the other two-thirds.[12] The latter was formerly controlled by the Uighur population and diaspora, but over the last 15 years, following the reopening of the border, it has increasingly been taken over by Han.[13]

The Emergence of the Shanghai Cooperation Organization

The Shanghai Cooperation Organization has provided an ideal vehicle to accomplish all of these goals. From its founding, the SCO has emphasized two principles that distinguish it from Western-dominated multilateral organizations. First, as has become an axiom in China's foreign policy, the SCO charter and public statements repeatedly underscore that it respects its members' sovereignty and rejects interference in their domestic affairs.[14] This can be contrasted with the economic conditionality imposed by Western donors (World Bank, IMF), the human rights criteria or political conditions of Western-led security organizations (NATO, OSCE human dimension), and the growth of the "responsibility to protect" norm, used to justify NATO's military actions in Kosovo and Libya, which sanctions external intervention on humanitarian grounds. Second, the organization's official documents are littered with references to rejecting "unilateral military solutions," a clear reference to the United States, and promoting the "democratization of international relations," multipolarity, and a new "cooperative spirit." Some Western commentators have interpreted the repeated references to the "Shanghai Spirit" as intentionally opposing the West or embodying authoritarian norms.[15]

Organizationally, the SCO's permanent bureaucracy is headquartered in Beijing, not Shanghai, and its Secretary General is appointed for a three-year term, rotating through the member states. Councils of the member states' heads of state and heads of government hold annual summits, while meetings of functional ministries target specific issues for cooperation. SCO national coordinators are tasked with domestically coordinating meetings and ensuring that SCO decisions are transmitted and implemented by the relevant national agencies and state organs. Distinct from these Secretariat-governed institutions is the Regional Anti-Terrorism Structure (RATS), which, since 2004, has been based in Tashkent and acts as a center for security cooperation, information pooling, and exchange and monitoring of the SCO's Anti-Terrorism Treaty. Typically, officials at RATS report directly to their respective ministries of Internal Security or Defense, not the Secretariat in Beijing.

Preference for Multilateralism, but De Facto Bilateralism

The public emphasis on multilateralism and regional harmony means that the SCO has not yet adopted a "problem-solving" or technocratic apparatus. Instead, the organization relies on intergovernmental ties and the operating principle of consensus, which Chinese officials view as critical to building the trust and "regional harmony" that they perceive to be the prerequisite for promoting closer regional integration in the future. But at the same time, the emphasis on consensus means that the forum has not been an effective vehicle for tackling problems or seemingly intractable regional disputes, such as the sensitive water management issue. In terms of membership, the original six countries remain the only full SCO members, while India, Pakistan, Iran, and Mongolia have observer status.[16] In 2010, Beijing sought to institutionalize the rules and principles for admitting new members, which included a clause that applicants not be under UN sanctions, a clear indication that Iran would be excluded from membership.

Western scholars have noted for some time that Beijing has demonstrated a willingness to play by international rules and even to be socialized into accepting the security norms embodied in major international treaties and regimes.[17] But the SCO seems to take this issue further, as it is China's attempt to establish, from scratch, a new organization that is neither controlled by nor beholden to Western interests and inputs.

The result is that Beijing has a considerable and growing stake in the international success of the organization, which, in turn, leads it to play up its accomplishments as a multilateral forum. As a result, even in cases in which the SCO as an organization has not advanced a common policy or adopted Beijing's proposals, China has continued to refer to its bilateral engagements with the Central Asian states as "SCO" projects or initiatives.[18] Such labeling causes confusion among regional observers and analysts, who often attribute Chinese accomplishments to the SCO's regional mechanisms. Finally, China's interests in a successful SCO have led the organization to prioritize securing recognition and partnership from other international organizations and multilateral institutions.[19]

Defining a Regional Security Agenda: The Changing Politics of the SCO

Over its first decade, the SCO has been most effective in the area of security cooperation, especially internal security. Member countries have successfully concluded and ratified a security treaty, established an anti-terrorism center and forum, and coordinated their efforts to combat transnational threats in the region.[20] Beyond dealing with such irregular regional threats, however, gaps have emerged in the broader security priorities of Russia and China, while the pressing question of securing Afghanistan has not yielded a robust or even a coherent policy response among SCO members.

Border Arrangements and the Shanghai Five

The SCO's predecessor, the Shanghai Five, was used by Russia, China, Kazakhstan, Kyrgyzstan, and Tajikistan from 1996 to 2001 as a forum for resolving disputes and demilitarizing borders. Such was the momentum and good spirit of the negotiations, the official history goes, that in 2000 the forum began discussing other security issues, such as cooperating to counter the transnational security threats of regional terrorists, separatists, and extremist groups. Soon after, the forum grew into a fully blown international organization, rapidly expanding its portfolio to include a number of security and non-security areas.[21] In reality, Chinese security services had already been cooperating with their Central Asian counterparts on apprehending and extraditing Uighur suspects in the late 1990s, but the 2001 SCO Charter formalized these activities.

Despite their formal resolution by these regional forums, border issues remain a sensitive issue within the Central Asia states. Notwithstanding Taylor Fravel's research that shows that China made significant territorial concessions in Central Asia in order to secure its territorial integrity, the popular view in

Central Asia is much different.[22] Across Kazakhstan, Kyrgyzstan, and Tajikistan, rumors and conspiracy theories abound that accuse local elites involved in border negotiations of being somehow corrupted or bought off by Beijing. In 2002, the Kyrgyz parliament, led by nationalist factions, initially refused to ratify the just concluded Kyrgyz-Chinese border agreement.

The "anti-China" card was also played quite heavily in 2005 by acting president and presidential candidate Kurmanbek Bakiyev to shore up his nationalist credentials. Bakiyev criticized Akayev and his foreign policy team for having sold out Kyrgyz sovereignty to Beijing. Interestingly, observers of China in Kyrgyzstan claim that, following his election, the Chinese Embassy put great pressure on Bakiyev to retract the criticism and to publicly reaffirm his commitment to China's territorial integrity and bilateral agreements.[23] The Kyrgyz president did so in November 2005 and was reportedly awarded a Presidential Summit in Beijing in June 2006, where the two heads of state reaffirmed these cooperative principles.[24]

Nevertheless, the perception that the SCO was a critically important actor in resolving border agreements remains at the foundational core of the organization and its official history. But, as a Central Asian borders expert cautions, "It would not be accurate to ascribe the cooperation in [border] security to the SCO. The SCO has certainly facilitated multilateral summits and bilateral talks on issues of border security, but it is not the cause of such cooperation. Initial talks and agreements between Kyrgyzstan and China predate the SCO as well as its predecessor, the Shanghai Five."[25] This "credit attribution" of bilateral agreements to the SCO has been a recurring theme in the organization's public image and self-promotion.

9/11, Counterterrorism, and the U.S. Military Presence

The regional U.S.-led Global War on Terror (GWOT) that followed the attacks of September 11, 2001, had two contrasting impacts upon Chinese policy thinking about Central Asia and the SCO's development. On the one hand, the U.S. campaign provided an opening for Beijing to escalate its security operations against separatists (or "splittists") in Xinjiang. By conflating the agenda of nationalist and separatist Uighur groups, such as the East Turkestan Islamic Movement (ETIM), with radical Islamic organizations, Beijing used the new norms and parameters of GWOT to frame its Xinjiang campaign.[26] Two months after 9/11, Chinese officials declared that "at least hundreds" of East Turkestan members had received training in Afghanistan.[27] Then, in a now often-cited January 2002 press release on "East Turkistan Forces," the Information Office of the State Council for the first time publicly acknowledged the extent of anti-state activity in the region and proclaimed that Osama Bin Laden and the Al-Qaeda network in South Asia supported the groups.[28]

Later in 2002, the United Nations, supported by the United States, placed the East Turkestan Islamic Movement on its list of terrorist organizations, while in September 2002 the U.S. Treasury placed the group on its blacklist of terrorist organizations. Beijing and Washington also expanded their working groups and senior-level dialogues on South Asia and cooperated on intelligence sharing, while the U.S. Federal Bureau of Investigations was allowed to open an office in China.[29] Within a few months, the issue of Uighur separatism was reframed from a local sovereign affair within China to a frontline in the new global war on terror.[30]

At the same time, the very entry of the U.S. military into the Central Asian theater also raised alarm throughout Chinese foreign and defense policy circles, especially after Russia initially endorsed the new U.S. basing presence. China feared that the American presence could become permanent, thereby adding to the array of US bases in Asia that encircle China, and that such a beachhead could be used to choke off Chinese energy supplies, conduct surveillance operations in Western China, and even provide a springboard for the U.S. government or its allies to destabilize Xinjiang.[31] Moreover, as in Moscow, Beijing viewed the establishment of military bases in Central Asia as part of a dangerous broader "unilateralist" turn in U.S. security policy under the Bush administration, something explicitly flagged by and opposed in China's New Security Concept from the same time.[32]

The U.S. military's entry into Central Asia also generated a greater sense of urgency for Beijing to institutionalize the SCO. Just a few months earlier, in June 2001, the SCO had been formally inaugurated on the fifth anniversary of the Shanghai Five, with Uzbekistan being admitted as a full member in the new organization. Rebecca Nadin has carefully documented how the SCO's initial tepid response to 9/11, compared with the United States' aggressive post–9/11 regional security cooperation, greatly alarmed Beijing, as it sought to rescue the organization from the brink of an early extinction.[33] In the first half of 2002, Chinese diplomats energetically scheduled a number of SCO coordination meetings and summits, covering the topics of Afghanistan, border guards, counterterrorism, and cultural and economic ties. At the pivotal June 2002 annual summit in Saint Petersburg, the members signed an agreement establishing the SCO regional antiterrorism structure (RATS) as well as the foundational SCO Charter. Instructively, Article 2 of the Charter both affirmed members' state sovereignty and the principle of non-interference in each other's internal affairs, rejecting any regional "unilateral superiority" in military affairs.[34]

The Color Revolutions and Chinese Alarm

U.S. defense policymakers viewed the growth of the organization with some distrust, but it was not until 2005 that the SCO was thrust onto the Washington's agenda for the first time as a potential challenger to U.S. and Western military operations in the region. The Color Revolutions, particularly the so-called Tulip Revolution of March 2005 that ousted long-standing Kyrgyz President Askar Akayev, caused great concern in China, albeit for slightly different reasons from those of Moscow. While Russia was convinced that these regime changes were directed against Moscow and were intended to bring to power pro-Western governments, China was concerned that such democratizing forces might spill over and destabilize its Western province of Xinjiang, as well as potentially empowering political dissidents and subversive groups in the rest of China.[35] Chinese scholars and think tanks devoted extraordinary attention to the political upheavals, focusing on issues such as economic inequality and poverty, the incendiary role of the Western media, electoral opportunism among opposition parties and, as in Russia, the undue influence of Western-backed NGOs.[36] Beijing also dispatched Chinese research teams composed of scholars and analysts to the sites of these revolutions to assess the causes and their potential to be replicated.[37] As in Russia, these events refracted back onto domestic policy, as Chinese officials introduced new regulations restricting the activities of domestic NGOs and the media.

By the summer of 2005, the onset of the Color Revolutions, regional fears of regime change, and the United States' increasingly vocal "freedom agenda" all contributed to an air of intense geopolitical competition and concern about U.S.-sponsored democratization. Chinese and Russian fears and countermeasures were also embedded in official SCO documents, policies, and proclamations.

These factors converged in the run-up to the July 2005 SCO summit in Astana and Uzbekistan's eviction of U.S. forces shortly after (see Chapter 3). Some U.S. officials, most notably Secretary of Defense Donald Rumsfeld, attributed the eviction from K2 to pressure brought by China and Russia on Uzbekistan through the SCO. The Astana episode also led to open speculation that the security organization was now evolving into an anti-NATO military bloc.[38] The biannual joint military exercises (or "Peace Missions"), conducted by China and Russia since 2003, also raised fears that the SCO would develop an advanced operational capability.[39] In academic circles, the SCO's Astana statement was pointed to as an example of emerging "soft-balancing" or "actions that do not directly challenge U.S. military preponderance but that use nonmilitary tools to delay, frustrate and undermine aggressive unilateral U.S. policies."[40] Central Asia was perceived as a front line in the geopolitical push-back against the Bush administration's unilateralism.

The Astana declaration on U.S. bases, while supported by China, was brought forward by Karimov and was endorsed by Russian President Putin—it did not originate in Beijing. All SCO members at the time feared growing regional instability and Western-sponsored interference. But Eurasian governments soon learned the Color Revolutions "playbook" and adopted successful countermeasures to ensure that the model of "election day" regime change would not be successfully used again.[41] As it turned out, the 2005 Astana declaration marked the peak of Sino-Russian security concerns and cooperative backlash against the West, not the beginning of an anti-U.S. alliance.[42]

Beijing and Moscow Split over "Splittism": Georgia and Urumqi Compared

Just three years later, the differences between Chinese and Russian regional security imperatives would be revealed in the aftermath of the Russia-Georgia War. In August 2008 the SCO's self-defined security goal to combat the "three evils" of terrorism, separatism, and extremism came into direct conflict with Russia's attempts to splinter Georgia and to recognize the independence of the breakaway territories of Abkhazia and South Ossetia.[43] Just a few days after President Dmitry Medvedev recognized the two territories, the Russian premier headed to Dushanbe for the 2008 annual SCO summit to secure support for the Russian position. It is still unclear how much backing Moscow believed it could obtain from the SCO states, but some Russian analysts and commentators suggest that Medvedev was fairly confident that he could secure Kazakhstan and Kyrgyzstan's recognition of Abkhazian and South Ossetian independence.[44] Instead, the Central Asian states, backed by Beijing, held firm and reaffirmed their commitment to preserving the sovereignty and territorial integrity of states. Though internally the Central Asian states all agreed that recognizing these territories ran contrary to their own national interests and concerns over territorial integrity, China's firm stance on the issue gave them some political cover to rebuff Moscow.[45]

China's refusal to accommodate Russia's recognition of the Georgian breakaway territories can be instructively contrasted with the SCO's immediate and strong support for China in the aftermath of the July 2009 ethnic violence that erupted between ethnic Uighurs and Han in Urumqi, the capital of Xinjiang. Immediately following the rioting, the Chinese Ministry of Foreign Affairs drafted a strong SCO statement that characterized the riots as "purely China's internal affair" and that supported Beijing's actions designed to "restore order in the region." Within just a few hours, all SCO countries signed on to the communiqué, and an official declaration was issued.[46] The episode's contrast with the Dushanbe summit also illustrates that China has been more successful than Russia in using the SCO to promote its regional security agenda.

The Question of Afghanistan and U.S. Withdrawal

Perhaps the most intriguing issue on the SCO's security agenda is whether it could play a more active role in stabilizing Afghanistan, either independently or in cooperation with the United States and NATO. From a distance, it appears that SCO members and the West both have a common interest in defeating the Taliban and ensuring the stability of Afghanistan. SCO summits on Afghanistan have been critical of both U.S. goals and strategies and have provided a forum for member states to emphasize the importance of a "regional solution." In November 2005, the organization created the SCO-Afghanistan contact group; one initiative, following the 2007 summit in Moscow, explored establishing an SCO-sponsored forum for promoting national reconciliation and dialogue, modeled on the Tajikistan peace process of the 1990s.[47]

Yet, as even SCO officials admit, the lack of consensus within SCO members about their own individual policies on Afghanistan has prevented the organization from developing a more robust or coherent set of proposals.[48] For example, since 2008, Russia has insisted that the CSTO, not the SCO, should be NATO's regional partner in the region, while the Central Asian states, with the exception of Uzbekistan, have balked at escalating their visible role in Afghanistan. Even in China, there are reportedly differences between officials in the Ministry of Foreign Affairs, who are more supportive of cooperating with international efforts, and the People's Liberation Army and security services, who favor maintaining China's more hands-off policy. The lack of consensus on Afghanistan means, in practice, that the organization's projects in Afghanistan are limited to narcotics interdiction, a consensus issue, though even here the credibility of the Central Asian states' commitment to the cause is in doubt.[49]

Moreover, though the United States and China both want a stable Afghanistan, their strategies on how to ensure regional stability diverge. Chinese doubts about the capacity of the United States to reconstruct Afghanistan and to oppose Taliban-supported Pashtun factions has led Beijing to adopt more of a hedging strategy.[50] China's deep and extensive relations with Pakistan's security services and intelligence agencies, which have covertly assisted the insurgency, also give Beijing an additional instrument of engagement. As a result, providing indirect pay-offs to areas and actors that might be allied with the Taliban is viewed as a more effective guarantee of China's investments and interests in the region, rather than exclusively supporting the Western-backed regime in Kabul.[51] Beijing fears that more active involvement in Afghanistan would actually destabilize its efforts in Xinjiang and could possibly attract undue attention to Chinese internal policies. The July 2009 Urumqi riots seemed to have convinced regional analysts and policymakers not only that stability in the province remains tenuous, but that more publicly active involvement by China in Afghanistan in support of U.S. operations could boomerang back on it.[52]

Yet U.S. officials, especially those in the Obama administration, have persistently tried to nudge Beijing toward playing a more active role, such as providing more money for Afghan reconstruction, sending peacekeeping troops or re-construction teams, and either contributing to the NDN or opening other logistical routes, possibly through the Wakan corridor, to supply NATO forces in the region. The latter requests were initially met with strict Chinese conditions, including that all transported goods should be non-lethal, should be made by Chinese companies, and, specifically, should be made in Xinji-ang.[53] In September 2011, the Chinese side did offer a more modest set of proposals in the areas of training diplomats, health care, and agriculture, sug-gesting that there might be room for some complementary, if not cooperative initiatives.

But as Beijing refocuses on its strategy to plan for the 2014 U.S. withdrawal, it faces a number of regional constraints that prevent it from taking a truly active regional role. Deteriorating U.S.-Pakistan relations have made Beijing cautious about being drawn into a proxy conflict in the subcontinent, while U.S.-Chinese relations themselves have the potential to be strained by a number of other is-sues, such as confrontations over East Asian security matters. Regionally, it is unclear why Central Asia's bordering states would be more amenable to an intensive SCO-driven Afghan engagement than similar U.S. regional proposals, while Moscow is unlikely to allow the SCO to develop a more high-profile role than the CSTO post-2014. Thus, despite public affirmations about the impor-tance of Afghanistan's stability and successful state-building, it seems unlikely that China, either bilaterally or through the SCO, will play a leading role in Afghanistan, even after the looming U.S. withdrawal.

The Economic Realm: China as a Provider of Regional Public Goods?

In contrast with China's skilful use of the SCO to promote its internal security priorities in Central Asia, Beijing has been less successful in developing its non-security agenda in the organization, especially in the areas of economic coopera-tion. According to Zhao Huasheng, a leading Chinese scholar of Central Asia, Chinese planners envisage a sequenced plan of economic engagement, beginning with providing investment and financing for infrastructure projects in Central Asia and eventually expanding into broader areas of trade and economic cooperation with a multilateral legal and regulatory framework.[54] Beijing's ultimate goal, reaf-firmed in a speech by Premiere Wen Jiabao in 2007, is to create a free-trade zone in the region. Such a zone would both facilitate Xinjiang's development by connect-ing it with the outside world, and, in the view of Chinese officials, politically stabi-lize the poorer parts of Central Asia by fostering economic development and reducing poverty.

China's Growing Regional Economic Activity

Despite a lack of progress on the SCO's economic agenda, China has expanded its bilateral economic activities in Central Asia over the last decade in remarkable fashion. As Figure 5.1 demonstrates, China's trade with the region has exploded over the last 10 years, and, during the financial crisis of 2008, it surpassed even Russia to become Central Asia's greatest trading partner. In actual terms, China's trading volume is significantly higher, as Central Asian customs officials tend to underreport, often by several multiples, their trade with China (see Chapter 9), especially the growing shuttle trade between the regions.[55] The figures for China's near-exponential growth in trade with Kyrgyzstan, a bordering country and fellow member of the WTO, have been most striking (see Figure 5.2), as the small Central Asian country appears to have become a hub for the reexport of Chinese goods to the rest of Central Asia and the CIS.[56] In 2009, China even became Turkmenistan's leading source of imports, vaulting ahead of Russia and Turkey, while China recently has become the leading foreign investor in Kyrgyzstan, Turkmenistan, and Tajikistan.[57] As Russia has retrenched from many of its commitments to projects and investments in Central Asia, China has strengthened its economic role.

But China's economic rise has raised concerns in nearly all of the Central Asian countries about the structure of the economic relationship, especially their terms of trade. Central Asia acts primarily as a market for Chinese manufactured and consumer goods (over 85 percent), while its exports are overwhelmingly raw materials, primarily commodities, metals, and energy (also over 85 percent).[58] And beyond these concrete measures of asymmetrical economic

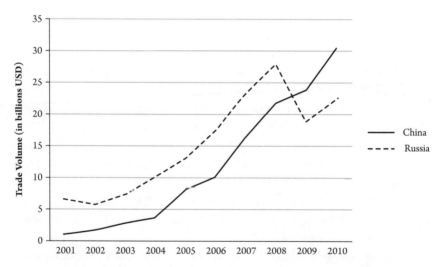

Figure 5.1 Central Asian Trade with Russia and China, Annual, 2001–2010 Source: International Monetary Fund (IMF), Direction of Trade Statistics (DOTS), 2001–2010

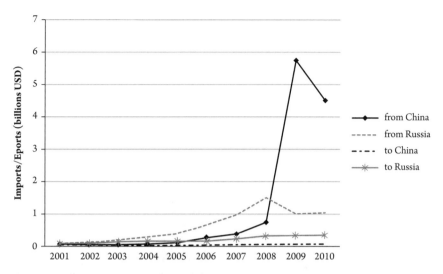

Figure 5.2 Kyrgyz Trade with China and Russia, 2001–2010 Source: International
Monetary Fund (IMF), Direction of Trade Statistics (DOTS), 2001–2010

relations, a high degree of paranoia about Chinese economic intentions still
dominates Central Asian public perceptions. The Central Asian media is filled
with stories of Chinese land grabs and plans for economic expansion, while in
Kazakhstan and Tajikistan, a common theme recounted by journalists is that
Beijing has somehow bought off its elite and law enforcement for "special access."
At bazaars across Central Asian border regions, the traditional markets for small
business owners and traders, the presence of Chinese merchants and store-
keepers has exploded over the last few years, stirring resentment among local
merchants who believe they are being undercut and driven out of business.[59]

Chinese migrant laborers, most of them working on Chinese construction and
infrastructure projects, are also increasing. In Tajikistan, for example, the number
of officially recorded Chinese workers increased from 30,000 in 2007 to 82,000
in 2010.[60] These migrant laborers tend to live in self-contained camps, away from
major cities, minimizing interaction with local communities though fueling a
sense of suspicion and estrangement. They typically earn low wages, equivalent
to $10 a day, while contractual clauses that mandate Chinese companies to hire a
certain percentage of local workers appear to be routinely ignored.[61]

The SCO as a Regional Public Goods Provider?

Russian and Central Asian fears of Chinese economic power have stalled most
efforts to promote greater economic cooperation and regional trade under the
auspices of the SCO. Curiously, a number of European-based scholars and

analysts have been promoting the impression that the SCO already has become a leading provider of "public goods" in Central Asia and that it actively facilitates cooperation in areas such as infrastructure investment, communications networking, and transportation building.[62] According to these commentators, such integration not only deserves to be supported by the European Union as part of its emerging Central Asia strategy, but necessitates that EU governments drop any normative reservations and engage with the SCO in order to avoid exclusion from the region's development planning.

Certain SCO initiatives that were announced but never implemented have contributed to this impression. In 2005 the SCO established the Business Council and an Interbank Association to coordinate regional investment among the member countries' national development banks. The association was envisioned as the precursor to a regional development bank that has yet to materialize. A list of 130 alleged "SCO projects" that the Council supervises are almost all preexisting Chinese bilateral and multilateral initiatives that have been given the SCO's stamp of origin. These include the flagship trans-Central Asian highway projects that the Asian Development Bank initiated in the 1990s through its Central Asia Regional Economic Cooperation (CAREC) program.

In fact, the original ADB program was started with seed money from Japan back in the 1990s, supplemented by the EU, and is now being directed to suit Chinese interests and infrastructural development.[63] The so-called SCO investments of $1 billion that were disbursed in 2006–2007 were entirely financed by Beijing. As one broader survey of Chinese infrastructure development across Asia observes, Beijing is quite eager to present its new wave of highway, railway, and airport construction as regional initiatives, supported by international organizations such as the ADB or ASEAN in the interests of multilateral integration, even though Beijing has intricately planned these new routes and will disproportionately benefit from them.[64]

New Chinese Investments: Benign or Colonial?

Chinese investments in Central Asia under SCO auspices also raise political questions. To be sure, Central Asia's infrastructure has suffered from decades of neglect, and new investment is desperately needed. At the same time, Chinese aid is designed to upgrade infrastructure to primarily serve the interests of Chinese companies and businesses, raising similar concerns that have been noted by observers of China-African relations.[65]

China's economic packages to target countries bundle investment and assistance, without a clear specification of loan terms, recipients, and repayments schedules. This aid lacks the types of domestic economic and political conditions imposed by the West, though the assistance does mandate the involvement of Chinese companies in managing these various projects. But with its entry into the area of project financing and assistance, it remains unclear how Chinese and SCO initiatives will interface with more established regional financial institutions such as the World Bank and the IMF. Beijing's more favorable conditions may undercut more traditional sources of financial assistance, as has been illustrated in certain African cases such as Angola. Indeed, a U.S official recounted that U.S. negotiations with Tajikistan over a possible World Bank loan in 2006 were undercut by China's decision to allocate $600 million in concessionary loans to the small Central Asian state.[66] Finally, the lack of transparency in Chinese loans, coupled with their lack of conditionality, raises the possibility that these funds may be misused by local elites.

Just such a possibility is raised by a recent report by the Crisis Group that, as part of a comprehensive study of the region's decaying infrastructure, which warns that Chinese (and Russian) bilateral aid programs need stronger mechanisms for oversight and accountability.[67] The report brings up the instructive example of the local management of the new Dushanbe-Chanak road in Tajikistan. The project was built with a $280 million loan from China; soon after the highway's opening in 2009, however, high tolls were imposed.[68] The company operating the tollbooths and managing the road's maintenance is Innovative Road Solution (IRS), a mysterious entity with no public history and offshore registration in the British Virgin Islands. IRS officials themselves contradicted the Tajik Minister of Transportation's claim that the company won an open tender. The estimated annual revenue from the road totals $48 million annually, though the government has yet to disclose the ultimate owner of IRS, or the total revenue flows and operating costs of the company.

The SCO Anti-Crisis Fund Episode

Finally, the financial crisis that started in the fall of 2008 magnified the regional economic imbalance between Beijing and Moscow and greatly increased China's role as a donor in the region. Early in the financial crisis, Beijing planners believed that the economic downturn would depress regional development and possibly destabilize the region politically. Beginning in October 2008, China proposed to establish an SCO anti-crisis fund for investing in Central Asian infrastructure.[69] Moscow refused the request and then proceeded to draft its own anti-crisis financial packages for CIS members Belarus and Kyrgyzstan under EurAsEC auspices. At the June 2009 SCO summit in Yekaterinburg, Chinese officials, once again, proposed to establish a $10 billion SCO fund, and suggested that Russia and China each contribute $5 billion and exercise joint control over its selected projects. Moscow once again refused, citing a legal barrier that prevents Moscow from contributing to multilateral organizations without explicit Duma approval.[70] However, Russian analysts uniformly believe that Russia's hesitance was driven by concerns about growing Chinese economic power at a time of relative weakness for Russia.

Instructively, China went ahead and announced that it would fund the entire $10 billion on its own. In 2010, the Chinese government solicited project requests from the Central Asian states and indicated that it would disburse funds over the course of the next couple of years. From a comparative perspective, $10 billion for infrastructure development would greatly exceed the funds committed by the World Bank, the European Bank for Reconstruction and Development, or Asian Development Bank (ADB) in the region and will crystallize China's new role as the region's leading external donor. It may also provide a significant new source of external funds for Central Asian elites to pursue their private agendas.

Hungry Giant, Eager Partners: China's Regional Energy Partnerships

The most dramatic area of new China–Central Asian relations is in the area of energy cooperation. Over the last several years, Chinese companies have made major forays into developing Central Asia's energy resources and have completed the construction of important new pipelines to transport Central Asia's resources eastward.

Historically, Chinese energy demand has been met adequately through domestic production of oil and, especially, coal, as China only became a net importer of oil in 1993. However, China's 10 percent annual growth rates, with accompanying industrialization and urbanization, require that China secure ever-increasing amounts of energy, much of which now must be secured from overseas. In November 2010, according to the International Energy Agency (IEA), Chinese oil demand surpassed 10 million barrels a day, requiring the imports of 4.8 million barrels a day of crude.[71]

Gas has constituted a smaller part of China's energy mix, about 80 bcm (billion cubic meters), or 3.3 percent of total demand in 2008, but is also expected to rapidly rise over the next decade.[72] The IAE estimates that in 2020 Chinese natural gas demand will be 216 bcm, with domestic supply totaling 137 bcm, requiring the import of 79 bcm. More strikingly, the China National Petroleum Corporation (CNPC) estimates that Chinese demand in 2020 will reach 350 bcm and that domestic sources will supply 150 bcm, leaving a 200 bcm shortfall. Central Asia will likely account for most of these imports, while Russia and Myanmar will also contribute additional supply.

China's Moves into Central Asian Energy

At the level of international politics, securing energy from Central Asia is also viewed as preferable, given that hydrocarbons can be directly piped in, thereby avoiding the chokepoint of the Strait of Malacca, a key transit corridor connecting the Pacific and Indian Oceans, which is vulnerable to naval blockade and disruption. In turn, China can secure pipelines and Central Asian's energy infrastructure through both current bilateral mechanisms, and, possibly in the future, the SCO superstructure.

China's interest in Central Asia's energy supplies has focused on both hydrocarbons and electricity generation. In terms of oil, most Chinese development has been centered in Kazakhstan. Excluded from entering the large international consortia at the Tengiz field and offshore Kashagan field, China marked its entry onto the scene in 2003 with the commissioning of the Atyrau-Alashankou pipeline and an assortment of CNPC deals. In 2005, CNPC acquired PetroKazakhstan, a Canadian-registered company, giving the Chinese giant control over Kazakhstan's second-largest oil producer and access to over 12 percent of the country's total production.[73] In addition, throughout the decade, Chinese companies have deliberately and strategically purchased a host of smaller and medium-sized fields throughout the country.[74] By 2007, analysts estimated that China controlled up to 26 percent of Kazakhstan's oil, making the Central Asian country the second single most important supplier of oil to China, after Sudan.[75] In 2010, one report revised this estimate to 50 percent, accounting for 40 million tons of Chinese outright production or as part of joint ventures.[76] These acquisitions have generated concern and also intense competition from other firms, especially Russia's LukOil. As Chapter 8 documents, Chinese oil companies have also been implicated in a series high-level corruption scandals involving leading Kazakh officials.

In the realm of electricity generation, China has invested in several joint hydropower projects in Kazakhstan, including one near the border city of Khorgos, along with proposed projects in Tajikistan and Kyrgyzstan.[77] These initiatives are intended to export power to support Xinjiang's regional economic development. However, as of 2010, China appeared to have tabled plans for the construction of hydroelectricity generators in Tajikistan, pending the resolution of water conflicts between Tajikistan and Uzbekistan.[78] Kazakhstan is also a critical supplier of uranium to Chinese nuclear plants and has discussed expanding its export of electricity.

Unlike hydropower and oil, which are mostly intended for the regional development of Xinjiang, Central Asian gas will supply the Chinese national market, especially the still-growing eastern coastal cities. China's growing demand for gas has elevated the overall importance of Central Asia as the main source of imported gas, especially Turkmenistan. Chinese energy firms have concluded a number of agreements with Turkmen state companies. In 2007 CNPC concluded a production-sharing agreement (PSA) to develop the Bagtyyarlyk field and to drill other exploration wells, making CNPC the only foreign company to conclude a PSA for onshore field development in the opaque country.

In the middle of the economic downturn, Beijing pressed home its interest in securing long-term supplies of energy by extending large official loans to the Central Asian states, which were secured by future hydrocarbon exports. In 2009, China's Development Bank extended a $4 billion credit to Turkmenistan to develop the South Yolotan field, estimated as the world's second largest natural gas field, close to the Afghan border, while in March 2011 yet another $4 billion credit was extended, this one to be paid off over 10 years and secured with supplies of gas. The loan also appears to have opened the door for CNPC's service contract for South Yolotan, announced in December 2009. Thus, within a short time frame, China appears to have become Turkmenistan's most privileged partner for gas development, providing new pipelines, investment, and credits to the Central Asian country.

The Turkmen deal was preceded by the announcement in April 2009 of a major $10 billion deal reached between Kazakhstan and China. The package included a $5 billion loan by China's Export-Import Bank to the Development Bank of Kazakhstan. In addition, Beijing provided $5 billion for investment by CNPC to acquire a 50 percent stake in KazMunaiGas, the largest Kazakh state oil company. The structure of these deals mirrors other similar "loans for energy" agreements that Beijing has concluded with other global energy producers during the financial crisis, including with Ecuador, Brazil, Russia and Myanmar.

The Eastern Connection: New Pipelines in Kazakhstan and Turkmenistan

China's growing role in Central Asia's energy sectors has been capped with the completion of two new pipelines, both traversing Central Asia to deliver energy to China (see Figure 5.3). The Kazakhstan-China oil pipeline spans the entire landmass of Kazakhstan, bringing oil from the Caspian at Atyrau all the way to the eastern border town of Alashankou. The pipeline was built throughout the 2000s in three distinct stages and it now offers Chinese companies with smaller holdings and investments a reliable export route that bypasses Russian territory. According to official Chinese customs data, data, since the pipeline's opening in 2005, export volumes to China have increased from about 25,592 b/d to over 200,000 b/d in 2010. [79]

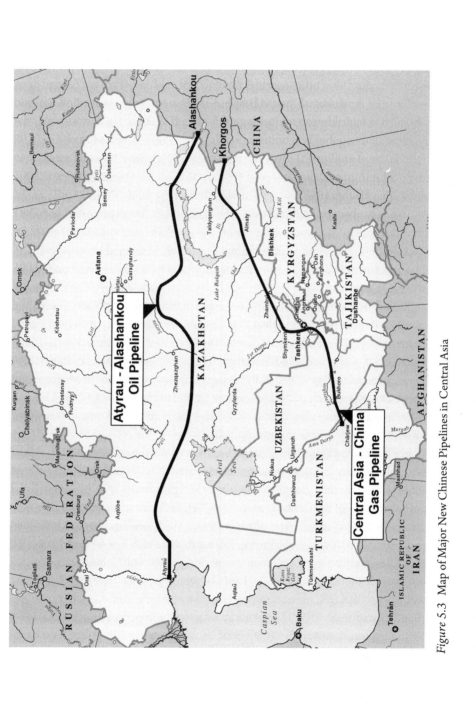

Figure 5.3 Map of Major New Chinese Pipelines in Central Asia

But perhaps the most significant, and politically intriguing, energy project is the new Central Asia–China gas pipeline, completed in December 2009 and designed to bring Turkmen gas to China. The pipeline represents the first major gas pipeline completed since the Soviet collapse to completely bypass Russian territory and the Gazprom-Transneft network. The pipeline originates in Turkmenistan, traverses Uzbekistan and Kazakhstan (both of which will also deposit gas into the network), before linking up with the newly constructed West-East China pipeline to take this gas to the Chinese eastern coast.[80] The original agreement, to supply 30 bcm a year, was subsequently increased to 40 bcm and then, in December 2011, again revised upward to 65 bcm. Of note, total Turkmen gas production in 2009 was 72 bcm, though the Turkmen government claims that it will expand its capacity to 200 bcm by 2030. Overall, the Central Asian pipeline is projected to provide the majority of China's imported gas needs over the next few decades. Even more impressive than these volumes of gas is the speed and purpose with which Beijing planned and executed the pipeline. The final agreement was reached in 2006, and production was finished on time in just over three years.

Though Russian officials maintain a nonchalant public attitude toward the opening of the pipeline, it is clear that China's aggressive entry into the Central Asian gas arena has undercut Moscow. The opening of the Central Asia–China pipeline not only breaks the Russian gas transit monopoly, it also affords Ashgabat additional leverage in negotiations over price and volume with Moscow; the possibility of securing additional supply from Turkmenistan, Uzbekistan, and Kazakhstan also provides additional leverage for Beijing in its negotiations with Moscow for future Russian gas supplies.

For the United States, the Central Asia–China pipeline, as well as its Kazakhstan oil counterpart, is a welcome development, consistent with U.S. energy strategy of expanding global energy supply and promoting the "sovereignty and independence" of the Central Asian states. Yet, there are some analysts who now claim that China's rapid rise might also have some downsides. For example, if all of Turkmenistan's gas starts flowing eastward, there may not be enough left for the Trans-Caspian projects, such as the long-proposed Nabucco pipeline to Europe.[81] Moreover, in a post-Afghanistan world, it is not clear whether China would view the U.S.-supported construction of a new Turkmenistan-Afghanistan-Pakistan-India (TAPI) pipeline as a strategic competitor or a complement; with its growing ties to Turkmenistan, including mounting Turkmen debt to China, Beijing would certainly be in a position to influence such decisions. China's entry has fundamentally rearranged the regional energy map, though so far Washington's traditional policy platitude of encouraging alternatives to Russian routes still seems to be its operating principle.

Conclusion: Whose Backyard?

China's decisive entry into Central Asia has achieved a number of foreign policy objectives. Through the SCO, Beijing has secured the cooperation of the Central Asian states with its security agenda and has found new energy partners to supply it with important reserves of oil and gas over the next decades. At the same time, this regional effort has become China's showcase of a non-Western regional organization that Beijing claims to embody the spirit of a new form of multilateralism.[82] China has achieved all of this without publicly alienating Russia, though its actions are causing increasing concern in some circles in Moscow.

Chinese officials now have an important stake in ensuring that the SCO is perceived as a success. The organization not only provides multilateral cover for a broad variety of Chinese projects and initiatives currently underway in the region, but embodies China's growing influence and role as a regional leader. Yet, Beijing will also have to deal with Central Asia's local rules, especially the graft and rent-seeking that have frustrated other external actors, from Western donors to Russian and United States security planners. Though Beijing may be more adaptive to such local environments—as demonstrated by its remarkable energy cooperation with countries such as Turkmenistan—it still faces substantial challenges and a lingering distrust about its long-term motives.

Moreover, Beijing will have to resolve the tension between promoting more effective integration and adhering to the SCO's stated goal of non-interference in the sovereign affairs of member countries. After all, in order to implement a legal and institutional foundation for achieving more extensive regional integration, successful regional organizations such as the European Union or ASEAN have had to adopt more supranational institutions and procedures that necessarily erode some areas of members' sovereign jurisdiction.[83] If Beijing actually wants to make progress on regional integration, it will also have to play a more active role in trying to influence the domestic affairs of its member countries.

Nevertheless, China's strategy in Central Asia reveals critical differences in how Beijing and Washington justify and manage their regional roles. In public, U.S. officials repeatedly stress the importance of promoting the sovereignty and independence of the Central Asian states and reject Russian claims of a privileged sphere of influence. But behind the scenes, U.S. officials, especially since the U.S.-Russian reset, have gone to considerable lengths to reassure Moscow about the limited nature of American regional ambitions.

Beijing does just the opposite; publicly, Chinese officials begin any discussion of Central Asia by acknowledging that the region is part of Russia's special sphere of interest and routinely invoke the importance of the China-Russia strategic partnership. But in practice, as we have seen, Beijing rarely concedes on any matter that compromises its security or economic interests, and its initiatives have clearly undercut Moscow's monopolies over a variety of Central Asian economic sectors and policy areas. Central Asia once may have been Russia's backyard, but China has redrawn the fences.

|| 6 ||

Anti-Terrorism, Democratization, and Human Rights

External great power engagement provided the Central Asian states with the opportunity to strengthen their regimes and stress their local rules, much to the detriment of the region's democratic development and human rights practices. During the 1990s, a variety of international actors engaged with the Central Asian regimes on democracy and so-called values issues.[1] Outside observers framed regional political developments in terms of the ongoing broader post-Communist political transitions and referred to the "human security" commitments that the countries had undertaken by joining the Organization for Security and Cooperation in Europe (OSCE) and ratifying the major international human rights conventions.[2] But by the end of the 1990s, as many of their post-Communist counterparts had implemented reforms and achieved sustained democratic gains, Central Asian governments were consolidating state power and had grown irritated with Western criticism of their political practices.

From 2001–2010, as U.S.-Russia-China regional engagement intensified, the trend in the quality of democracy in the region clearly declined (see Figure 6.1). According to the Freedom House composite scores for democracy, both Turkmenistan and Uzbekistan began at high levels of authoritarianism and have only gotten worse, while the quality of democratic institutions in Kazakhstan and Kyrgyzstan, widely perceived as generally more open than their regional counterparts, also steadily declined from the "Partly Free" to the "Not Free" categories. Of course, correlation is not necessarily causation, as these regimes may have become more repressive even in the absence of external engagement. Moreover, throughout their post–9/11 security engagement, the United States and the European Union continued to fund democracy assistance programs, maintained a public commitment to support human rights in the region, and sometimes even exerted effective pressure on Central Asian governments on certain individual cases and issues (such as improving election procedures in Kyrgyzstan or pressing Uzbek authorities to abolish the death penalty).[3]

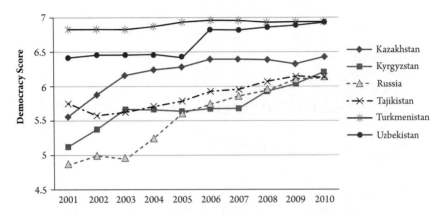

Figure 6.1 Democracy Trends in Central Asia, 2001–2010 Source: Freedom House, Nations in Transit, 2001–2010. Note: Higher scores indicate lower levels of democracy. Worst possible rating = 7.

Despite these good intentions and selected successes, the West also inadvertently contributed to the region's overall democratic erosions. External engagement did not directly cause these trends, but rather played into the hands of local elites, who over the decade became more adept at using external agendas, including the concerns of intensifying geopolitical competition, to solidify their domestic political standing. Three particular external-local interactions had deleterious effects on the region's political rights. First, the onset of the West's Global War on Terror (GWOT) allowed Central Asian regimes to blur the line between anti-terror campaigns and the targeting of political opposition, as external actors equipped Central Asian security services, mutually recognized each other's designations of "transnational threats," and offered novel legal justifications for their cross-border renditions of terror suspects and extremists. Second, the Color Revolutions of 2003–2005 allowed Central Asian regimes to conflate democratization with externally promoted regime change, thereby triggering a widespread regional backlash against international actors engaged in democratic monitoring and advocacy. Third, in reacting to the perceived threat to regime integrity posed by so-called Western-style democracy and human rights appeals, the Central Asian states grafted a set of alternative norms, practices, and institutions, supported by Moscow and Beijing, which stressed the importance of sovereignty and cultural relativism; practices such as the rise of alternative election monitors sent by the CIS and the SCO mimicked the form of their Western counterparts, but opposed critical assessments of their elections, helping the Central Asian governments to push back against Western criticisms and value judgments.

Engagement on Anti-Terrorism and Human Rights

First, the intensifying engagement between all three external actors and the Central Asian states on security issues, especially counterterrorism, severely damaged the region's already challenging human rights landscape. All of the governments had ratified the major international human rights conventions early in their independence,[4] but as regimes consolidated their control over the judiciaries and national security services, a wide gap quickly emerged between these formal constitutional protections and their actual defense.[5] However, the regional and international environment that compelled the Central Asian governments to at least publicly commit to upholding these standards and international legal obligations in the 1990s would give way to a decade in which political crackdowns and human rights violations were routinely justified in the name of counterterrorism and security.[6]

At the most basic level, cooperation in the 2000s on counterterrorism provided Central Asian security services with U.S., Russian, and Chinese training, military hardware, surveillance instruments and, in the Chinese case, even censoring software. These external transfers enhanced their capacity to not only fight regional terrorist groups, but also to more effectively serve the presidency. The resulting so-called "securitization" of regional politics—or the expansion of anti-terrorism campaigns into criminal law—has been noted by a number of regional observers.[7] The GWOT provided an ideal opportunity for the Central Asian regimes to frame their internal security practices as part of a broader international coalition and to justify coercive practices as part of a "permanent international state of emergency."[8]

None of the external powers conditioned their security assistance, nor did they adopt strict safeguards to ensure that hardware and training for the purposes of counterterrorism would be used appropriately. For example, in the case of U.S.-Uzbek cooperation, an investigative report found that elements of the Uzbek law enforcement and security services involved in the May 2005 Andijan crackdown had received training and equipment from U.S. counterterrorism projects.[9] A more detailed analysis by RAND in 2006 observed that, over the course of U.S. security assistance and engagement, Uzbekistan "remained a repressive regime" and that Uzbek internal security forces did not generate measurable improvements in either political stability or human rights.[10]

Logrolling and Expanding the Pool of Transnational Threats

Less obvious than the direct training and transfers of hardware, the "Big Three" also pioneered new forms of extralegal arrangements throughout the region in the name of counterterrorism. First, the intersection of various security agendas in the name of anti-terrorism—U.S. interests in combating the Taliban and its allies, Russia's crackdown in Chechnya, China's interests in clamping down on Uighur groups, and the Central Asian states' interests in outlawing regional militant groups and political opponents—quickly expanded the pool of organizations and individuals that were classified as regional "terrorists" and "extremists."

As all three external powers strengthened their regional anti-terrorist efforts, they "logrolled" their recognition of these transnational threats—that is, they accepted each other's blacklisting of certain organizations in exchange for a reciprocal act of recognition.[11] In 2002, for example, the U.S. government, in its effort to attain Chinese backing for the Global War on Terror, agreed to list the Uighur organization the East Turkestan Islamic Movement on the UN's Consolidated List of terrorist organizations with Al-Qaeda links; in exchange for being allowed basing rights in Uzbekistan, U.S. officials placed the Islamic Movement of Uzbekistan on its own list of terrorist organizations and agreed to target its leadership in its Afghanistan operations.[12] China and Russia publicly supported each other's efforts to combat their own separatist groups in Chechnya and Xinjiang. In October 2004 they issued a joint statement that called for international support of their efforts, stressing that "China understands and firmly supports all measures taken by Russia to resume the constitutional order of the Republic of Chechnya and to fight against terrorism. Russia firmly supports all measures taken by China to fight against the terrorist and separatist forces in 'East Turkestan' and to eliminate terrorist jeopardy."[13] The Central Asian states all responded to China's requests to list Uighur groups, while in 2005, at the request of the Uzbek government, Russia placed the much discussed Islamic group Hizb ut-Tahrir organization on its national list of terrorist groups.[14]

Regional Blacklisting

The now common practice of blacklisting reinforced this political logrolling.[15] The United Nations first accepted blacklisting in Resolution 1267, adopted by the Security Council in 1999, which created the Consolidated List of individuals and entities associated with Bin Laden, Al-Qaeda, and the Taliban. That resolution was strengthened after September 11, 2001, when the Security Council passed Resolution 1373, which established the Counter-Terrorism Committee of the Security Council and encouraged states to create their own national lists and to cooperate on other counterterrorism measures.[16] The 1267 regime, in particular, obligates states to freeze the assets of entities on the list and to "bring proceedings" against those entities on the list within their jurisdiction. The United States, Russia, and China all expanded their own national lists and participated in these multilateral efforts to craft common lists.

Despite the acceptance of blacklisting as a legitimate anti-terror tool, its domestic and international use over the last decade has raised a number of human rights concerns.[17] Questions about the transparency in procedures of listing and delisting, the lack of judicial oversight, unclear grievance and appeals procedures, and insufficient presentation of evidence all have plagued the development of national and multilateral terrorist blacklists.[18] At the UN level, international law scholars have criticized resolution 1373 for failing to provide a common definition of terrorism and for not specifying how to reconcile new anti-terrorism requirements with mandatory concurrent compliance with human rights norms.[19]

In Central Asia, the SCO has played a critical role in the identification and blacklisting of transnational threats under the mantra of combating the three evils of terrorism, extremism, and separatism. Specifically, the SCO's Regional Anti-Terrorism Structure (RATS), established in Bishkek in 2002 and moved to Tashkent in 2004, created the basis for regional information sharing and a common database of extremist individuals and organizations. An earlier attempt by Russia to establish an anti-terrorism center for pooling intelligence among CIS countries had foundered, but the wave of Color Revolutions provided the SCO members with a renewed impetus to establish a regional body that would not be subject to Western influence. Unlike the SCO's Secretariat, which is based in Beijing and emulates a supranational organizational form, the RATS participants report directly to their respective Ministries of Interior.

Despite numerous pledges to make the consolidated list public, RATS officials have yet to do so. Though the group's activities are shrouded in secrecy, a recent report on RATS practices found evidence of a considerable ratcheting of the number of groups and individuals on the consolidated list.[20] In 2006, the first RATS Council agreed to place 15 organizations and 400 individuals on the list. In 2007, the unified list had grown to include 42 organizations and 944 individuals; in an April 2010 meeting, RATS Director Dzhenisbek Dzhumanbekov revealed that the database named 42 organizations and 1,100 persons sought in connection with "extremist and terrorist activities." UN Special Rapporteur on Counter-Terrorism Martin Scheinin expressed "serious concerns" about these SCO data-sharing practices, observing that "this sharing of data and information is not subject to any meaningful form of oversight and there are no human rights safeguards attached to data and information sharing."[21]

In addition, the SCO also has adopted ad hoc resolutions at its summits that expanded its categorization of what or who constitutes a regional "extremist." According to a Human Rights Watch brief, the 2005 Astana summit, held in the wake of the Andijan crackdown, produced a number of resolutions that seemed to target the Uzbek refugees who had fled to camps in southern Kyrgyzstan.[22] Not to be outdone, in the spring of 2011 the CSTO Secretariat announced that it, too, would create a similar common database of extremist and terrorist organizations among member countries.[23]

New Institutions, Practices, and Cooperative Norms

In addition to expanding the scope of entities and individuals considered "transnational threats," external anti-security engagement with the Central Asian states also created new practices and legal arrangements to execute these policies. In pursuit of the Global War on Terror, the United States rejected many of the standards mandated by international laws of war as inapplicable to its antiterrorism efforts. The U.S. government used the extraterritorial status of its naval base in Guantanamo Bay, Cuba, to justify the indefinite detention of over 550 people captured in the battlefields of Afghanistan and northern Pakistan. U.S. officials classified many of these detainees as "illegal enemy combatants" so that they would not be afforded U.S. Constitutional due process or the protections of the Geneva Conventions.[24]

Dozens of detainees at Guantanamo were either Central Asian citizens or of Central Asian origin, with most of them accused of fighting on behalf of the Islamic Movement of Uzbekistan (IMU). The *Washington Post*'s list of past and present detainees shows citizens of Kazakhstan (3), Tajikistan (12), Turkmenistan (1), and Uzbekistan (7), as well as Russian (9) and Chinese (22) citizens.[25] According to the Center for Constitutional rights, China, Tajikistan, and Uzbekistan all sent interrogators to Guantanamo.[26] Former Uzbek prisoner Zakirjan Hasam reportedly tried to commit suicide the evening of his interrogation out of fear that he would be returned to Uzbekistan and tortured, along with his family. After being hospitalized, he was once again placed in front of Uzbek interrogators.[27] At his subsequent Combatant Status Review Board, Hasam denied even knowing what the IMU was and claimed that he had been forcibly transferred from Tajikistan to Afghanistan, where he could not afford to pay a $3,000 bribe to local villagers to avoid being handed over to U.S. forces.[28] His "enemy combatant" designation was subsequently removed, and in November 2006 he was transferred to Albania.

A web of so-called "black sites," secret detention facilities that were scattered around the world and were jointly operated by the U.S. Central Intelligence Agency and host governments, supplemented Guantanamo. In the post-Communist sphere, such sites were probably operated in Poland, Romania, Lithuania, and Uzbekistan. In the Uzbek case, terror suspects appear to have been detained in a facility outside Tashkent and possibly in the restricted penal colony of Jaslik in remote Karakalpakstan.[29] As a result, the United States and its allies routinely gathered information from Uzbek counterparts that had been extracted through the use of torture.[30] As we will see with the issue of "extraordinary renditions," the U.S.-Uzbek security relationship occupied a legal void; domestically, Uzbek officials invoked international anti-terrorist efforts to justify their increasingly repressive tactics, while the United States specifically argued that international law did not apply to many of its anti-terrorism practices.

While the United States created extralegal categories and procedures to justify its counterterrorism cooperation with Central Asian security services, the SCO elevated its pioneering security arrangements to the treaty level, ensuring that its new practices and procedures formally superseded national laws and legal safeguards. The SCO Anti-Terror Convention (2009) allows official agencies involved in security matters to apply their own national standards and procedures to other signatory countries, regardless of whether the specific elements of a crime, burden of proof, or legal procedure meet the standards of that host country.[31] The convention allows for the rapid handover between security services of suspects, thereby bypassing certain national constitutional guarantees to due process, formal extradition procedures, and international commitments to political asylum and refugee status.[32] Moreover, under the SCO's Convention on Immunities and Privileges (2005), all official SCO structures and country officials, including those at RATS, are protected by diplomatic-style immunity and are immune from criminal prosecution.[33]

Perhaps the most controversial SCO initiative to date, from a human rights perspective, has been the broad regional acceptance of the need to fight the "three evils"—terrorism, extremism, and separatism—as a new security norm. The very elevation of "separatism" and "extremism" to the level of terrorism has been widely criticized, from a legal and human rights perspective, as overly vague and inappropriate, as it bundles groups and individuals with political and ideological agendas into the same category as actual terrorists who have inflicted harm on civilians. Governments can easily blacklist and malign political opponents and dissidents, without actual proof of extremist activities or ensuring consistency with national criminal law.[34] Moreover, the reciprocal acceptance of these categories has led all SCO members to now repress certain types of political activity that previously were not considered threats under national law. For example, prior to the SCO convention, Russian law did not regard the practice of "separatism" as an inherently extremist activity or ideology.

Case Study: Comparing Extra-Territorial Security Cooperation

One of the most striking aspects of Central Asia in the 2000s was how quickly it became a space in which the United States, Russia, and China, in collaboration with Central Asian governments, all routinely conducted renditions and forced transfers of individuals accused of terrorist and extremist activity.

CIA Extraordinary Renditions to Uzbekistan

In an "extraordinary rendition," suspects are forcibly detained and removed from a country, and are taken to a third country, where they are detained and interrogated without representation or even a legal process. The crimes or plots of which rendered persons are accused could be against the host country or the sending country, effectively making extraordinary rendition a way to outsource torture to the security services of a third country. Renditions conducted by the CIA actually began during the Clinton years; renditions to Egypt, for instance, had been taking place since the mid-1990s, officially for the purposes of returning suspects to stand trial.[35]

But after 9/11 the practice was quickly established as an important component of U.S. global counterterrorism efforts. To do so, Bush administration officials developed novel and contorted legal readings of its international legal commitments, especially Article 3 of the Convention Against Torture that prohibits renditions when there is "substantive ground for believing" that a suspect will be tortured abroad, also known as the international legal principle of *non-refoulement*. However, hundreds of suspects were rendered to the security services of states in the Middle East and Central Asia with scant consideration given to whether their lives or freedoms would be threatened.[36] According to Dick Marty, special investigator of the European Council, the CIA operated a global "spider's web" of renditions, involving at least 1,245 flights throughout European airspace.[37]

From the very onset of the War on Terror, Uzbekistan seemed like a natural candidate for the application of what Vice President Cheney referred to as the methods of the "darker side."[38] The CIA had a history of quiet cooperation in Uzbekistan with its Predator drone project,[39] while Uzbek authorities had granted the United States basing rights and intelligence sharing to support its mission in Afghanistan. The axis between Tashkent and Kabul was reportedly well known as a route for detainee transfers,[40] but flights to Uzbekistan also routinely passed through European countries such as the United Kingdom, Germany, and Poland.[41] Stephen Grey's investigation of the CIA rendition network revealed that Tashkent became "a vital hub in the CIA's world operations. No other destination east of Jordan had received so many flights from the CIA fleet, nor from the particular planes like the Gulfstreams that were used in renditions."[42]

At a presidential press conference in March 2005, President Bush responded to a question about the rendition program by providing a boilerplate assurance that U.S. officials send suspects "back to their country of origin with the promise that they won't be tortured." A follow-up question asked specifically about what Uzbekistan could accomplish in its interrogations that the United States could not, to which Bush tersely responded, "We seek assurances that nobody will be tortured."[43] Of course, the State Department's own human rights reports from the time detailed that prisoners were commonly tortured in Uzbekistan. According to a former major in the Uzbek National Security Service (SNB), Ikrom Yakubov, American officials, who he assumed to be CIA agents, observed the abuse of rendered prisoners in Uzbekistan's prisons.[44]

Not only did the United States outsource the interrogation of Central Asian terrorist suspects to Uzbekistan, but it further "outsourced" its own role in the renditions by relying on private contractors for many, if not most, of the actual rendition flights and prisoner transfers. The renditions to Uzbekistan likely involved the participation of contractors, especially the controversial private security firm Blackwater, which was awarded over $1 billion worth of contracts by the Bush administration. The company was tasked with routinely flying between Afghanistan and Uzbekistan, and, according to Jeremy Scahill's investigative study, the Central Asian state was "one of the 'key destinations' for both U.S. military and CIA renditions."[45] Furthermore, according to an internal company memo obtained by *Der Spiegel*, Blackwater was contracted by the CIA to fly terror suspects from Guantanamo to a secret prison camp in Uzbekistan (in addition to Pakistan and Afghanistan), where the detainees faced "special treatment" in detention.[46] The magazine also claims that the Department of Defense in 2003 cleared Presidential Airways and Aviation Worldwide, both owned by Blackwater's owner and founder Eric Prince, to conduct rendition flights. According to another investigative report, between 2004 and 2008 Presidential Airways was awarded at least $192 million worth of contracts by the U.S. Department of Defense; according to its 2007 terms of reference, the airline was tasked to perform for CENTCOM "passenger, cargo and combi Short Take-Off and Landing air transportation services between locations in the Area of Responsibility of Afghanistan, Kyrgyzstan, Pakistan and Uzbekistan."[47]

Though Uzbekistan was the most important regional destination for renditions, other flights within the region have been documented. Flight logs examined by the European Parliament also indicate that Baku and Ashgabat were frequent regional destinations, with one particular aircraft, contracted to Premier Aircraft Management, logging 50 flights between Frankfurt and the capital of Turkmenistan from June to November 2005.[48]

The SCO Anti-Terror Treaty and Regional Renditions

The SCO also facilitated the transfer of accused extremists and terrorism suspects across borders. It sanctioned these new practices, not by denying the applicability of international law, as the United States did, but by codifying transfers within a new supranational convention. The most controversial, and secretive, of these SCO activities has been facilitating cooperation among regional security services in detaining and transporting suspects. According to one critical Russian newspaper account, RATS' "main objective is helping special services of the states-members to bypass the obstacles presented by national legislation and by the norms of international law on giving up suspects."[49] The convention essentially prohibits member countries from offering political asylum or refugee status to any individuals accused by another signatory country of extremism. For example, Russia, Kazakhstan, and Kyrgyzstan have all been accused by human rights organizations of forcibly returning to Uzbekistan refugees who were accused of being involved in Andijan events, despite their internationally recognized refugee status and pending asylum applications.[50]

Ascertaining the exact number of people transferred under the SCO treaty is difficult, given that the treaty is usually not officially invoked by authorities, but it appears as if the two most important directions of transfers have been from Central Asia and Russia to China and from Russia to Uzbekistan.[51] Over the 2000s, dozens of Uighurs appear to have been rendered from Russia, Kazakhstan, Uzbekistan, and Kyrgyzstan to China, including the much-publicized case of Huseyin Celil, a Uighur refugee with Canadian citizenship who was forcibly transferred to China in 2006 while visiting relatives in Uzbekistan; he subsequently was sentenced to life imprisonment by a Chinese court.[52] The renditions from Russia to Central Asia, especially to Uzbekistan, appear to have intensified around 2005, when Russia was courting Central Asian governments in its bid to counter U.S. regional influence. In a March 2006 meeting at RATS, Russia's FSB director noted that Russia had transferred 19 suspects to Uzbekistan, all of them accused of membership in the Islamic organization Hizb ut-Tahrir.[53] Prior to 2005, the religious organization had been legal in Russia.[54]

The case of Alisher Usmanov dramatically illustrates this changing practice of extraterritorial cooperation between Russian and Uzbek security services.[55] Originally from Uzbekistan, Usmanov was awarded Russian citizenship in 1999 and worked as a Sharia teacher in a madrasah in Kazan. In 2000, when Hizb ut-Tahrir was still legal, Usmanov attended meetings of the organization; Uzbek authorities later demanded his extradition on the grounds of fomenting religious extremism. Russian prosecutors initially refused these requests on the basis that Usmanov was a Russian citizen, but in April 2005, his citizenship was revoked for allegedly submitting false documentation. In June 2005, Usmanov was abducted in Kazan the morning of his scheduled release from a remand prison and was flown directly to Uzbekistan in what the Head of Public Affairs of the Uzbek National Security Council explained was part of "a joint plan with the Russian Federal Security Service to combat international terrorism."[56] In November 2005 he was convicted in Namangan of extremist activities and was sentenced to eight years in prison.

In what appears to be an example of an even more politically motivated detention and transfer, Mahmadruzi Iskandarov, leader of the Democratic Party of Tajikistan and outspoken critic of President Rahmon, was abducted in April 2005 outside his home (in exile in Russia) just two weeks after a Russian prosecutor had refused to extradite him to Tajikistan.[57] According to a Russian investigative report, he was transported by military plane to Tajikistan, where he entered the country under the alias Gennady Balanin at Dushanbe airport.[58] Iskandarov was met by officials from the Tajik Ministry of Interior, and, in October 2005, was sentenced to a prison term of 23 years.[59] According to one account, following the Russian refusal for Tajik extraditions, the Tajik president had met with Russian Defense Minister Sergei Ivanov for three hours.[60] Though Russian officials deny any official involvement in the episode, Tajikistan's response to requests for details from the European Court of Human Rights stressed that Iskandarov was turned over by law enforcement authorities from the Russian Federation.

Russian media accounts and Russian human rights organizations have indicated that the SCO treaty has provided the legal and cooperative framework for this wave of renditions. But whether it was the SCO treaty, the CSTO, or simply ad hoc bilateral arrangements, it is clear that midway through the 2000s the Russian Federation had ceased to be a "safe space" for Central Asian political dissidents or exiled opposition figures. In exchange for trying to woo Central Asian governments such as Uzbekistan and Tajikistan, the Kremlin allowed the politically motivated renditions and abductions of dissidents, effectively turning Russia into "a hunting ground for the security services of the most authoritarian states in Central Asia."[61]

Comparing Renditions in the Name of Anti-Terrorism

All three major countries violated international human rights laws and norms in actively participating in regional renditions, though they often used different justifications and instruments. Of all the states enacting these new anti-terrorism measures in Central Asia, Russia has faced the greatest international legal scrutiny and constraints due to its commitment, as a member of the Council of Europe, to uphold decisions of the European Court of Human Rights (ECHR). Under Article 3 of the European Convention of Human Rights, to which Russia is a party, signatories are prohibited from extraditing or transferring individuals who would face the risk of torture upon return.

In perhaps the most famous case of regional extradition, in May 2005 Russian officials arrested 14 men in the city of Ivanovo, close to Moscow, 12 of whom were Uzbek nationals, on accusations that they were involved in the Andijan uprisings.[62] The men were granted refugee status by the United Nations High

Commissioner for Refugees (UNHCR), but Russian prosecutors pressed forward with efforts to extradite them. Following their release from custody in April 2007, the ECHR stayed the extradition request and then, in 2008, found that extraditing the men to Uzbekistan would violate Russia's commitment to the European Convention. Others have not been as fortunate. On October 26, 2006, Rustam Muminov, an Uzbek citizen accused of "anti-constitutional activities" by Uzbek security services, was forcibly transferred from Moscow to Tashkent, even though the ECHR had sent an indefinite restraining order against the transfer just two hours before.[63] Though Russian officials have not always abided by the court's rulings, the ECHR mechanism is a high-profile venue for legal recourse, providing a spotlight and public exposure that defendants in other countries lack.

Returning to the central themes of this book, this section also reveals the effects that the trilateral security engagement had across the region. For the United States, the global anti-terrorism campaign justified secretive bilateral cooperation, the outsourcing of torture, and extralegal practices such as renditions and the running of "black sites." For China, the anti-terrorism agenda was less informed by events in Afghanistan, and more by its rekindled campaign against Uighur separatists in Xinjiang and the fear that sudden regime change and regional chaos might spill over and destabilize its western province. Russia's motivations and calculations were even more complex: the threats posed by Afghanistan and the Color Revolutions necessitated active balancing against Western influence in the region, leading Moscow to support the Central Asian regimes and the politically motivated actions of their security services. As a result, in the name of anti-terrorism, Moscow accepted and assisted with the operations of Central Asian security services not only within the region, but within the boundaries of the Russian Federation itself.

Securitizing Civil Society: Targeting NGOs

A second mechanism through which external competition adversely affected democratization occurred in the wake of the Color Revolutions. As Central Asian elites increasingly conflated external support for democracy with regime change across Eurasia, local rulers took aggressive countermeasures to treat external actors engaged in democracy promotion and monitoring as security threats. In this area, Central Asia's rulers took some cues from Moscow. As concern about the Western-backed electoral revolutions peaked in 2004 and 2005, the Kremlin's pushback against Western interference in the domestic politics of the post-Soviet states quickly became a model for the Central Asian states to emulate or, more craftily, to strategically invoke. Though some commentators have pointed to Moscow's actions as motivated by an ideological affinity for supporting authoritarianism, the timing of the effort suggests that the motive was more pragmatically geopolitical.[64]

NGOs as Vehicles for Revolution

Of particular concern was the role of Western NGOs that promoted civil society and monitored democratic standards in the region. In the wake of Ukraine's Orange Revolution, where Western NGOs were perceived to have played a critical role in training and mobilizing political opposition, Moscow acted decisively to curtail their activities domestically and to publicly denounce them as geopolitical agents.[65] These efforts were immediately and gratefully emulated across Central Asia. Throughout 2005, state television and radio channels provided a platform for Russian commentators and analysts to issue warnings about the perils of U.S. democracy-promotion activities in the region. Responsibility for registering and monitoring NGOs was transferred from Ministries of Culture and Information to Ministries of the Interior, thus underscoring that the actions of NGOs had become "securitized."

During this period, all of the Central Asian governments took rapid steps to legally restrict the activities of foreign NGOs.[66] Though the Central Asian states had already begun to push back against NGO activities in their own nuanced ways, Russia's efforts gave them the backing and a high-profile model upon which to graft their local efforts. Uzbekistan was the most aggressive, closing 300 NGOs in the country between 2004 and 2007.[67] In the wake of the uprising in Andijan, local authorities expelled a number of international groups, including Freedom House, Amnesty International, and the National Democratic Institute, and on January 1, 2006, the Uzbek government adopted a new restrictive criminal code that made it illegal for individuals to engage in any activities with unregistered NGOs and criminalized public gatherings involving registered NGOs without prior official approval. In Kazakhstan, tax authorities in 2005 audited over 30 NGOs and adopted new national security legislation that allowed the government to close NGOs that contributed to "aggravating the political situation" or "stratification of society." In late 2005, authorities in Tajikistan similarly drew up a new law that increased reporting and re-registration requirements, particularly for international groups, and restricted the political activities of NGOs. Even in Kyrgyzstan, with one of the most vibrant of Central Asia's civil societies, state investigation into foreign-funded NGOs increased, paving the way for a similarly restrictive law, introduced by President Bakiyev in 2007. As Appendix 1 suggests, within a few months all of the Central Asian states either passed or drew up their own versions of Russian laws designed to clamp down on the activities of NGOs.

A leaked cable from the U.S. Embassy in Tajikistan in 2005 underscores both how the role of Western NGOs in the Color Revolutions became perceived as a security issue and how Central Asian rulers pragmatically invoked Russian pressure to justify their new appetite for pushback.[68] In a meeting of the U.S. Ambassador to Tajikistan James Hoagland and the Tajik Ambassador to the United States, Homrahon Zaripov, the Tajik official explained that the pressure to clamp down on the activities of NGOs had come directly from Moscow, both through the Russian media and via the Russian-infiltrated Tajik Ministry of Interior. However, as if to emphasize Dushanbe's political leeway, Zaripov also stressed that Tajik President Rahmon had not acquiesced to Moscow's demand to evict the "big three" NGOs—Freedom House, the National Democratic Institute, and Internews—and would hold their status in abeyance, presumably to use as future bargaining leverage in bilateral consultations. Zapitov also recounted Rahmon's meeting the previous month with George Soros, founder of the Open Society Institute, which supports a foundation in Tajikistan. The Tajik president warned that, although he had found "no fault" with the organization so far, he was, "prepared to shut down the Soros foundation immediately if any 'irregularity' came to his attention."

The Assault on the OSCE's Human Dimension

The Central Asian states also enthusiastically backed Russia's campaign to curtail the election-monitoring activities of the OSCE's Office for Democratic Institutions and Human Rights (ODIHR), the main international organization that has conducted election monitoring missions in the post-Communist region since the mid-1990s. Throughout the region, the ODIHR was already perceived with suspicion and even hostility, having publicly criticized a national election in each of the Central Asian countries in the period of 1999–2000. During the Color Revolutions, the monitoring body's Election Day pronouncements that these votes had not been "free and fair" triggered anti-government mobilizations and accusations of electoral fraud by defeated opposition candidates. As a result, the ODIHR was viewed as a critical political tool of the West for implementing regime change.

In response, Russia and the Central Asian states launched an all-out assault on the organization's activities, as well as the broader so-called human dimension, or "values agenda," of the OSCE. Central Asian states stopped agreeing to undertake projects focused on political reform and monitoring human rights abuses, and directed the organization to focus on capacity building and training.[69] Mounting opposition came to a head at the 2007 OSCE summit, when Russia threatened to withhold funds from the international organization and proposed a number of reforms that would weaken the ODIHR's monitoring work. In a confidential memorandum circulated around the OSCE in 2007, Russia proposed—and was backed by all of the Central Asian states, Armenia, and Belarus—significant changes in the activities of the ODHIR.[70] These included capping the number of foreign monitors at 50, mandating that the ODHIR team issue its assessment in consultation with the host country, and transferring the responsibility for assigning the Director of Mission from the Warsaw ODHIR office to the OSCE Parliament in Vienna. Collectively, these proposals would have gutted the practice of election monitoring. In 2008, both Uzbekistan and Russia refused to grant visas to ODIHR missions in a timely fashion, but the dispute was temporarily shelved as part of the deal that awarded the OSCE's rotating chairmanship to Kazakhstan in 2010.

The backlash against NGOs and fears of "external interference" reinvigorated the tactic of associating political opposition figures and groups with destabilizing "outside interests." As external competition accelerated across the region, such official claims gained wide plausibility among the public.[71] Over the decade, the conflation of democracy promotion with Western geopolitical agendas seems to have significantly dampened broader public attitudes toward Western-backed democracy promotion efforts. According to one public opinion survey, by 2007 support for U.S. democracy assistance in Kazakhstan and Uzbekistan had dropped to almost negligible levels. In Uzbekistan, only 6.5 percent of respondents regarded U.S. support for democracy as the "most valuable" or "valuable" type of foreign assistance, while in Kazakhstan this figure dropped to just 4.5 percent.[72] By comparison, support for U.S. economic assistance stood at 32 percent and 24 percent, respectively, with public health topping the list of respondents' priorities at 42 percent and 44 percent.

Competing Democratic Norms and Institutions

Finally, as the Central Asian governments pushed back against the external actors they perceived as threatening and destabilizing, they also adopted new norms, practices, and institutions to justify their actions and democratic backsliding.

The Rise of Sovereign Democracy and Competing Norms

Chief among these strategies was the adoption of the Kremlin's emerging doctrine of "sovereign democracy," developed in the wake of the Color Revolutions, particularly Ukraine's Orange Revolution of November 2004. The concept was coined by Vladislav Surkov, deputy head of the presidential administration, and was originally used in a speech in February 2006 for political activists from

Russia's ruling party, United Russia.[73] Soon, a variety of government officials routinely referred to the concept, while President Putin used it to publicly justify tough new restrictions on the registration and activities of foreign NGOs.

The concept of sovereign democracy has two principal meanings for Russian elites: first, the source of the sovereign legitimacy of the Putin era elite is found within Russia, as opposed to the West and the ill-fated Yeltsin era model that allegedly crippled Russia in the 1990s; and second, the regime will actively guard against foreign attempts to influence Russia's domestic politics through international or transnational actors.[74] Both of these pillars of the "sovereign democracy" concept proved popular among Central Asian elites. They not only used the concept to justify their own crackdown against NGOs, but also copied Moscow's strategy to de-universalize democratic standards and values. As a result, Central Asian leaders spoke openly of their own particular "democratic models" and culturally specific national political projects.

Kazakhstan's President Nazarbayev has been one of the leading proponents of this cultural relativism, consistently attempting to carve out a political justification for his rule that opposes Western models, but that signals a commitment to incremental reforms that are consistent with Kazakhstan's "paternal political culture." In one speech Nazarbayev noted that, "We need time for the universal principles of democracy to truly sprout on our soil and find its national-historical specificity. Democracy—it is not just a system, but also a culture."[75] Later, in the wake of the Color Revolutions, the Kazakh president cautioned, "Kyrgyzstan—is suffering, as are the poor people of Georgia; we are seeing what is happening now in Ukraine. Of course, we need to consider good advice, but we also must recognize what is specific to democracy in our country, which never in history has had a democratic tradition."[76]

Nazarbayev's presidential counterparts in Tajikistan and Kyrgyzstan made similar claims, while Turkmenistan's Niyazov painted with a broader brush, accusing all external efforts to raise issues of democracy or human rights as unacceptable infringements on Turkmen sovereignty. In its foundational statement and subsequent public statements, the SCO repeatedly stressed that the organization embodied the "Shanghai Spirit" of its members, defined as "mutual trust and benefit, equality, consultation and mutual respect for diverse civilizations," a thinly veiled contrast to the universalizing tendencies and intrusive demands for political liberalization made by Western political organizations.[77]

Along with adopting "sovereign democracy," Central Asian governments also adopted the meme of highlighting U.S. "double standards" and hypocrisy, emphasizing that the rhetoric of democracy was only used to mask U.S. geopolitical agendas. In this spirit, the Russian and Central Asian media played up the use of Guantanamo Bay as an extralegal detention facility and the scandal at Abu Ghraib to emphasize U.S. selectivity and instrumentalization in its democratic commitments. As revealed by the U.S. Embassy cables, President Karimov of Uzbekistan would routinely refer to U.S. "double standards" to deflect criticism about the state of political rights whenever U.S. officials broached the topic.[78]

A series of fascinating field experiments conducted by Edward Schatz and Renan Levine across Tajikistan and Kyrgyzstan in 2007 seem to underscore the effectiveness of the media campaign.[79] The political scientists examined whether positive images of the United States as a place of religious tolerance and respect for rights varied according to the messenger making the claim. They found that, when such positive statements were attributed to official U.S. diplomatic sources, especially President Bush or the U.S. Ambassador, the message of the United States as a positive guardian of rights was not only discounted, but was actively resisted and opposed by Central Asian participants. The authors conclude that, in Central Asia, "the legacy of the global controversies that arose during the Bush administration may limit the capacity of U.S. government officials to engage in effective public diplomacy."[80]

The Entry of Alternative Election Monitors

The rise of alternative election monitors on the Central Asian political scene illustrates how Western promotion of democracy has lost much credibility and has been challenged by a "multiple principals" problem. Throughout the 1990s, election monitoring was considered a relatively low-key and technocratic practice, while the ODIHR was allowed to conduct its short-term and long-term missions in relative calm. But following the Rose Revolution, Russian and Central Asian officials publicly accused the election division of promoting double standards and unnecessarily meddling in the internal affairs of member countries.[81] In September 2004 at a CIS summit in Astana, 9 of the 12 CIS leaders endorsed a statement that accused the OSCE of unnecessary interference in the domestic affairs of countries under the pretext of promoting democratic values.[82]

The aftermath of the Color Revolutions saw the rise of alternative election monitors sent by the CIS and the SCO. Not surprisingly, these monitoring missions reached strikingly different conclusions about the quality of elections in Eurasia than the ODHIR. As Appendix 2 suggests, the CIS and SCO verdicts in the Central Asian cases consistently have been far less critical than the ODHIR assessments. For example, for the 2007 Uzbek presidential elections, the CIS team observed that the elections were "free, open and transparent," and "a major factor in further democratization of social life in Uzbekistan," while the SCO mission stated that the poll was "legitimate, free and transparent and fully corresponded to the requirements of the national legislation and international election standards In the Central Asian cases, the CIS and SCO."[83] By contrast, the ODIHR final report observed that the "presidential election took place within a tightly controlled political environment and failed to meet many OSCE commitments for democratic elections."[84]

The presence of alternative monitors also provided ready-made favorable media coverage opportunities for these countries on and immediately following Election Day. As election-monitoring specialist Judith Kelley has argued, "The ability of governments to manipulate the election monitoring experience increases as the number of organizations available for monitoring grows."[85] Consistent with this hypothesis, throughout the latter half of the decade, the Central Asian governments have developed media strategies that quote these more friendly observers and their positive assessments in their election day coverage, while minimizing more critical coverage from groups such as the ODIHR. But neither the CIS nor the SCO election-monitoring divisions have signed on to the United Nation's "Code of Conduct for International Election Observers," a UN-backed regime created in 2005 to institutionalize certain standards and best practices in international election observation.[86] And despite promises to release a handbook of monitoring best practices, the CIS group has yet to do so.[87] In short, the CIS and SCO monitors who began monitoring elections in Central Asia in 2005 seem to be emulating the form, but not the substantive approach and practices of the OSCE/ODIHR monitors.

Conclusion

To be sure, the Central Asian governments all exhibited authoritarian tendencies and repressive practices well before they became objects of geopolitical influence. However, external engagement with the United States, Russia, and China provided local elites with new material, political, and normative opportunities to consolidate their regimes and quash opposition. New security cooperation in the name of terrorism by all three powers trained and equipped the security services of these regimes, while creating the new normative environment of anti-terrorism that allowed them to effectively erase distinctions between defending state security and silencing legitimate political opposition. In the related field of democracy promotion, the Central Asian governments, with the backing of Moscow and Beijing, successfully recoded Western-backed NGOs and democracy promotion actors as security threats and treated them as such, shutting down major organizations and criticizing the authority of the OSCE's election-monitoring division and values agenda. Finally, by grafting their own domestic pushback against Western democratic standards onto Russia's "sovereign democracy" concept, Central Asian elites mounted an ideological and normative counteroffensive against the West, accusing Washington of promoting double standards and hidden geopolitical agendas.

As such, it was the interaction between external players and Central Asia's local rules that over the course of the decade contributed to the deterioration of political rights across the region. Though the West did not intend for its "values" agenda to be eroded in this fashion, it increasingly came to accept this new difficult environment as a permanent characteristic of the region and adjusted its policies and expectations accordingly.

Geopolitical Competition and Political Stability: Kyrgyzstan's Base Bidding War

Even as Washington, Moscow, and Beijing have differed in their strategic goals and in their support of democratization and political reform in Central Asia, all the outside powers publicly agree that they have a common interest in promoting "political stability." But the term is overused and poorly defined, having become inextricably entangled as a rationalization for upholding local rules. The Central Asian regimes themselves justify their hard-line tactics and survival strategies in such terms, playing to outside fears about the security threats posed by looming state collapse, fragmentation, and militant Islam.[1] Similarly, along these lines, external actors have funded projects to develop state capacity or have supported these regimes' self-styled anti-terrorism efforts and political crackdowns. Over the course of a decade, political stability—initially understood as an "outcome"—has morphed into a reason to validate the political status quo.

The dramatic events of 2010 in Kyrgyzstan challenged the external consensus about the fundamental durability of the Central Asian regimes and their patrimonial structures. The sudden collapse of the Bakiyev government in Kyrgyzstan in April 2010 and the outbreak of mass ethnic violence two months later emphasized the fragility of Kyrgyzstan's political institutions. The regime collapse was preceded by intensifying U.S.-Russia rivalry over the fate of the Manas military base, leading some analysts to speculate that Moscow had deliberately sought to take down Bakiyev to punish his disloyalty to Moscow.[2]

This chapter focuses more closely on the role played by external competition in destabilizing the Kyrgyz government during the Bakiyev era (2005–2010). On the surface, the Kyrgyz case appears to challenge some of the arguments made in this book about the importance of "local rules" in structuring the interactions among the great powers in Central Asia. But even in this dramatic, and perhaps exceptional, case of geopolitical push and pull, a closer examination reveals that local actors played a pivotal role in driving these external dynamics; President Bakiyev and his ruling circle actively drummed up a bidding war between Moscow and Washington, making increasingly brazen demands for economic pay-offs. This bidding war provided Bishkek with non-transparent revenues that fed elite predation, eroded institutional capacity, and limited Western actors' willingness to criticize deteriorating political and economic trends in the country. After briefly examining the determinants of "political stability" in patronage-driven systems like the Central Asian states, this chapter explores how the Bakiyev government actively fueled U.S. and Russian competition and why Kyrgyzstan's patrimonial regime during this time proved more fragile than its regional counterparts.

How External Actors Maintain Central Asian "Political Stability"

The definition of *political stability* has varied considerably across the scholarly and policy communities. Classically, the term has been used to define the absence of political violence (civil war, violent demonstrations, organized crime, and militia conflicts), as described in Samuel Huntington's pioneering work on political institutions and political order.[3] Others have used the term as shorthand for the longevity of a specific government or regime, as a code word to justify political loyalty (i.e., the once "stable" regimes of the Persian Gulf), and/or to refer to the persistence of certain policy-making processes and institutions, despite changes in government.[4] Still others maintain that the term is inherently "relational," always defined in opposition to prevailing government concerns and therefore not measurable.[5]

For the purposes of this analysis, this chapter provisionally accepts Huntington's view that stability is the endurance of a political equilibrium, as measured by the absence of political violence and unrest. In the subset of states under consideration—patrimonial systems with strong parallel networks of informal authority—regime survival is paramount, and a breakdown in the patronage channels often precedes the collapse of political order.

Political Stability across Central Asia's Patrimonial Regimes

A cursory examination of the political stability of the Central Asian countries in the post-independence period reveals important variation. Kazakhstan and Turkmenistan have experienced the endurance of Soviet-era rulers who have effectively consolidated their control over state institutions, balancing informal interests and social networks. Kazakh President Nazarbayev has emphasized international legitimacy and openness to the outside world, thereby tempering some of his excesses, whereas the more repressive Turkmen President Niyazov completely isolated his country from almost all external contacts and influ-ences.[6] But in both cases, political systems have remained mostly unchallenged, with Ashgabat witnessing the orderly transition of power from the rule of Saparmurat Niyazov to Gurbanguly Berdymukhamedov in late 2006.

By contrast, in Kyrgyzstan, we have witnessed sudden regime collapses in 2005 and 2010, as well as an explosive ethnic conflict in the south of the country in June 2010 (and in the late Soviet era).[7] Tajikistan began its independence from a baseline of the extreme instability of civil war and moved toward greater state consolidation following the 1997 settlement. Finally, Uzbekistan occupies a position somewhere between these more and less stable country clusters. The repression demonstrated by Tashkent in defense of the regime has chilled polit-ical opposition and dissent, yet, as the events in Andijan showed, the legitimacy and long-term sustainability of the government is more vulnerable than it is in Astana and Ashgabat.[8]

If we accept that, in institutional composition, all of the Central Asian coun-tries are characterized by similar local patrimonial rules—including the preva-lence of informal politics, repression (mild to strong), institutional weakness, corruption, and elite predation—then there must be other reasons that account for why regimes and their accompanying patrimonial structures have endured unchallenged in some cases, but not in others.

External Flows, Competition, and Institutional Stability

A key factor in explaining these differences lies in examining the comparative fiscal composition of states and the varying external sources of revenue that feed their distributive institutions. External flows differ in some inherent characteris-tics, including their transparency, institutional targets, monitoring, condition-ality, and reliability.[9] For example, Western financial assistance from groups such as the IMF or World Bank tend to be transparent, are highly monitored and conditional, generally flow to the Ministry of Finance of the recipient country, and are subject to a clear schedule of disbursals and renewals. Bilateral security assistance, in contrast, tends to be opaque, less monitored, targeted to a state's security apparatus, controlled directly by the president, and more ad hoc in nature.

Accordingly, different types of external revenues may channel elite predation in significantly different manners; revenues that flow into state institutions, such as the Ministry of Finance or the Ministry of Oil and Gas, should be distributed within existing state-mediated patronage networks, thereby bolstering the state's authority and institutional structure. On the other hand, other revenue streams that bypass existing state institutions and agencies altogether, either by having elites directly appropriate them or by transferring them offshore, will tend to erode intra-systemic patrimonial practices. Patronage systems that suffer a loss of revenues will themselves risk precipitating distributional conflicts, political violence, and even their own collapse.[10]

In the cases of Kazakhstan and Turkmenistan, both have relied heavily on inflows of revenues from the sale of oil and gas, though Kazakhstan is also a far more diversified economy that is integrated into world financial markets. Such rental income is well documented to simultaneously contribute to state corruption, but also to forge and expand key domestic political coalitions and patronage networks that strengthen the legitimacy and mediating power of the state.[11] In these cases, then, external competition has mostly taken the form of competition among foreign oil and gas companies to win contracts to develop these resources and promote their preferred transit routes. These companies have perpetuated similar patterns of elite corruption across U.S., Russian, and Chinese energy investments. However, with the exception of Turkmenistan in the late 1990s, when gas exports and resulting revenues were at a low point, energy sales have provided a bedrock of steady revenues that encouraged state consolidation and augmented these governments' bargaining leverage over individual foreign oil companies.[12]

The more unstable and weaker Central Asian states are not only poorer, but have depended upon international financial organizations and external NGOs to effectively provide state-like functions and social services.[13] In the 1990s, Kyrgyzstan's self-styled image as a reformer helped it to secure large amounts of foreign assistance, especially from the West (while at the same time incurring huge amounts of external debt), while international organizations promoted and funded Tajikistan's initial reconstruction and state-building after its postwar national reconciliation.[14]

But over the last decade, both Kyrgyzstan and Tajikistan increasingly have leveraged intensifying external competition and their geopolitical positioning to secure more direct military and security assistance from the United States, Russia, and China, while ignoring external demands for deeper economic and political reforms. Unlike the steady inflows of foreign direct investment (FDI) experienced by Kazakhstan and Turkmenistan, these security-related revenues have tended to be ad hoc, short in duration, unmonitored, and often targeted at elites themselves, as opposed to broader state agencies or institutions. They have empowered national elites to grab as much as they can, as quickly as they can, shortening their political discount rates and concentrating these benefits outside the distributional networks of the patrimonial state.[15] As a result, in these cases international competition has eroded the development of broader institutional capacity and has undermined state-building.

Geopolitical Competition and Political Stability in Bakiyev's Kyrgyzstan

The rest of this chapter provides a case study of how external competition and revenues served to simultaneously enrich elites and destabilize the patrimonial state under the regime of President Bakiyev in Kyrgyzstan (2005–2010). Under Bakiyev, U.S.-Russia perceptions of zero-sum geopolitical competition intensified, as did the eagerness of the Bakiyev regime to leverage this competition for its own private benefit. The types of external revenues provided by these external actors—military assistance, emergency bilateral grants and loans, military basing payments, and contractual kickbacks—engendered naked self-interest that circumvented Kyrgyz state institutions. The apex of this competition was the "bidding war" over the status of the U.S. base at Manas, initiated by Bakiyev in 2009, which secured hundreds of millions of dollars from Moscow and Washington.

The Bakiyev Years and Intensifying U.S.-Russian Competition

During the rule of President Askar Akayev, the Manas base provided a steady income of private revenues to the ruling family, but its overall status was not publicly questioned or politicized excessively. Base-related issues and disagreements tended to be handled quietly by U.S. and Kyrgyz officials, as details were often kept hidden from the media. Perceived U.S.-Russia competition, while growing, also was partially mitigated by the Kyrgyz president, who tried to reassure Moscow of the limited purposes of Manas. For example, in 2003 Akayev readily agreed to a Russian request to establish a Russian base in the town of Kant, under the auspices of the CSTO, just 30 kilometers away from Manas.

After Akayev's ouster in March 2005, the Manas facility took on a new significance. Bakiyev himself proved a capable populist who almost immediately positioned himself as a champion of Kyrgyz sovereignty. He criticized Akayev and the Kyrgyz Foreign Ministry for compromising Kyrgyz sovereignty, including conceding too much territory to China during final border demarcation talks, and openly stated that the Manas base had served the interests of the United States and Kyrgyz elites, not Kyrgyzstan as a whole. In July 2005 in Astana, Bakiyev signed the SCO declaration about removing foreign military bases from the region. The U.S. eviction from K2 just a few days later gave the Kyrgyz president the confidence that, having the only remaining official U.S. base in the region, he could demand a much greater quid pro quo for continuing to provide basing rights to the United States.

Bakiyev and the Beginning of Hard Base Bargaining

Upon replacing Akayev, Bakiyev quickly took over the complex network of base-related fuel and service contracts, but he also sought to greatly increase the official $2 million rental payment for the base, a fee he considered a preposterously low "symbolic amount," given the base's obvious value to U.S. defense planners. After Astana, the Kyrgyz president began to talk publicly of renegotiating the agreement and increasing the rent; during an October 2005 visit by U.S. Secretary of State Condoleezza Rice, the Kyrgyz president also demanded a formal accounting of all base-related payments made during the Akayev regime and compensation for lost or embezzled funds.

Over the course of the autumn and winter, Bakiyev and his foreign representatives communicated to U.S. officials that they were seeking a hundredfold increase in the annual rent, from $2 million to $200 million. U.S. officials had little interest in opening discussions on the issue, but Bakiyev pressed on, strategically invoking external pressure and domestic political considerations. In January 2006 the Kyrgyz Foreign Ministry issued a formal request to the U.S. Embassy in Bishkek that demanded significant payment increases, with requests for a $50 million payment just for leasing and parking fees, as well as separate compensation for base-related environmental damage and the Akayev-era fuel contracts. On February 15, 2006, Bakiyev stated in an interview to the Russian newspaper *Kommersant* that he was seeking a $207 million rental payment for Manas, as Kyrgyzstan remained a poor country that could ill-afford the presence.[16] Just prior to an April 2006 visit to Moscow to meet with Russian President Vladimir Putin, Bakiyev issued an ultimatum to the United States on concluding a new deal by June 1.[17] Throughout these episodes, U.S. officials considered Kyrgyz demands excessive and threatened to secure alternate multiple regional basing arrangements for well below the new $200 million price tag.[18]

The two sides finally reached an agreement in July 2006, though the negotiations were both tense and revealing of both sides' differing interests and political agendas. According to a long-standing and perhaps misguided policy, the United States does not pay "rent" for its overseas military facilities. Rather, it encourages common security cooperation and provides economic and military assistance for such purposes.[19] In this spirit, U.S. negotiators offered a number of types of military cooperation and assistance as part of any new Manas deal, but their Kyrgyz counterparts were reportedly disinterested in anything but actual cash payments as quid pro quo.[20]

The July 2006 Accord

For the U.S. side, the resulting deal may have been legally astute, but politically it was too clever by half. The U.S. agreed to issue a public "Joint Statement" that stated the

U.S. side "expects to provide over $150 million in total assistance and compensation over the next year," thereby allowing Bakiyev to claim that he extracted a great deal of the $200 million that he demanded from the Americans. However, the actual lease payment for Manas only rose from $2 million annually to $17 million, with the "compensation package" bundling an array of various bilateral assistance programs (many of them already in place), as well as more general base-related economic contributions. To emphasize the U.S. point, the statement stressed that the base deal was part of a "larger, robust bilateral relationship" between the United States and the Kyrgyz Republic; it also pointed out that, since independence, the United States had provided more than $850 million in total aid to the Central Asian state.[21]

The legal distinction between base-related rent and bilateral aid may have satisfied the principals on the U.S. side, but the Kyrgyz government quickly soured on its terms. For one, Kyrgyz negotiators claimed that they were promised "more liquid" forms of assistance as part of the compensation package, in addition to the $17 million in rent.[22] Kyrgyz negotiators also resented that humanitarian programs such as the Peace Corps were counted in what they viewed as the basing rights package. Just a few months after supposedly signing the deal that would resolve the issue for at least the next five years, the Kyrgyz government was privately calling for another renegotiation.

Bishkek's resentment was fueled by a series of base-related accidents and scandals that received large-scale media attention, especially in the Russian-language press. In September 2006, a U.S. major deployed at Manas claimed to have been kidnapped from a large department store in Bishkek and kept captive for several days, though local Kyrgyz media claimed, instead, that she had faked the story, while local police also cast doubt on her narrative. Then, on December 6, 2006, the base was thrown into the national media spotlight when U.S. serviceman Zachary Hatfield shot and killed a fuel truck driver at the base's main checkpoint. The victim, Alexander Ivanov, was an ethnic Russian, but a Kyrgyz citizen, and long-time contractor at the base. Hatfield claimed that the driver had threatened him with a knife (only a nail file was found on Ivanov) and the incident soon spiraled into a media and public relations feeding frenzy.

The Manas base's public relations took a further hit after U.S. authorities clumsily offered Ivanov's widow the small sum of $1,000 as compensation (it was actually a symbolic payment but was mischaracterized in the press), and Hatfield was shortly thereafter whisked from the country.[23] Some U.S. and Kyrgyz observers claim that Moscow fueled the incident by paying for Ivanova's legal representation and generating inflammatory media coverage about the event. But U.S. officials, for their part, were slow to blunt the public relations disaster for both the base and the Embassy, focusing, instead, on the narrow questions of legal responsibility and the provisions of the United States' Status of Forces Agreement with the Kyrgyz government.

The Audacity of Access: Bakiyev's 2009 Manas Gambit

By the end of 2008, Kyrgyz dissatisfaction with the Manas deal, a spate of negative stories about the base, and the general deterioration of U.S.-Russian relations (including the August 2008 Georgia-Russia War) had placed the base in jeopardy. Tensions also characterized relations between U.S. diplomats and base officials, as Manas personnel dwarfed the Embassy in size and seeming influence, often simply ignoring or bypassing regular diplomatic channels in their dealings with Kyrgyz officials.[24] In retrospect, the imbalance of military and diplomatic interests also seems to have blinded DOD officials to the precarious nature of Bakiyev's rule and growing popular dissatisfaction with the regime. Defense planners placed a "K2" lens on Kyrgyz domestic developments, reasoning that the Uzbek eviction of the United States from K2 in 2005 resulted from Washington pressing Tashkent too hard on human rights concerns.

In the autumn of 2008, the primary challenge confronting Bakiyev was economic. The financial crisis had already devastated Russia, and its spillover effects threatened to sink Central Asia's economies with it. The hundreds of thousands of Kyrgyz labor migrants in Russia would be unable to send back critical remittances, while doubts also arose as to whether Moscow would be able to deliver on promises of investment in regional energy and infrastructure. Making matters worse, the Bakiyevs had accelerated their domestic plundering, privatizing the Kyrgyz national electricity company for reportedly a fraction of its value and taking major stakes in banks, restaurants, department stores, and most other profitable businesses.[25] Rumors also appeared that the Bakiyev family, from Kyrgyzstan's south, was intimately connected to exploding organized crime and the southern routes of the Afghan drug trade. Around this time, Maksim Bakiyev, the president's son, gained notoriety for his entrepreneurial activities and high visibility within the country; a year later, he would be appointed head of a special national investment fund, designed to mediate all foreign flows of foreign aid and FDI. With revenue at a standstill, a projected budget deficit widening, and most major national assets already seized, Bakiyev planned what can only be described as one of the most audacious geopolitical gambits contrived by a ruler of a small, nominally weak state—the plot to initiate a bidding war between Washington and Moscow over the future of the Manas base.

The Russian Role

Russia, of course, also played an important role in initiating the 2009 Manas eviction.[26] U.S.-Russian relations had reached a low point during the Russia-Georgia war in August 2008, and Central Asian diplomats themselves informed

U.S. officials that Russia was plotting to evict the United States from Manas to punish it for its support of Georgia. According to one report, Moscow had asked Uzbekistan at the fall 2008 meeting of the CIS to challenge the legal basis of Manas in exchange for supporting to support Tashkent's position on regional water disputes with its upstream neighbors.[27] At the same time, despite facing what they termed "enormous pressure" from Moscow, Kyrgyz officials in their bilateral meetings with U.S. representatives positioned themselves as willing to buck the Kremlin if given adequate incentives. For example, shortly after Russia reached an agreement with the Kyrgyz leadership in January 2009 to provide an aid and investment package to Bishkek in exchange for closing Manas, Kyrgyz Presidential Chief of Staff Danyar Usenov informed the U.S. Embassy that the "situation could still be saved" if the U.S. increased its payments.[28]

So the plot to close Manas served both the interests of both Bishkek and Moscow. At a joint press conference in Moscow in early February 2009, President Bakiyev first announced in public that the small Central Asian state had taken the decision to close down the U.S. air base, citing its domestic unpopularity. At the same event, Medvedev announced that Russia would be granting a special emergency assistance package to the Central Asian state, comprised of a $150 million grant, a $300 million soft loan, and $1.7 billion in credits to invest in the Kambarata-2 hydroelectric plant project. As part of the deal, Russia also assumed control of a number of Kyrgyz defense industries, including a 48 percent controlling stake in the Dastan torpedo manufacturing plant near Lake Issyk-Kul.[29] Though Russian and Kyrgyz officials denied that the aid package was in any way tied to the announcement on the closure on Manas, the quid pro quo was clearly implied, and the move was interpreted as a significant geopolitical victory for Moscow. A few days later, the Kyrgyz parliament supported Bakiyev's decision by voting to evict the United States from Manas, with only one deputy voting against the move.

Behind the Scenes Negotiations and Local Intermediaries

The announcement of the Manas closure occurred at a particularly bad time for Washington. In February 2009, many appointees of newly inaugurated President Barack Obama in the State Department, National Security Council, and Department of Defense were either new to their positions or had yet to be confirmed. Principals scrambled to understand the history of Manas realpoliticking and were hastily briefed regarding Manas's indispensability to the Afghanistan campaign. But the episode also raised an important political challenge: having been pounded by his Republican opponent in the presidential campaign for his foreign policy inexperience and plans to engage in dialogue with countries such as Iran and Russia, President Obama and his team could now ill-afford to hand Moscow such a high-profile victory so early.

Almost immediately after the announcement, U.S. officials sought to open back channel communications with Kyrgyz officials, while publicly stating that they would respect Bishkek's sovereign decision to terminate the agreement. U.S. Ambassador Tatiana Gfoeller noted after the announcement in a February 6 cable that the size of the Russian package was effectively only $450 million (without the pledge for investment) and was wanted by Bakiyev for his short-term political survival, specifically "as a war chest for presidential elections...With a $450 million slush fund in hand, Bakiyev can raise salaries, fund social housing, ensure there will be no shortages of food in the markets, buy off local officials, and buy the votes needed to engineer a successful re-election."[30] One week later, Gfoeller observed that "it is clear that Moscow purchased Kyrgyz President Bakiyev's decision to close Manas," and that "it is also clear that Bakiyev views the Base exclusively as a commercial commodity."[31] The U.S. ambassador further speculated that if the Russians could be reassured that the base would be closed in a couple of years, then the United States might convince Bakiyev to re-open the base for around $150 million, "if the U.S. pledge provided the money Bakiyev wants for his political purposes in a timely manner."[32]

A U.S. negotiating team was sent to Bishkek to try to conclude a new deal, while U.S. officials intensely lobbied Russian counterparts to agree to respect a renegotiated deal. Not coincidentally, in early April the Kyrgyz finally agreed to the parameters of a new agreement—which involved raising the rent to $60 million and renaming the facility—just after Moscow had wired its promised $300 million in credits.[33] How the Russian disbursal was spent remains a subject of intrigue, as Maksim Bakiyev is rumored to have laundered the funds through his offshore bank accounts, via the Asia Universal Bank in Bishkek (later nationalized).[34]

During the crisis, the president's son seems to have been one of two Kyrgyz individuals who positioned themselves as brokers between the U.S. Department of Defense and the Kyrgyz government. Maksim had grown increasingly active and influential in Kyrgyz politics over the previous year, in addition to pursuing his business activities. A frequent visitor to the United States, the 32-year-old presented himself as a potential ally to the United States and, in his meetings with U.S. officials, played up his dislike for Russian attempts to influence Kyrgyz politics. As early as February 18, just days after the initial closure announcement in Moscow, Maksim appears to have reached out to U.S. officials about saving the base through an intermediary;[35] he later claimed to have persuaded his father to reverse course on the base closure and took credit for the decision to rename the facility "Manas Transit Center" to emphasize its logistical, as opposed to operational, military role. In a leaked U.S. Embassy cable, the U.S. *chargé d'affaires* describes a dinner conversation with Maksim just a few days after the new Manas agreement was publicly announced:

Maxim indicated that his support for the turnaround on Manas entailed some risk, but said his background as a futures trader made him comfortable with risk. "I saw that a deal was needed, and stepped in to set it up," he said. He claimed the Russians were mad, and were trying to punish Kyrgyzstan, but they were in a box, given Medvedev's statement in February that the future of Manas was a sovereign decision of Kyrgyzstan.[36]

Though the Embassy remained skeptical of the younger Bakiyev's self-proclaimed importance, his posturing as an interlocutor reflects just how strategically the Kyrgyz regime was courting its external suitors. The posturing seems to have worked, as the same cable concluded that, despite his unofficial status, "Maxim's favorable disposition towards the United States could be of benefit to our interests."[37] Similarly, a leaked cable by the U.S. Embassy in Bishkek two months later described the president's son as "smart, corrupt and a good ally to have," reasoning that, "while this is a relationship which must be cultivated carefully, we believe it is also a relationship which can pay important dividends for the USG [United States Government]."[38]

The other key broker during the Manas crisis appears to have been Erkin Bekbolotov, co-founder and owner of Mina Corp, the mysterious company providing fuel to Manas, who would stand to lose hundreds of millions of dollars in fuel contracts if the eviction was carried through. According to the Tierney report (see Chapter 8), Bekbolotov called Maksim Bakiyev shortly after the February announcement with his own proposal for how to save the base.[39] After proposing the "raise the rent, rename the base" solution to a receptive Maksim, the owners of Mina on February 19 emailed Mark Iden, Director of Operations for DLA Energy. As described in the Tierney report, "just days after Mr. Iden received the call from Mr. Bekbolotov, DLA Energy issued a non-competitive solicitation to directly award Mina a follow-on contract worth almost $600 million to supply fuel to Manas." At a Mina-DLA Energy meeting in March 2009, Iden agreed to pass on the proposal to the Department of Defense, but by that time Maksim had already been in direct contact with U.S. Ambassador Gfoeller with his similar plan.

The 2009 Agreement and the U.S.-Russia Reset

The terms of the new deal were concluded in April, though not publicly announced until early July for political purposes. Perhaps not coincidentally, Kyrgyz television throughout May and June 2009 ran heavy coverage of the situation in Afghanistan, emphasizing its deterioration and possible regional consequences. In late June the two sides announced the new deal, with the increased rent and renaming of the facility, and, as Maksim had predicted, Moscow had little choice but to publicly support the new agreement as Kyrgyzstan's "sovereign right."

In an immediate reaction to the double-cross, Russian Defense Minister Anatoly Serdyukov and Deputy Prime Minister Igor Sechin were dispatched to Bishkek. Shortly after, Moscow announced that it would be opening a second base in Kyrgyzstan in the southern Osh district, to be used by CSTO Rapid Reaction forces. Though Kyrgyz officials commented that the new base was needed in the fight against growing extremist activity in the Ferghana Valley, the timing of the measure seems to suggest that the new base was, at least in part, Bishkek's concession to Moscow for the Manas fiasco. Yet, even this face-saving announcement quickly backfired, as Uzbekistan was not consulted on the proposal, and Tashkent interpreted the base announcement as a possible hostile intervention in its ongoing dispute with Kyrgyzstan over water rights.[40]

With the high-profile success and new revenues secured from the Manas bidding war, Bakiyev mobilized his election campaign in July 2009 and handily won re-election in a ballot deemed particularly problematic by OSCE observers.[41] Tellingly, U.S. officials remained quiet, issuing a tepid statement a few days after the poll, much to the dismay of the Kyrgyz political opposition. In fact, throughout 2009 the political climate deteriorated, with journalists and political analysts being beaten and harassed, and opposition politicians intimidated and arrested on trumped-up charges. The political watchdog NGO Freedom House downgraded Kyrgyzstan to "Not Free" from its previous designation as "Partly Free."[42]

But reconciliation on the Kyrgyz issue was also on the agenda for President Obama and Medvedev's warming relations. At their Moscow summit in early July 2009, the two leaders cemented the "reset" of relations by announcing a new bilateral accord allowing for the transit of American weapons and lethal cargo through Russian territory and airspace. Following the reset and the expansion of the Northern Distribution Network, Russia appeared to have abandoned its attempts to overtly block U.S. access to Manas.

Moscow's Soft Power Barrage and Bakiyev's Fall

If the Manas renewal signaled a political victory for the new U.S. administration, Russia would soon extract a modicum of revenge when the regime of Kurmanbek Bakiyev suddenly collapsed in April 2010, following a series of protests across Kyrgyzstan's northern cities. On April 7, these protests spread to Bishkek, as demonstrators clashed with security services, killing 80 people on the streets and injuring hundreds of others. Mercifully for the city of Bishkek, within 24 hours the security services and police folded, prompting Bakiyev to flee to his home city of Osh. As he tried to regroup, a group of opposition figures declared themselves the interim government. A few days later, following consultations with the presidents of the United States, Russia, and Kazakhstan, Bakiyev left Kyrgyzstan for exile in Belarus, hosted by President Alexander Lukashenko.

Much has been made of Russia's active involvement in the toppling of Bakiyev, with several Russian actors appearing eager to take credit, just as Western NGOs had done following the collapse of Akayev's regime in March 2005.[43] Moscow's actions have been viewed as an incensed and direct response to the Bakiyev regime's double-cross on the promised Manas closure in spring 2009. However, as we have noted above, bilateral U.S.-Russian relations actually had improved in the summer of 2009, while the two presidents had reached an understanding on the operations of Manas. Over the course of summer 2009, news stories in the Russian media about Kyrgyzstan remained neutral in tone, downplaying the significance of the Manas saga and highlighting the more cooperative tone of the reset. A closer look also reveals a critical temporal gap between Bakiyev's Manas gambit in spring 2009 and Moscow's use of its soft-power mechanism against the Kyrgyz president, which began in earnest in late 2009.

Various explanations have been advanced to explain this timing gap. Some credit Moscow for taking its time to intensify its contacts with the Kyrgyz opposition in the fall of 2009 in anticipation of later instability. Another possibility is that the Russian military and the Kremlin became increasingly concerned with growing military-to-military cooperation between Kyrgyz security services and CENTCOM, which went well beyond what was needed at Manas. In November 2009, Maksim requested that the United States fund the construction of an "international counterterrorism center" in the remote southern Kyrgyz province of Batken;[44] just a month earlier, a U.S.-funded special forces training center in Tokmok became operational.[45] Still others claim that it was the visit of a high-level Kyrgyz delegation to China in November 2009 that finally prompted the Kremlin to concentrate its soft power against Bakiyev.

Russian Soft Power at Work

Regardless of the exact trigger, Moscow seems to have mobilized its instruments of soft power in a concerted effort to weaken the Kyrgyz ruler. Negative news stories about Kyrgyzstan began to appear in the Russian press in fall 2009 and then intensified in spring 2010, highlighting the Bakiyev family's power ambitions and corruption.[46] For example, the widely read *Nezavisimaya Gazeta* ran a prominent feature on Bakiyev and his son, titled "Father and Son," which detailed how Maksim was positioning himself for an Azeri-style takeover of power and featured critical quotes from members of the Kyrgyz opposition.[47]

A less visible, but even more effective lever was Russia's decision to introduce a new export duty of 100 percent on fuel exports to Kyrgyzstan on April 1, 2010. Officially, the action to impose a $193.50/ton tax had been scheduled to take place as part of the strengthening of the Russia-Belarus-Kazakhstan Customs Union, but Moscow easily could have deferred the action or granted an exemption. The more convincing explanation, as advanced by Bazarbai Mambetov, head of the Kyrgyz Oil Traders' Association, was that the Kremlin wanted to end a scheme through which massive quantities of Russian jet fuel for Manas were being falsely certified as for civilian use, thereby depriving Russian coffers of hundreds of millions of dollars in excise taxes.[48] The punitive tax immediately spiked inflation throughout Kyrgyzstan, especially on the costs of energy and transported goods. The announcement of impending price increases also was a major grievance that helped mobilize the anti-Bakiyev demonstrations on April 6 in Naryn and Talas, which soon snowballed into a broader anti-regime revolt.

Counting the Cost: The Aftermath of April 2010

Base Backlash

The aftermath of the Bakiyev collapse did few favors for U.S. standing and influence in Kyrgyzstan. Members of the Kyrgyz interim government claimed that during Bakiyev's last year in tenure, U.S. Embassy officials lost all interest in maintaining contacts with Kyrgyz opposition members and civil society.[49] U.S. Ambassador Gfoeller was particularly singled out as unresponsive and even dismissive of the possibility that the Bakiyev regime was in any way threatened, favoring a strategy of increased cooperation with the government. The fact that Gfoeller was married to Michael Gfoeller, who at the time was a State Department Policy Advisor to CENTCOM, further heightened criticisms that the Embassy had become a political tool of the base and had failed to provide an independent assessment of Kyrgyzstan's deteriorating political environment.

The status of the base, the most important concern of U.S. officials, was a source of cynicism and irritation among most of the interim government, either because of their ties to Moscow or because of their perceptions that the U.S. had abandoned political criticism of the Bakiyev government in order to maintain access to Manas. Kyrgyz interim officials extended the 2010 lease out of obligation, but also claimed that the Bakiyevs themselves had been holding up the 2010 renewal, demanding that the State Department organize a U.S. visit for Maksim.[50] Interestingly, Maksim was scheduled to visit Washington later in April 2010 for a series of official and business events, but the program was canceled following the regime's collapse.

Almost immediately, Kyrgyz attention turned to the fuel contracts that were servicing the base and the role played by the mysterious Mina Corp. In June 2010, the Pentagon rebid the tender for the Manas fuel contract (though this would be won again by Mina), while high-level U.S. envoys such as Assistant Secretary of State Robert Blake and National Security Council senior director for Russian and Eurasian affairs Michael McFaul made several trips to Bishkek in an effort to repair relations and the United States' image. In July 2010, the United States pledged $45 million to Kyrgyzstan at an international donors conference, including paying for the cost of a new constitutional referendum and parliamentary elections in October 2010. U.S. officials now adopted the public position of insisting that Washington wanted to develop multiple contacts with the Central Asian country and not focus exclusively on Manas. But the trials and tribulations of the last few years seem to have severely damaged U.S. standing in Kyrgyzstan. According to the latest Gallup Survey, only 30 percent of Kyrgyz held a positive view of the United States, though Russia's numbers were even lower, at 23 percent.[51]

The Question of Parliamentarianism

Despite Russia's apparent political victory, it too faced its own challenges in the wake of Bakiyev's toppling. Moscow moved quickly to solidify its new close relationship with the interim government, as Russia became the first state to acknowledge the government of interim premier Roza Otunbayeva. President Medvedev invited Otunbayeva to a CIS summit as the official Kyrgyz head of state, even though in her new position she was viewed as unconstitutional by a number of the other CIS heads of state, most vehemently by Belarus's President Lukashenko.

According to Kyrgyz officials, nearly every Russian envoy who visited Bishkek following the collapse of the Bakiyev regime stressed that the Russian government did not think it feasible or appropriate for the Central Asian country to pursue an experiment in parliamentary democracy, as the Kyrgyz were intending to do.[52] Kyrgyz interim leaders received similar messages from the other Central Asian states, chief among them Kazakhstan. Regardless, Kyrgyz officials pressed ahead with a June 2010 referendum on the country's new political system and then held parliamentary elections in October 2010. In the October poll, six parties emerged over the voting threshold, with eventually three forming a coalition government, though the durability of the new mixed system remains in doubt heading into new presidential elections.

Violence Erupts in the South

The fragility and weakness of the interim government would be revealed just a couple of months after it assumed power, when ethnic-based violence erupted in

June 2010 in southern Kyrgyzstan at a level of ferocity not seen since late-Soviet times.[53] Interethnic violence had first broken out in May between factions loyal to Bakiyev and Uzbek groups backing the interim government. After the June 9 clashes in the markets of Osh and Jalalabad, members of local communities immediately mobilized into armed gangs along ethnic lines. Uzbek neighborhoods were raided and torched by Kyrgyz gangs, while Uzbek homes and businesses in mixed neighborhoods were also targeted. Law enforcement ceased to function, and, according to some reports, some Kyrgyz security officials actually aided the gang violence against Uzbek groups. There were also reports of widespread sexual violence, as well as broad discrimination against Uzbeks in the administration of relief supplies and medical attention to the injured.

On June 12 the interim government declared a state of emergency and appealed to Russia to intervene militarily in the south to restore order, a request that was denied by Moscow. One day later, authorities in Bishkek started calling up reservists to send to the south, though these recruits' general lack of training and ethnic Kyrgyz background further signaled that the interim government lacked both the capacity and credibility to adequately restore order. The International Commission investigation estimates that around 470 people were killed, most of them Uzbeks, and 1,900 injured, while up to 400,000 residents, again mostly Uzbeks, were displaced from their homes, with over 100,000 fleeing to neighboring Uzbekistan.[54] By the end of June a tense calm had returned to the south, but the visible signs of the conflicts remained, with entire neighborhoods abandoned and the two ethnic communities now effectively separated.

As with the last outbreak of Uzbek-Kyrgyz violence, the so-called "Osh riots" of 1990, the cause of the violence seems to have been the lack of central authority in the south. Bakiyev's main base of support was in the south; after his collapse, the interim government in Bishkek had a tenuous hold on state institutions there, especially the police and security services. Following the change in government in Bishkek, Otunbayeva's interim government disbanded the Bakiyev era parliament, and the governance of the south reverted to the local mayors, governors, and criminal networks, encouraging Uzbek factions to oppose Bakiyev supporters in clashes that took ethnic dimensions.[55] Supporters of the Otunbayeva government counter that the violence was clearly premeditated and triggered by pro-Bakiyev factions. Vice-Prime Minister Azambek Atambayev accused Maksim Bakiyev of paying out $10 million to various gangs to instigate the riots. But whatever havoc the Bakiyevs planned and spread through their allies and cronies, the ferocity of the violence and the incapacity of state structures to adequately protect minority communities—as well as the numerous reports that Kyrgyz security services actively partook in the violence—exposed the weakness of the new government in Bishkek and the precarious state of political order in the impoverished Central Asian state.

Conclusion: Political Stability and Geopolitical Competition in Central Asia

Though the concept of "political stability" is often difficult to pinpoint and is highly politicized, this chapter has argued that external competition in Bakiyev's Kyrgyzstan played a critical role in destabilizing the country. At the same time, this competition followed "local rules" as the Kyrgyz regime initiated the Manas bidding war and broke promises to both sides so as to maximize its bargaining leverage and increase private economic benefits. Despite conspiracy theories and rumors, it is highly doubtful that either Washington or even Moscow intended to destabilize Kyrgyzstan to the point of breaking, as it seemed to be following the June 2010 ethnic violence. Rather, the types of opaque, ad hoc, and narrowly targeted revenues that the two external powers provided, along with their aggressive manipulation by the Bakiyev regime, combined to feed extreme predation by the Kyrgyz government to the detriment of internal state-building and broad-based patrimonial redistribution. Once again, it was the interaction between external powers pursuing their strategic agendas and elites playing by local rules that resulted in these dysfunctional outcomes.

Given its peculiar characteristics, it is not clear whether the Kyrgyz case travels well, as the conditions that encouraged this rapid destabilization in Kyrgyzstan may not be present to the same degree elsewhere in the region. Kyrgyzstan's extreme poverty, state weakness, and susceptibility to Russian influence may well be distinct, while the presence of a major foreign military installation, viewed as critically important by at least one great power, was a necessary condition for the bidding war. The types of private goods that emerged from these forms of external support—base-related payments and contracts, unconditional bilateral economic transfers, and military assistance—were readily appropriated by the Bakiyev regime for their own private purposes. Perhaps Tajikistan is the closest analogous case, as it has hosted a number of military facilities of a variety of external powers (Russia, France and India); however, in the Tajik case, Rahmon has not been able to leverage any of these other minor interests against Russia to the same degree, while his attempts to extract additional material concessions from Russia for basing rights have proven difficult, given that Moscow holds the trump card of controlling the status of hundreds of thousands of Tajik migrant workers.

Finally, this type of material analysis of external influence and political destabilization does not account for the potential impact of the Arab Spring on the region. In Tunisia, Egypt, Libya, Bahrain, Syria, and elsewhere, it is clear that anti-government protestors fueled each other's activities and copied each other's mobilization tactics. Whether these dynamics will diffuse to Central Asia, a region where social media remains less widely used, remains an open question. But as we will see in the next chapter, Central Asia's levels of corruption and governance problems rival and exceed many of those that seemingly drove popular revolts in the Middle East and North Africa.

‖ 8 ‖

The Price of Access: Contracts and Corruption

Central Asia continues to face severe governance and corruption problems. Do-mestically, patronage politics and informal networks channel unofficial eco-nomic activity, while the use of state resources for personal profit by elites remains a "local rule" throughout the region. Corruption is so pervasive within Central Asian state institutions that some have referred to it as a sanctioned and prevalent informal tool of administrative control, allowing rulers to blackmail and effectively sanction subordinates who fall out of line.[1] Moreover, the types of external revenues that have flowed from the international economy and com-munity into the Central Asian countries—security assistance, international aid, rents from the sale of natural resources—are also among the types of revenues most susceptible to graft, misappropriation, and corruption on the part of ruling regimes.[2]

The magnitude of the problem warrants some quick comparisons. Over the last decade, international anti-corruption watchdogs, such as Transparency In-ternational and Global Integrity, have consistently ranked the Central Asian countries at the bottom of their global indices. Figure 8.1 presents a time-series of the World Bank's indicators on "control of corruption," a bundle of available corruption surveys. The Central Asian states rank in the bottom 10 percentile in the world, with the exception of Kazakhstan, which, in recent years, has improved modestly to rank in the bottom 20 percentile.

Figure 8.2 shows how unfavorably Central Asia compares even to the Middle Eastern states that experienced the so-called Arab Spring. Even though public discontent about corruption and accountability were important drivers of the 2010 anti-government protests in Tunisia, Egypt, and Jordan, these countries still rank considerably *higher* than their Central Asian counterparts, with only Libya and Syria recently dipping below the 20-percentile mark. Interestingly, Djibouti, which hosts the largest U.S. military base in Africa, scores considerably better than its Central Asian–base hosting counterpart, Kyrgyzstan.

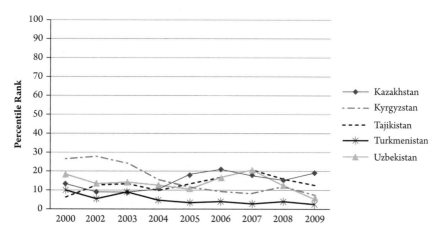

Figure 8.1 Control of Corruption, Central Asia, 2000–2009 Source: D. Kaufmann, A. Kraay, and M. Mastruzzi (2010), *The Worldwide Governance Indicators, Methodology and Analytical Issues*

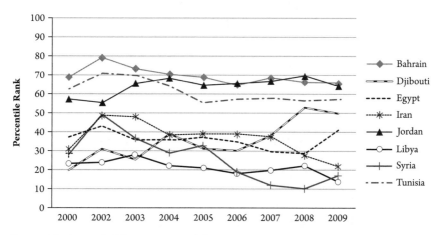

Figure 8.2 Control of Corruption, Middle East, 2000–2009 Source: D. Kaufmann, A. Kraay, and M. Mastruzzi (2010), *The Worldwide Governance Indicators, Methodology and Analytical Issues*

As with our study of democratization and human rights, this chapter does not (and cannot) argue that U.S.-Russia-China competition and engagement have been primarily responsible for causing Central Asia's acute governance problems. However, in their pursuit of economic and security engagement with the Central Asian states, external powers have had to bargain with and curry favor with local elites in order to obtain and maintain access to the host country. This chapter explores some of the specific arrangements that have structured and mediated these interactions, as well as how they have fed local graft and rent-seeking; in both economic and security issues, local elites have actively evoked a heightened sense of geopolitical competition to secure favorable contractual terms and private deals for themselves.

These access arrangements have been embedded in new transnational networks that link local elites, deal brokers, foreign companies, government actors, and offshore financial vehicles. These networks have simultaneously structured arrangements to benefit local elites, while allowing foreign companies and governments to maintain "plausible deniability" and to distance themselves from accusations that they actively feed graft and corruption. They are the most concrete embodiment of how great power interests are channeled by local rules. The chapter illustrates these themes with case studies that compare corruption scandals, and the accompanying transnational networks that they generated, involving U.S. and Chinese oil companies in Kazakhstan and the controversy surrounding fuel contracts at the U.S. airbase at Manas.

The Impact of External Engagement on Central Asian Corruption and Governance

The interaction among the United States, Russia, and China in the security and economic spheres has abetted corruption among Central Asian elites in two main ways.

Multiple Principals and the Price of Access

First, and in line with one of the overall arguments of this book about the negative impact of multiple suitors vying for influence, Central Asian rulers have cited the shady actions of one external actor to encourage others to engage in similar questionable behavior. In their bids to secure contracts, the governments and companies of the United States, Russia, and China have accommodated these local demands, which, in turn, have encouraged even more brazen forms of external rent-seeking. In the security realm, we have already recounted the 2009 Manas bidding, which allowed the Bakiyev regime to extract payments from both Russia and the United States that they subsequently embezzled from national accounts. The Northern Distribution Network developed by the United States has been predicated on offering economic incentives to the Central Asian governments to support the Western resupply effort for Afghanistan, thereby blurring the lines between offering economic contracts and encouraging graft.

Turning to the oil and gas sector, foreign investment in Central Asia's hydrocarbon development has been riddled with corruption, not unlike the extractive industries in other parts of the developing world. However, what distinguishes, at least in part, the politics of oil and gas deals in Central Asia is that local officials

routinely have used the potential interest of energy companies from rival countries as a tactic to augment their bargaining leverage and to demand private pay-
offs. The political context of these negotiations has also changed. In the 1990s,
Western companies were welcomed by the Caspian energy producers as the
bearers of desperately needed foreign investment and technical expertise, but
over the 2000s, the return of a resurgent Russia and the entry of China into the
Central Asian energy market created a competitive environment that has
empowered more aggressive negotiating behavior by Central Asian governments vis-à-vis Western companies.[3]

International maneuverings to secure oil concessions in Kazakhstan during
the last decade provide several instructive examples. In 2003, the Western members of the Kashagan consortium exercised their right of first refusal to block the
Chinese companies CNOOC and Sinopec from buying BG Group's 17 percent
stake in the consortium. The announcement so incensed President Nazarbayev,
who had personally supported the deal and viewed Chinese entry as an important geopolitical hedge, that within hours he retaliated by withdrawing the consortium's pre-production exemption from paying Kazakhstan's value added tax.[4]
CNPC's 2005 purchase of the Canadian company PetroKazakhstan, also targeted by Russia's Lukoil, was rife with behind-the-scenes interference by Russia
and China in Kazakh domestic politics.[5] And, according to a leaked U.S. Embassy cable, in a 2010 meeting with the U.S. ambassador to Kazakhstan, an executive of KazMunaiGas described Chinese and Russian companies as circling the
country's major concessions "like vultures," hoping to pick up whatever pieces
might be left by Western partners if these deals imploded.[6] Local elites skillfully
both leveraged and invoked these perceptions of external competition.

Central Asia Goes Offshore: New Global Networks of Transactions

Second, by using the legal protections and opportunities afforded by offshore
financial vehicles, Central Asian elites have joined with these external private
and public actors to create new complex transactional networks that have concealed their misappropriation of state-owned assets. The region has become an
excellent illustration of how corruption and money-laundering in this globalized
world grow in tandem, as the "presence of one tends to create and reciprocally
reinforce the incidence of the other."[7]

Since independence, what had been one of the most economically isolated
areas of the world has selectively integrated deeply into global finance.[8] In addition
to money-laundering, the offshore world has proven to be an invaluable tool for
splitting the legal personas and activities of state companies, creating chains of shell
companies and financial vehicles designed to avoid national regulations and tax
obligations. Central Asian elites have used these new offshore vehicles to facilitate

and structure their external transactions. For example, the Tajikistan Aluminum Company (TALCO), Tajikistan's largest enterprise with reported ties to the ruling family, has used a web of offshore registries to conduct and hide its dealings;[9] in one set of court proceedings bought forth in the controlling legal domain of the British Virgin Islands, TALCO alleges that a former manger conspired with the Russian Rusal, the world's largest aluminum company, to divert over $500 million in profits between 1996 and 2004, stashing them in offshore bank accounts.[10]

Though data on the geographic origin of regional foreign direct investment (FDI) is sparse and unreliable, some documented trends in Kazakhstan suggest that offshore companies and financial intermediaries are becoming routine conduits for external investment. According to Kazakhstan's National Bank, in 2010 total FDI from the British Virgin Islands (BVI) to Kazakhstan had reached $712.5 million, a total that actually surpassed China's official FDI in 2009 ($708.7 million).[11] In 2008, the total value of inflows from entities registered in the Cayman Islands ($608.5 million) approached the $692.5 million of official Chinese FDI. The Caymans and BVI are themselves among the leading sources of FDI to China and destinations of Chinese FDI abroad, suggesting that a good proportion of these offshore flows to Central Asia may actually originate in China.[12]

These offshore vehicles also have allowed external patrons to structure deals in which local elites have been granted private benefits, while maintaining "plausible deniability" about their own role in encouraging graft and corruption. Though, as we shall see, there have been some instances of external actors making overt bribes or direct payments to Central Asian officials, most of the personal profiteering has been concealed within legitimate corporate entities and business transactions, such as financial holding companies, intermediary trading companies, and contractors with offshore registration. As such, within the broad parameters of conducting legitimate international business transactions, these offshore tools have allowed ruling elites the means to divert or siphon off state revenues for their own private use. For example, an investigation of the structure of Turkmenistan-Russia fuel deals by the NGO Global Witness found that much of the graft and kickbacks was channeled through Itera, an intermediary trading company that for many years exclusively handled Turkmenistan's gas exports to Ukraine.[13]

Foreign Oil Companies, Contracts, and Corruption in Kazakhstan

The unfolding of two high-profile corruptions scandals involving senior local elites and energy companies from the United States and China illustrates broad similarities in how oil companies use complex offshore vehicles to structure these deals and to disguise private payments.

Kazakhgate and the Giffen Affair

The most publicized corruption scandal in Central Asia involved the dealings of James Giffen, an American operator who in the early 1990s became a close advisor to President Nazarbayev after he had cultivated senior Soviet officials during the Gorbachev period. After the Soviet collapse, Giffen and his consulting company, Mercator, became indispensable to Kazakhstan's leadership by organizing introductions to international energy companies, brokering large deals, and picking up international travel expenses.[14] Giffen's self-styled position as gatekeeper to Kazakhstan's oil wealth eventually earned him a Kazakh diplomatic passport, while his power within Kazakhstan reportedly grew with his ability to help Nazarbayev and his elite cronies to benefit personally from new international oil deals.[15] Giffen and his company reportedly took cuts of successful transactions, including a success fee from Chevron's Tengiz field that netted him 7.5 cents on every barrel the company produced.[16]

After a lengthy investigation of Swiss financial transactions by U.S. and Swiss officials, Giffen was finally arrested at JFK Airport in New York on March 30, 2003, and was indicted for wire and mail fraud, money laundering, and violations of the Foreign Corrupt Practices Act (FCPA).[17] According to U.S. prosecutors, since 1995 Nazarbayev and two of his senior colleagues had received hidden payments totaling $78 million through six large oil deals involving American oil companies, including Texaco, Amoco, Philips Petroleum, and Mobil Oil, all of them negotiated by Giffen.[18] Giffen allegedly used a complex network of over 30 offshore bank accounts and shell companies to direct unlawful payments from these oil companies to the personal Swiss bank accounts of "very senior" Kazakh officials, later identified as the former prime minister and oil minister Nurlan Balgimbayev, as well as Nazarbayev himself. The funds were reportedly used to buy lavish gifts including jewelry, luxury vehicles, vacations, and tuition payments at overseas universities.[19]

The indictment also accused Giffen of using Mercator to conceal transactions and launder money. Between 1995 and 2000, Mercator collected at least $67 million in success fees from brokering these international oil deals. In one instance, the indictment alleged that Mobil paid Mercator a $51 million fee for negotiating Mobil's 1996 acquisition of a 25 percent stake in the vast Tengiz oil field.[20] Brian Williams, a Mobil Oil lawyer who had assisted Giffen and had received a kickback of $2 million for his services in negotiating Tengiz, pled guilty to tax evasion on June 12, 2003.[21]

Though the case dealt with a set of transactions that had taken place from 1995 to 2000, it hung over U.S.-Kazakh relations for the next decade. Nazarbayev was consumed by the case's status and became obsessed with its potential to damage his reputation. In his meetings with U.S. President Bush and Vice President Cheney, Nazarbayev and his representatives repeatedly asked that the investigation be limited or dropped.[22] One visit to the United States by the Kazakh president in 2006 seemed particularly ill-timed, coming just a month after the Bush administration announced a high-profile new "National Strategy to Internationalize Efforts Against Kleptocracy."[23] In 2007, the U.S., Kazakh, and Swiss governments agreed to use the $84 million case-related funds in the discovered Swiss bank accounts for the benefit of underprivileged Kazakh children; the World Bank sanctioned the deal, though Astana never admitted that these were the personal accounts of the Kazakh president.[24]

The case itself took a number of curious twists and turns that revealed a complicated web of U.S. private and state interests. Soon after his indictment, Giffen's lawyers mounted a novel "public authority defense," claiming that his actions had been authorized and encouraged by a number of U.S. government agencies, including the Central Intelligence Agency, the National Security Council, the State Department, and the White House, all of which were eager to obtain information about the Central Asian country.[25] The defense bogged down court proceedings for years, as lawyers and government attorneys argued over Giffen's right to access classified documents.[26]

To the surprise of many observers, the defense worked. In August 2010, Giffen pleaded guilty to one misdemeanor of failing to disclose on a 1996 tax return that he was a signatory to a Swiss account, and his lawyer, on behalf of Mercator, pled guilty to one count of an FCPA violation for gifting speedboats worth $16,000 to a senior official.[27] In a remarkable opinion, presiding Judge William Pauley accepted Giffen's claims to be an indispensable player advancing U.S. geopolitical interests. Pauley thanked Giffen for "his service" to the United States and described him as "a conduit for secret communications to the Soviet Union and its leadership during the Cold War," who later became a "trusted adviser to Kazakhstan's president." [28] Giffen was sentenced to time already served (one night in jail).

The judge's comments were striking, not only for actually allowing the national interest defense, for which there is no actual exemption in the FCPA statute, but also for his seeming conflation of the Soviet era, when Giffen facilitated U.S.-Soviet business deals, and the 1990s, when the alleged crimes actually took place. Thus, the decade-long saga drew to a close, with the Justice Department closing the case with a whimper and other branches of the U.S. government breathing a collective sigh of relief that the issue would cease to be raised at future U.S.-Kazakh bilateral meetings.

The Chinese Connection: CNPC and Aktobe MunaiGaz

A no-less explosive scandal broke out in early 2010 involving Timur Kulibayev, Nazarbayev's second son-in law and rumored possible political successor. Over Nazarbayev's tenure, Kulibayev has positioned himself as one of the most powerful men in Kazakhstan and has become one of the richest men in the world, controlling several energy and resources companies and managing Kazakhstan's national sovereign wealth fund, which controls up to 90 percent of the country's prized companies.

Charges of major acts of bribery and corruption in a number of energy deals were leveled against Kulibayev by Mukhtar Ablyazov, the politically estranged oligarch and former chairman of BTA, Kazakhstan's largest bank, which was forcibly nationalized in 2009. The most dramatic of these, published in February 2010 in a series of open letters in Kazakh opposition and independent newspapers, alleged that Kulibayev made a personal profit of $166 million from CNPC's 2003 acquisition of the Kazakh government's 25 percent stake in Aktobe MunaiGaz. The oil company was Kazakhstan's fourth-largest producer and since 1997 had been 60 percent owned by CNPC, the first big deal made in the country by a Chinese energy company.

Investigative reports into the deal detail its elaborate structure.[29] On May 28, 2003, Kazakh officials offered their 25 percent stake for the unit at $300 million, but were unable to find any purchasers at the asking price. Just a day later, CNPC bought the same stake for $150 million, a net company valuation of $600 million, which seemed to be a fraction of the company's true worth. That very year, CNPC-Aktobe MunaiGaz reported a profit of $240 million, while just two years later, CNPC acquired the company PetroKazakhstan, which boasted only half of the reserves of CNPC-Aktobe MunaiGaz, for over $4 billion.

Like the alleged Giffen deals, the transactions and the alleged personal payments were executed through a complex web of offshore companies and financial vehicles. In its purchase of Aktobe MunaiGaz, CNPC used a company titled CNPC International Caspian Limited (CICL), which had been formed by one of its subsidiaries in April 2003 and was registered in the British Virgin Islands. CICL's start-up capital was just $100 and soon after its founding the company sold a 49 percent stake (for $49) to Darley Investment Services, another BVI-registered firm owned by Arvind Tiku, an Indian national and known business partner of Kulibayev.[30] Subsequently, CNPC loaned CICL the entire $150 million required to purchase the 25 percent stake in Aktobe MunaiGaz. After the sale, CNPC bought back 29 percent of Darley's stake for $25.9 million; over the next two years, CNPC subsidiaries bought Darley's remaining 20 percent stake in CICL for $140 million,[31] netting Darley a total of $165.9 million from an initial outlay of $49 after the company's founding.[32]

In response to the allegations, Kulibayev filed a libel lawsuit against the Kazakh newspapers that had published Ablyazov's letter, while Kazakh officials seized all the editions of five Kazakh newspapers. A Kazakh court also ordered the media to stop publishing "any information damaging to the dignity and honor" of Kulibayev, leading to an outcry among Kazakh journalists and media organizations.[33]

Among other scandals, Ablyazov also accused CNPC of colluding with Kulibayev to avoid paying tax on the 2009 sale of MangistauMunaiGas (MMG) to KazMunaiGas (on the board of which Kulibayev served as the chairman of directors) and CNPC. The purchase was presented as an open tender on the Kazakh stock exchange, thus legally avoiding the need to pay a 20 percent tax to the Kazakh National Treasury. However, according to Ablyazov, CNPC had issued a press release announcing the acquisition in April 2009, thereby signaling that it was the known buyer well in advance of the transaction, and, as a result, subject to tax.[34] Ablyazov also alleges that the total value of the deal—$2.8 billion—was less than half of the market value of MMG. Thus, according to Ablyazov, the deal avoided paying at least $652 million and perhaps up to $1.8 billion in taxes.

CNPC has denied breaking any laws or engaging in bribery in these matters.[35] But the timing, structure, and sequence of these deals suggest careful planning and local collusion. In the Aktobe MunaiGas deal, CICL had been established over a month before the unsuccessful tender that was held on May 28, 2003. The deal also must have involved a fair amount of mutual trust, as payments were deliberately and sequentially transferred among these various entities over a period of a couple of years.[36] The end result of these transactions is that CNPC paid $315.9 million for its additional 25 percent of the company, $150 million for what was offered on May 29, 2011, and the additional $165.9 million to buy Darley's stake in CICL. This figure appears close to the $300 million valuation that Kazakh authorities initially placed on their 25 percent share of the company.

The Murky Fuel Contracts at Manas

Though formally a part of U.S.-Kyrgyz security cooperation, the U.S. military presence at the Manas base also has been the target of allegations of high-level corruption.[37] Since its establishment as a staging and logistical support hub in December 2001, Manas has come to play a vital role in U.S. operations in Afghanistan. All U.S. troops transiting in and out of Afghanistan (about 55,000 a month in 2010) pass through Manas, while the airport also hosts the aircraft that conduct about 30 percent of all in-air refueling operations over the Afghanistan theater.

These air operations require massive quantities of fuel. Every day, U.S. forces operating out of the Manas Transit Center consume about 500,000 to 600,000 gallons of TS-1 jet fuel, the rough equivalent of an Olympic-size swimming pool. Stored in 20 massive bladders that look like giant hot water bottles, every day about 50 fuel trucks replenish the Manas "fuel farm."[38] Within Kyrgyzstan, the base's fuel contracts have long been perceived as sources of graft and corruption among the ruling families of Presidents Askar Akayev and Kurmanbek Bakiyev. As U.S. Representative John Tierney, the chair of the U.S. congressional investigation into the Pentagon's fuel deals at Manas, observed, "Real and perceived corruption in the fuel contracts has now been linked to two revolutions [in Kyrgyzstan] and seriously strained U.S.-Kyrgyz relations."[39]

Contracting during the Akayev Era

The initial fuel contract at Manas was awarded to the Maryland-based logistics company AvCard in November 2001, weeks before the formal announcement of the initial Manas deal, as a sole-source contract. Just two months later, the U.S. Defense Logistics Agency (DLA) awarded the company another contract, and, by 2003, AvCard had been paid $56 million.[40] In 2003, a new company, Red Star, took over the main fuel contract.

Both AvCard and Red Star relied on two main subcontracted suppliers for the fuel, both with ties to the family of Kyrgyz President Askar Akayev. The first was the airport-run Manas International Services Ltd, a fuel provision unit that had been privatized from the rest of the state-run airport entity and was owned and controlled by Aidar Akayev, President Akayev's son. The second fuel company, Aalam Services Ltd., was owned by Adil Toiganbayev, Akayev's son-in-law. The Manas Airport Authority, under whose jurisdiction the Manas basing facilities were located, mandated that these two entities provide all fuel to the base. In turn, DLA contracts required that all prospective Manas fuel contractors demonstrate that they would deal with these suppliers.

The mandate proved lucrative for the Akayev family. A *New York Times* investigative story revealed that, out of a total of $207 million spent by U.S. Department of Defense on fuel contracts during the Akayev era, Manas International Services received $87 million and Aalam Services $32 million in subcontracts from Avcard and Red Star.[41] According to NBC News, a subsequent FBI investigation, later classified, uncovered that the Akayev clan had embezzled tens of millions of dollars of these base-related revenues through a network of offshore and U.S. accounts.[42] When the Akayev regime collapsed in March 2005, acting president Kurmanbek Bakiyev criticized the base for having benefited the narrow private interests of the deposed elite, rather than supporting the general budget of the Kyrgyz Republic. Bakiyev vowed to make the Manas-related contracts more transparent and shift them into a national budget; however, the subcontracting structure remained essentially unchanged.[43]

The Rise of the Mysterious Mina Corp

The complex web of local subcontractors tasked to procure the fuel concealed a network of local business and political interests that claimed pieces of the Manas business. However, the main contracting entities, Red Star, and, as of 2007, Mina

Corporation also remained mysterious and opaque companies with unusual ownership structures and international ties. Notwithstanding the insistence of their owners that the companies are not connected, Red Star and Mina share remarkably similar profiles. Both were registered offshore at the same address in Gibraltar and both maintained official offices in a housing complex in London from 2004 to 2009 and shared offices in the Bishkek Hyatt.[44] Neither company maintained a web site or released details of its basic corporate structure, employees, shareholders, or operations.[45] The three founders of Mina are Douglas Edelman, a California businessmen who had opened a hamburger restaurant in Bishkek in the 1990s, Erkin Bekbolotov, a Kyrgyz businessman, and retired U.S. Lieutenant Colonel Chuck Squires. Intriguingly, Squires served as U.S. Defense Attaché to Bishkek in the late 1990s and 2000s, though he had left his post before 9/11.

Over the course of the U.S. military's use of Manas, the DOD has paid Mina and Red Star more than $1.5 billion in fuel contracts, most of them awarded as sole-source tenders (see Table 8.1). After a one-year initial contract in 2003, bid openly and competitively, Red Star exercised two consecutive extension options and then, beginning in July 2006, was awarded five consecutive extensions with no competitive bidding. Red Star then shifted its application as an incumbent to Mina, which was awarded a one-year contract to deliver 156 million gallons of TS-1 that was extended through June 2009. In 2009, DLA invoked reasons of national security to avoid "full and open competition" procedures, awarding Mina yet another sole-source one-year contract, with two additional options for one-year extensions.[46]

According to a representative of IOTC, a competitor to Red Star and Mina that bid for these contracts, in 2007 Mina beat out IOTC's bid, which was 3 percent lower, while DOD officials refused to make pricing information of the successful bid available, even after multiple Freedom of Information Act requests.[47] The favoritism and secrecy with which DLA treated Mina in Kyrgyzstan was replicated with Red Star in Afghanistan, where the company was allowed to construct and exclusively operate a pipeline that directly transported jet fuel to the Bagram airbase, effectively locking in its role as monopoly supplier to the base.[48]

Mina officials have vigorously denied accusations that the fuel company and its network of suppliers maintained ties to the Bakiyev family. The fuel deals were the subject of an investigation by the U.S. House of Representatives Subcommittee on Security and Foreign Relations, Committee of Oversight, chaired by Representative John Tierney.[49] Though the investigation's final report of December 2010 discovered no direct evidence of corruption or bribery involving Mina Corp and the Bakiyevs, it found that the DOD had "failed to properly oversee the political, diplomatic, and geopolitical collateral consequences of its contracting arrangements," and "had turned a blind eye [along with the State Department] to glaring red flags in the fuel contracts."[50] The report cautions that its focus was narrow; House investigators did not conduct a forensic audit of the accounting documents that were

Table 8.1 **Manas Primary Fuel Contracts**

Contractor/ Vendor	Federal Contract #	Contract Duration	Contract type	Value (US$)
AvCard	02-D-0024	12/2001–2/2002	One-year base	24,763,305
AvCard	02-D-1005	2/2002–8/2002	One-year base	31,796,438
		8/2002–2/2003	Extension (no bid)	
Red Star	03-D-1000	2/2003–2/2004	One-year base	509,217,358
		2/2004–2/2005	One-year option	
		2/2005–2/2006	One-year option	
		2/2006–7/2006	Extension (no bid)	
		7/2006–9/2006	Extension (no bid)	
		9/2006–1/2007	Extension (no bid)	
		1/2007–5/2007	Extension (no bid)	
		5/2007–7/2007	Extension (no bid)	
Mina Corp	07-D-1007	7/2007–6/2009	Two-year base	525,555,704
		6/2009–8/2009	Extension (no bid)	
Mina Corp	09-D-1009	8/2009–8/2010	One-year base	450,713,178
		8/2010–9/2010	Extension (no bid)	
		10/2010–11/2010	Extension (no bid)	
		11/2010–12/2010	Extension (no bid)	
Mina Corp	11-D-1000	12/2010–12/2011	One-year base	315,180,960*
			Total	$1,857,226,943

Source: Mystery at Manas, 12.

*Estimated

sent to them by Mina, nor did they interview the Kyrgyz personnel who worked for the company's main subcontractors.[51] The report also notes that Mina's principals were generally uncooperative with the investigation, failed to show up for scheduled interviews, stated that they would invoke Fifth Amendment privileges if compelled to testify, and sought immunity for any congressional testimony.[52]

What the report did find was extensive behind-the-scenes collusion among Mina, Red Star, and Russian officials to fabricate Russian export certificates. Under Russian law, the export of fuel for external military use is prohibited and would have required a special exemption and export license. When procuring Russian fuel, subcontractors for Mina and Red Star had to certify that it was for domestic civilian use, providing a supporting letter from the Kyrgyz Civil Aviation Authority. In turn, Russian refineries would transmit this information to the Russian Exporting Agency, which granted final approval. Mina's principals argue that, given the quantities of fuel involved, Russian authorities and Gazprom senior officials must have known about the scheme, while DOD officials were informed about the practice.[53] Thus, even while the competitive bidding war between Moscow and Washington over the fate of Manas heated up in early 2009, behind-the-scenes collusion between American and Russian traders, authorities, and local officials kept ample fuel supplies flowing to the base.[54]

The Political Fallout

The collapse of the Bakiyev government in April 2010 unleashed a wave of political hostility against Mina by members of the interim government. Some members suggested that Maksim Bakiyev skimmed up to $8 million every month from these fuel contracts.[55] Edil Baisalov, Chief of Staff to the interim Kyrgyz President Roza Otunbayeva, described Mina and Red Star as "an indirect way for the Pentagon to bribe the ruling families of Kyrgyzstan."[56] Mina and Red Star were also accused of running a broader reexporting business, shipping the procured Russian jet fuel on to Uzbekistan and Afghanistan.[57] Though, under the U.S.-Kyrgyz basing agreement, Mina was exempt from paying Kyrgyz excise taxes, the company failed to pay any domestic taxes for its Kyrgyz employees.[58] The Kyrgyz president also accused Mina of having attempted to bribe her son at a meeting in Istanbul in the summer of 2010 by attempting to hire him as a consultant.[59] Over the spring and summer of 2010, Kyrgyz officials demanded that the fuel contract be revoked from Mina and be given instead to a state fuel company from Kyrgyzstan.

On the U.S. side, the toppling of Bakiyev and the interim government's hostility toward Mina divided the White House and DOD regarding the future role of Mina. Bucking increased political pressure from Washington to distance itself from Mina, in November 2010, DLA Energy awarded Mina yet another contract worth $300 million over several contending bids. However, following a furious outcry from Bishkek and threats to reconsider the status of the base, U.S. officials agreed to allow a Kyrgyz-run state entity to acquire part of the fuel contract. Following a meeting between Secretary of State Hilary Clinton and President Otunbayeva on December 3, 2010, the two announced that a Kyrgyz state company, most likely as part of a joint venture with Gazprom, would acquire a small stake that could, upon satisfactory performance, be increased to 50 percent.[60] By May 2011, the new solicitation for the Manas fuel contract was structured in such a way that it could allow the new venture Gazpromneft-Aero Kyrgyzstan to eventually control 90 percent of the contract, prompting Mina officials, according to one report, to speculate that they might pull out of the 2011 bidding altogether.[61]

The Manas Contractor and Sub-Contractor Pyramid

Though the exact structure of the Bakiyev-era fuel deals may never be uncovered, one final recent set of reports offers important insights into the fuel procurement contracting chain. Documents about the Manas fuel chain obtained by Central-Asia.ru since the fall of Bakiyev reveal plenty of opportunities for graft through the presence of several intermediary companies (see Figure 8.3).[62] In June 2010, the interim Kyrgyz government formed a national fuel company—TZK Manas—to act as the new primary supplier to Mina, but the company still appears to have been only one of many suppliers. At the front end, fuel sourced from the Omsk refinery in Russia was sold by the Russian company Gazprom Aerofuels to the Kyrgyz firm and trading intermediary Mega Oil for $670 per metric ton. After incurring $110 per ton in transportation costs, Mega then sold the fuel to TZK Manas for a price of $850–$890 per ton, which, in turn, sold the same fuel to Mina, the main fuel vendor for Manas, for $1,030 per ton. Finally, Mina sold the same fuel to DLA for final use at Manas for an estimated price of about $1,268 per ton.[63]

Despite the establishment of TZK as the sole supplier of fuel, the mysterious Mega Oil, with apparent connections to both Kyrgyz and Russian officials, managed to retain its role as an intermediary supplier for most of 2010. TZK was not granted

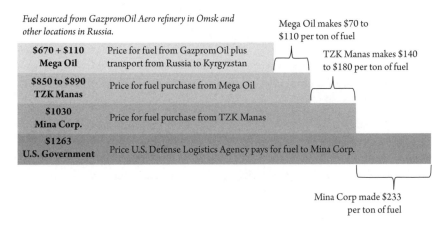

Figure 8.3 The Manas Fuel Chain, Late 2010 Source: Author's calculations based on information from Manas Transit Center and Centralasia.ru, "Korruptsionnye skhemy pri postavkakh aviatopliva na aviabazu Manas v Kirgizii," February 8, 2011

an actual license to transport fuel across the border until late September 2010, allowing Mega a number of months to operate as the exclusive trading company.[64]

With the political controversy surrounding Mina, the future of the Kyrgyz fuel contracts in 2011 remained uncertain. U.S. officials publicly discuss the positive impact that the new Kyrgyz-Russian joint venture is likely to have on the Kyrgyz economy, and the DLA placed its first order with the Kyrgyz-Russian joint venture in September 2011. However, it remains to be seen whether this fuel supply arrangement will truly increase revenues to the general Kyrgyz budget more than previous arrangements.

Conclusion: The Price of Access

Though the intensification of U.S.-Russia-China interaction in 2000s did not cause Central Asia's considerable corruption and governance problems, certain forms of security and economic engagement fed the region's informal networks and provided pay-offs to local elites. In the scandals involving foreign oil companies in Kazakhstan and the Manas fuel deals, external actors turned a blind eye to shadowy schemes and opaque contracts. As long as deals were successfully negotiated or, in the case of the Pentagon, fuel was provided, these principals had little cause to question their underlying arrangements.

Local elites profited handsomely from many of these international transactions and invoked geopolitical competition as a means to leverage their position and demand more private goods. The conclusion of the Giffen case brought an even more remarkable twist to these "Great Game" dynamics, as the American broker and trusted advisor to the Kazakh president successfully used his clandestine ties to the U.S. intelligence and foreign policy communities as a legal defense against charges that he bribed Kazakh elites on behalf of Western oil companies and laundered money.

Another similarity across the cases was that local elites, while using state assets for personal gain, embedded their deals within broader transnational networks of offshore vehicles, trading companies, and financial intermediaries. The fact that key actors in the Gibraltar-registered Mina Corp—a U.S. businessman, a Kyrgyz-Canadian trader, and a former U.S. defense intelligence official—all colluded with Russian oil traders and regulators to smuggle fuel to Kyrgyzstan attests to the complexity of networks and diverse interests embodied in many of these transactions. Moreover, these transactional forms have allowed U.S., Chinese, and Russian external actors the space to deny allegations that they directly promoted corruption, while giving local elites the means to personally benefit from these deals. They remain the most tangible embodiment of how the great powers and local elites have interfaced and cooperated.

9

Chasing the Shadow of a Region

For two decades, international actors have viewed Central Asia as a distinct and coherent region. External actors such as multilateral institutions, donors, and NGOs have sought to promote greater regional integration and have poured money into projects for common resource management, infrastructure upgrades, and economic cooperation. These countless initiatives have yielded few lasting successes, yet the international community remains fixated on developing these regional ties.

Similarly, each of the great powers that we have studied has advanced its own strategy, instruments, and institutions in support of Central Asian regionalism. China has pushed for a greater role for the SCO, while Russia has promoted the Moscow-led CSTO and EurAsEC–Customs Union as mechanisms for integration. U.S. policymakers have promoted north-south linkages between the post-Soviet states and Afghanistan and Pakistan and have argued that developing the NDN could revive the trade routes of the ancient Silk Road. Such forays into "strategic regionalism" certainly have strengthened bilateral ties between Moscow, Beijing, Washington, and the Central Asian states, but they have not deepened intraregional integration, nor have they addressed the area's most pressing problems, such as the management of common resources.[1]

In fact, two decades after independence, Central Asia arguably displays few tangible indicators of actual regional coherence. In the economic sphere, trade between the Central Asian states, on the one hand, and Russia and China has dramatically increased over the past decade, but these growing volumes have not spurred similar increases within the region; a partial exception was the growth in Kazakh-Kyrgyz trade and investment, but that was halted, and then reversed, in 2010 by the closure of the border following the collapse of the Bakiyev government and Astana's accession into the Customs Union with Russia. The mobility of people within the region is also severely restricted, as the vast majority of labor migrants go to Russia in search of employment. Central Asian public agencies still refuse to share information with each other, let alone coordinate policy concerning regional challenges. The common cultural and linguistic legacy bequeathed by Soviet rule is also fading, as national languages replace the use of Russian and national myths and state identities now take root over new generations; regional cultural and educational exchanges, youth contacts, and even sports events remain minimal.

Despite these trends, outside states and international organizations press for more "regional cooperation" with an almost metronomic regularity. This push is not exclusively Western; it is common for Russian and Chinese analysts, when assessing the future development of organizations such as the Customs Union or the SCO, to make comparisons with the European Union, citing the EU's long history as evidence that successful regional integration has taken place incrementally. In practice, however, Central Asia has proven to be the "anti-EU"; it is an area that collectively identifies, and is perceived by outsiders, as a distinct region, yet whose governments steadfastly refuse to actually cede their sovereignty to regional bodies or supranational authorities.

Central Asia's local rules, particularly its patrimonial structures, have proven significant barriers to more robust economic cooperation. Integration would make these countries better off in the aggregate, but private elite interests regularly trump national ones, as elites sign bundles of regional agreements, but implement few of them. The only significant drivers of actual integration are the ground-level actors who pursue the unofficial shuttle trade and benefit from illicit networks; otherwise, state elites continue to profit from the arbitrage opportunities provided by the endurance of national boundaries and regulations.

Regionalism: Virtual, Strategic, and Imagined

Though substantive regional integration may be in short supply, over the last 20 years, the Central Asian states have joined a plethora of organizations dedicated to promoting regional integration in both the economic and security spheres. Since independence, the Central Asian states—with the exception of Turkmenistan, which maintains its policy of neutrality—have all joined the Commonwealth of Independent States, the OSCE, the CSTO and SCO, the Economic Cooperation Organization (ECO), the Eurasian Economic Community/Customs Union, and the Asian Development Bank's Central Asia Regional Economic Cooperation Initiative (CAREC). Regional cooperation has also been promoted by outside organizations such as the World Bank, the European Bank for Reconstruction and Development (EBRD), the European Union, and several divisions of the United Nations, including the United Nations Development Program (UNDP), the United Nations Office on Drugs and Crime

(UNODC), and the United Nations Economic and Social Commission for Asia and the Pacific (UNESCAP). Notwithstanding the best efforts of these organizations and the individual efforts of China, the United States, and Russia, effective regional cooperation, integration, or even problem-solving mechanisms remain weak. This has led scholars to label such regional initiatives as "virtual regionalism."[2]

However, when judged from the perspective of Central Asia's ruling elites, these virtual agreements play critical political functions. Most important, they provide opportunities for Central Asian elites to acknowledge each other's authority, legitimacy, and territorial integrity, also known as "juridical sovereignty."[3] Not dissimilar to arguments made about post-colonial African leaders' propensity to enter symbolic regional agreements to compensate for their internal weakness, the Central Asian rulers have used regional forums to reinforce external support for the political status quo.[4] A steady diet of regional summits and cooperative initiatives also allow these leaders to regularly emphasize their foreign policy profiles and agendas to a domestic audience and captive media.

Central Asia's rulers themselves are highly selective about how their countries fit into the broader region. For example, officials from Kazakhstan frequently complain about being grouped with its relatively weaker and poorer neighbors, while Uzbekistan consistently expresses a preference for addressing regional problems through bilateral means, rather than multilateral or regional organizations. Turkmenistan's long-standing "policy of neutrality" allows Ashgabat to altogether avoid making formal commitments to outside powers, regional forums, or international organizations. Even relatively minor associations can carry important symbolic and cultural weight. For example, in 2002 the Kazakhstan Football Association left the Asian Football Confederation to join the more prestigious Union of European Football Associations (UEFA). But other times, especially when the topic is democratic standards, human rights practices, or issues of transparency, Central Asian elites and diplomats quite willingly frame their performance within an overall "Central Asian" regional standard, which on these issues is consistently lower or more culturally specific than its Western counterparts.

Central Asian elites also remain acutely aware of regional political developments and their potential demonstration effects. As we have seen with the region-wide reaction against the Color Revolutions or the compromising of human rights for the sake of counterterrorism, elites are extremely sensitive that a development in a neighboring state may serve as an example that might undermine their own authority. Most recently, all of the Central Asian governments (and Russia) expressed their concerns about the Kyrgyz interim government's decision in 2010 to construct a parliamentary democracy, parroting Moscow's line that such efforts at political experimentation might destabilize the region.[5]

The Need for Greater Regional Cooperation

The lack of substantive success of these regional forays is all the more lamentable given that Central Asia faces important challenges that require more robust cooperation. These include improving the conditions for cross-regional trade, managing disputed resources such as water, confronting environment degradation, protecting public health, coordinating border management, and upgrading regional infrastructure.

Twenty years after independence, the Central Asian states still confront the peculiar organizational legacies of Soviet regional planning, which governed common issues according to the logics of the Soviet system as a whole, not regional developmental needs.[6] As we have seen in the realm of energy, this meant that Central Asian hydrocarbon production was routed toward Russia, rather than regional markets. Similarly, under the Soviet system of electricity production and distribution, the Central Asian states were placed on a common grid, supplied by each other and by Russia, and followed a set of intricate norms, seasonal adjustments, and barter arrangements to secure adequate supply.[7] Extricating themselves from these Soviet-era arrangements and creating national electricity companies have disrupted these supply chains and heightened disagreements over payments and arrears. Similarly, the politically volatile issue of regional water management has escalated tensions among Kyrgyzstan and Tajikistan—the upstream countries that wish to construct dams to produce hydroelectric power—and downstream countries, most notably Uzbekistan, which still relies on these water flows to support its cotton monoculture.[8] Persistent external calls for greater cooperation over regional resources have not produced a new standing body or supranational authority, or even a routinized set of rules to govern these contentious issues, which every year become more acute and now have the potential to trigger a regional skirmish or even a conflict.[9]

Another pressing regional challenge is its deteriorating Soviet-era infrastructure. Roads, energy plants, and public buildings are in general disrepair and even crumbling, while many of the technicians with the requisite skills to maintain these antiquated systems are nearing or past retirement age.[10] Despite two decades of international initiatives and donor-sponsored projects, investment in improving the region's infrastructure has been inadequate and frequently mismanaged. The situation has even affected U.S. attempts to operate and expand the NDN; a leaked cable reveals the assessment of an international railroad expert who described the problems of the Uzbek train system: "Obsolete locomotives with inadequate brakes result in multiple delays and wheels that glow red hot by the time a train has completed the mountain crossing," with the cable concluding that, "a train wreck is possible in the literal sense."[11]

Moreover, nearly every Russian, Chinese, and U.S.-led attempt to upgrade the region's infrastructure—such as constructing new transmission lines or investing in a dam—is viewed as a ploy by the other great powers to strategically reorient the region in a favorable fashion.[12] For example, Moscow looks at U.S. proposals to connect the Central Asian electricity transmission lines to Afghanistan and South Asia with deep suspicion and was doubtful that the U.S. military's construction of a $37 million bridge in 2007 over the Panj river to link Tajikistan and Afghanistan was conducted for the officially given reason of stimulating trade between the countries.[13] Political analysts in all three countries perceive foreign investment in Kyrgyz and Tajik dam construction and hydropower projects as gambits to secure control of regional water sources. In this highly charged political environment, even seemingly technical issues carry strong geopolitical overtones. For example, Chinese railways, similar to European ones, run on wider gauges than their Russian counterparts. As a result, Beijing's plans to lay new Central Asian tracks for high-speed rail connections using the Chinese standard are perceived by some Russian observers as evidence of mounting Chinese colonization.[14]

The Local Barriers to Regional Cooperation

Most frequently, regional observers point to the national rivalries among the Central Asian countries, such as Uzbekistan and Kazakhstan's bids for regional hegemony, or the personal animosities held by the Central Asian presidents, as the main factors that foster regional distrust. If only Central Asian rulers could set aside their personal agendas and muster the necessary political will, they could achieve significant mutual gains. But below the surface lie more intractable difficulties that are embedded in the region's local rules.

Patronage Politics, Rent-Seeking, and Economic Structure

First, Central Asia's patronage politics continues to be a major barrier to more formal economic integration. Western approaches to regional integration typically take the state as their starting point, and then explain how overall gains from economic integration lay the foundation for governments to pursue regional free trade agreements and other related forms of cooperation.[15] But in political systems where power is controlled by authoritarian elites, national economic systems are already configured to benefit private interests and their rent-seeking activities, not the state as a whole.

Even if greater cooperation improves overall economic welfare, elites will be hesitant to agree to integration if eliminating "red tape" such as licensing requirements and other national regulatory barriers undermines their private revenue sources.[16] In practice, many of the areas proposed by the great powers to improve cooperation are sectors monopolized by the Central Asian elites. For example, SCO consultations to improve regional integration on issues such as electricity, transportation, and telecommunications inevitably run into the fact that these sectors are controlled by governing elites, or their families, who have no interest in liberalizing them or otherwise ceding control over their revenue streams.

Borders as Tollbooths

A second barrier to regional economic cooperation is that Central Asian authorities, both ruling elites and security services, continue to profit handsomely from borders and border crossings.

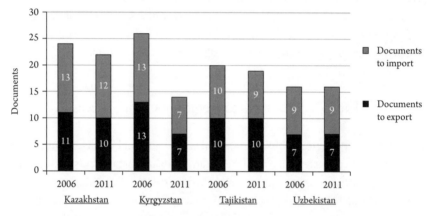

Figure 9.1 Number of Documents Required for Import/Export, 2006 & 2011
Source: Doing Business Project Data, World Bank Group

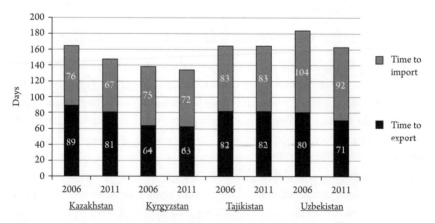

Figure 9.2 Time Required for Import/Export, 2006 & 2011
Source: Doing Business Project Data, World Bank Group

According to the World Bank, the Central Asian states continue to erect the most cumbersome barriers to trade, compared to almost anywhere in the world. As available data for the four Central Asian countries suggest (and with the inclusion of Turkmenistan, these findings would likely be strengthened), officially clearing borders, whether importing or exporting, can take over 100 days and requires a cumbersome stack of documentation (see Figures 9.1 and 9.2). Empirically, none of the initiatives promoted by the great powers over the last decade, be it the SCO's economic platform or the NDN, has notably improved the time required for cross-border transactions. For example, during this time Kyrgyzstan impressively halved its required number of formal documents, but this did not alter average import/export times, which suggests that informal barriers, not formal requirements, remain the core problem. Some modest gains were demonstrated by Uzbekistan, where the average time required for importing and exporting decreased by slightly over 10 percent from 2006 to 2011. However, Uzbekistan's baseline was extremely high, and within a global context, as Figure 9.3 shows, Central Asia as a region performs significantly worse than other developing areas, or even the other post-Communist states.

The World Bank data are supported by a number of studies that have tried to measure border corruption and indirect fees in Central Asian regional transport. A 2006 survey by the Asian Development Bank found that informal payments and bribes added $1,200–1,800 to the total cost of a truck transiting from Central Asia to Moscow, along with eight additional days of transit time, while rail transit could even double "ideal world" shipping costs and add up to 15 days in

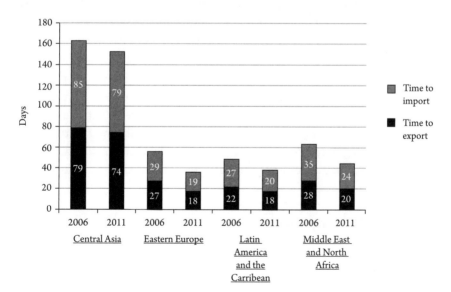

Figure 9.3 Comparative Time Required for Import/Export, 2006 & 2011
Source: Doing Business Project Data, World Bank Group

transit time.[17] A 2008 survey conducted by the U.S. Chamber of Commerce of over 200 companies doing business in Central Asia found that very high percentages admitted to routinely paying bribes to clear customs and to deal with border regulations.[18] Of those surveyed, 100 percent of respondents perceived a "high" or "very high" level of corruption among customs officials in Uzbekistan, 90 percent in Kazakhstan and 80 percent in Kyrgyzstan, compared to the Eurasian average of 57 percent.[19] Another study conducted the same year by the Congress of Business Associations of Central Asia in conjunction with Tajik shipping groups found that trucks carrying cargos along the China-Kazakhstan-Uzbekistan-Tajikistan corridor paid an average of $433 in unofficial payments to customs officials, traffic police, transportation inspectorate and phytosanitary services, with a monitored driver being stopped 221 times during the journey.[20] Over 50 percent of total transport time was spent crossing borders and haggling with customs officials.

Perhaps the most compelling evidence of the rampant corruption and organized local interests on the Central Asian borders can be found in comparing the discrepancies in official trade statistics recorded by the Central Asian and Chinese authorities. The most striking differences are those measuring trade volumes between China and Kyrgyzstan. For example, in 2006, according to data provided to the IMF by Kyrgyz customs authorities, Kyrgyz exports to China totaled $38 million, while imports were valued at $245 million.[21] However, according to the Chinese Ministry of Commerce, during the same year Kyrgyz exports to China totaled $111 million, while Chinese exports to Kyrgyzstan totaled $2.1 billion, a discrepancy of nearly tenfold. For the same year, Chinese trade statistics for Tajikistan were double those figures reported by their Tajik counterparts. And, according to one investigation, in 2007 Kazakh customs recorded about 3,000 trucks crossing the border at the entry town of Khorgos, while their Chinese counterparts put the figure at over 36,000 for the same year.[22] Though Central Asian government agencies attribute these discrepancies to differences in methodology, their sheer magnitude suggests that black market activity must account for a significant portion of these differences. Strikingly, a detailed study by Moscow-based researchers estimates that in 2008 unrecorded trade from China to the Central Asian states may have reached $15 billion.[23]

Informal Regional Networks: The Shuttle Trade and Drug Trafficking

This high level of border activity suggests that there is some evidence of growing regionalism in Central Asia, though it originates from the bottom up, not from decisions made by policymakers in the capitals. More precisely, it is not so much "virtual" as it is informal. In both the growing shuttle trade and drug trade, we see activity by networks of state and non-state actors which act autonomously or, in the case of some border guards, even defy official dictates to facilitate this informal economic exchange.

The Growing Shuttle Trade

Since the mid-2000s the shuttle trade taking place across Central Asia's borders, especially to its east, has exploded. Goods from the shuttle trade are quickly resold near the crossing points on the other side of a border or make their way to Central Asia's major urban open-air markets, such as Karasu (Osh), Dordoy (Bishkek) and Barakholka (Almaty). Agricultural goods, electronics and appliances, textiles, and consumer items constitute the bulk of this exchange. Most of the manufactured goods originate in China, and it is no coincidence that the shuttle trade has increased in parallel with China's growing regional economic activity. Typically, shuttle traders are local inhabitants of the border regions and operate on their own or with their families.[24]

The vast majority of this shuttle trade goes unrecorded, but traders must still negotiate borders, national regulations, and customs officials, whose demands for informal payments must be kept small enough to keep their operations profitable. The intergovernmental border arrangements that govern the shuttle trade range from the creatively legal and ad hoc to the informal and purely illicit. At the Khorgos and Jeminay border areas (China-Kazakhstan border), Kazakh businessmen are allowed, by agreement between the two countries' Ministries of Foreign Affairs, one-day visas to cross the border and purchase a limited amount of goods from Chinese vendors to bring back for resale.[25] In December 2011, the two sides inaugurated the new International Center of Boundary Cooperation at Khorgos, designed to become a transit and transportation hub for Kazakh-Chinese trade.[26] But we have also seen massive increases in the volume of unrecorded trade along the Kyrgyz and, more recently, along Tajik border posts with China in the absence of such bilateral agreements.

The case of Uzbekistan, which does not border China, is particularly revealing. Over the last decade, the Uzbek government, in a bid to protect its autarkic economic practices and secure the border against militant raids (such as the IMU infiltrations of 1999 and 2000), has officially maintained closed border policies, militarized its border patrols, and placed an increasing amount of legal restrictions on shuttle traders.[27] The border closure stifled official trade with Kyrgyzstan and Tajikistan, and ushered in a new era of cross-border smuggling.[28]

In practice, however, Uzbek border guards routinely defy these central directives and facilitate the shuttle trade in exchange for collecting informal payments. At Karasu, on the Uzbek-Kyrgyz border, Uzbek border authorities help maintain an unofficial crossing used by 40,000 people every day, most of them visiting the large market on the Kyrgyz side.[29] At other border spots, such as the Burgandiya crossing, traders and laborers routinely cross close to official checkpoints and in full view of the guards.[30] And reports from the 2,350 kilometer Uzbek-Kazakh border suggest that smuggling is booming as traders and gangs routinely set up new makeshift bridges and crossings along the frontier, while Uzbek guards are paid to look away.[31] In all of these cases, Uzbek border guards have failed to implement the strict border policy dictated from above.

The Regional Drug Trade

The second major economic activity that has created a vast array of regional informal networks is the drug trade. According to the UNODC, Afghanistan grows 99 percent of all opiates grown in the region. Central Asia is a transit region, hosting a series of "northern routes" for Afghan narcotics on their way to Russia and Europe.[32] The most popular routes traverse Tajikistan, via the relatively unguarded border with Afghanistan, and southern Kyrgyzstan, though Turkmenistan has also been reported to serve both the "northern route" and the "western route" destined for Iran.

Central Asian security services, border guards, and law enforcement are intimately involved in the drug trade. A 2003 U.S. interagency government report on narcotics trafficking in Central Asia concluded that "increasing heroin transit through Central Asia is contributing to endemic political and bureaucratic corruption, including in the security services and law enforcement agencies, throughout the region."[33] In Tajikistan, for example, trafficking is the largest source of economic revenue, by some estimates totaling 60–70 percent of official GDP, and high-ranking Tajik officials have been caught in Kazakhstan and Russia with large quantities of money and drugs.[34] Drug trafficking is also an economic staple of southern Kyrgyzstan, where authorities are closely tied with organized crime networks.[35] Finally, throughout its independence, Turkmen opposition members and government defectors have accused high-level government officials, including the president himself, of profiting handsomely from the transit of Afghan opiates.

Since trafficking in narcotics remains a vital source of government revenue, albeit unofficial, it is subject to local rules and tacit sanction. Though all of the Central Asian countries over the last decade have established dedicated counternarcotics agencies, law enforcement divisions, and specialized personnel, mostly through international assistance, government officials remain key players in the drug trade. Their interdiction efforts appear to concentrate more on targeting individual trafficker or smaller networks, rather than high-value, high-volume rings with strong ties to organized crime, with seized opiates estimated at only 4 percent of total flows.[36] Along these lines, a leaked U.S. Embassy cable from Dushanbe in 2007 recounts how Tajik President Rahmon fired a Tajik senior anti-narcotics officer for intercepting a car packed with 60 kilos of heroin that was driven by Tajik state security services, including a distant relative of the president.[37]

Implications for External Engagement

The growing informal sector and its ties to Central Asia's patrimonial politics have important implications for how international actors assist the region with border management. Acting mostly in good faith, external donors have provided significant border assistance to the Central Asian states; however, many of these projects and equipment purchases have been mismanaged or used for other purposes. For example, drug-sniffing dogs donated by the European Union and the United States to Tajik border authorities were used instead for breeding,[38] while night-vision technology designed to target smugglers has been used by security services against political opposition.[39]

With weak oversight, heightened competition, and donors eager to prove relevance in the field, Central Asian border guards and security services have received a bonanza of international assistance and projects, with little follow-up assessment of their performance; in their bid to court external assistance, as with engagement on counterterrorism, they have emphasized the security threats posed by the participation of militant Islamic movements and other clandestine movements in these illicit activities.[40] Of course, as with most clandestine economic activities, counter-narcotics efforts are difficult to measure and politically contentious.[41] For example, the increase in volumes of seized drugs over the last decade can be interpreted as evidence of better border capacity; or it may indicate a significantly greater overall volume of trafficking.

Central Asian security services and border guards also benefit from the engagement of multiple organizations. The OSCE, the SCO, the International Organization on Migration (IOM), the CSTO, the European Union, and the U.S. military have all funded border management or counternarcotics projects. With the intensification of geopolitical rivalry in the mid-2000s, such border assistance was infused with competitive overtones. For example, in 2004, when Tajikistan evicted Russian border guards from its border with Afghanistan, Tajik officials courted and received support from the United States military for the transition, much to the irritation of Russian authorities.[42] Over the course of the decade, U.S. CENTCOM has increased its border management assistance with all of the Central Asian countries, even building new border exchange posts in Turkmenistan (including one on the Iranian border).[43] For its part, strengthening regional counternarcotics efforts has become a platitude for the SCO at its meetings about Afghanistan, yet it is unclear how greater intergovernmental co-operation will fundamentally change the active stake that Tajik and Kyrgyz offi-cials have in promoting the drug trade. And potential U.S.-Russian cooperation on counternarcotics efforts have been hampered both by differences in philos-ophy—Moscow would prefer more aggressive eradication of the poppy crop in Afghanistan—and by U.S. and NATO refusals to formally partner with the CSTO, Moscow's preferred regional security organization.[44]

Conclusion: Waiting for a Region to Gel

The great powers and other external actors routinely call for more regional coop-eration and integration in Central Asia. Yet, despite the "strategic regionalism" practiced by Moscow, Beijing, and Washington, Central Asia's formal trade, movements of peoples, and the commitment to tackle common challenges remain remarkably low. The failure of most regional initiatives in Central Asia is rooted in local rules and in the very nature of patrimonial political systems. Cen-tral Asian governments maintain high barriers to integration, not because they lack the necessary technical expertise or capacity, but because elites privately benefit from the region's enduring system of national regulations and border re-strictions. The fact that external patrons all eagerly promote regional coopera-tion only heightens local perceptions that regionalism is a vehicle proposed by external actors to advance their own influence and control.

Regional security cooperation has fared only slightly better. Organizations like the SCO and CSTO have managed to pool individual Central Asian country efforts in the name of counterterrorism or, more accurately, regime survival; however, their limits have also been exposed. For example, the SCO, CSTO, and OSCE proved unwilling or unable to intervene or otherwise play a constructive role to stem the interethnic violence in June 2010 that followed the collapse of the Bakiyev regime.[45] And despite regular calls to improve counter-narcotics ef-forts throughout the region, substantial elements of the Central Asian states' se-curity forces and elites actively profit from, and probably manage, spurs of the drug trade. The presence of multiple regional security organizations has frag-mented border management and counter-narcotics efforts, while providing Cen-tral Asian authorities with a steady stream of unmonitored external assistance.

In the West, we tend to think about regional integration in functional and sequential terms: first, countries cooperate on trade and liberalize economic ac-tivity, while in the more successful cases, such as the EU and ASEAN, additional areas of political cooperation build upon these initial economic steps. Common defense or security policies are viewed as the most difficult and final stages in the integration sequence.

The Central Asian region follows a quite different pattern: rulers have proven willing to support regional security initiatives that guard their regimes from transnational threats and political opposition, but have proven reluctant to take greater steps to institutionalize the movement of goods, capital, and people that might undermine their control over resources and private revenue streams. Though the international community continues to promote regional cooperation in Central Asia, the preservation of national borders, as it turns out, is a key part of the region's local rules.

10

The New Regional Contests of a Multipolar World

After a period of calm and seclusion during the 1990s, Central Asia became the site of a new contest that actively engaged three great powers, empowered local governments to use this geopolitical environment for their domestic benefit, and gave rise to novel institutions, practices, and norms in international politics. In this final chapter, I begin by evaluating the record of the "Big Three" in terms of their regional goals. Next, I examine the trials and tribulations of European states and India in dealing with the region and find similar patterns of contentious "base politics," as well as tensions between pursuing security cooperation and promoting a values agenda. Finally, I consider some of the broader lessons that Central Asia holds for the emergence of other regional orders, focusing on the nature of U.S. power, the rise of China, and new regional efforts to counterbalance these external suitors.

The Scorecard: Partial Winners and a Big Winner

Ten years into the new great power contest for Central Asia, it is time to tally the scorecard. Though it will disappoint some, the record suggests there have been no real "losers" in the new "Great Game." In part, this has been the result of Washington, Moscow, and Beijing pursuing strategic goals that were mostly non-exclusive; but it has also been a function of these powers adjusting their strategies to more successfully play by the region's local rules. In this sense, the "Big Three" have also converged into supporting the Central Asian regimes and their local practices in order to secure cooperation and access.

The Eagle: Mission Accomplished?

Despite some important bumps—such as the 2005 eviction from K2 and the February 2009 announcement of the closure of Manas—the United States has successfully navigated the demands of the Central Asian countries and has secured the bases and logistical supply chains that it required to conduct its operations in Afghanistan, including the surging of forces that was ordered by President Obama in 2009–2010. Washington has mainly done so by providing economic benefits to the Central Asian states in exchange for their security cooperation. As we have seen with the Manas bidding war and the establishment of the NDN, U.S. planners have offered both public benefits and private payments to the Central Asian regimes. As of this writing, the U.S. Congress had just waived the ban on foreign military sales to Uzbekistan that had been in effect since 2004, when the Congress failed to certify that Tashkent was in compliance with minimal human rights standards. Uzbekistan demanded the resumption of U.S. Foreign Military Financing (FMF) as a quid pro quo for the United States' expansion of the NDN; thus the Pentagon, the State Department, and the White House lobbied hard for the exemption. U.S. policymakers will only hope that the Uzbek security services that receive this new hardware do not controversially use it on their population in another incident like that at Andijan.

Over the decade, CENTCOM also has invested in its relationships with the Central Asian militaries and security services by training their counterparts and completing a number of low-profile projects, including new anti-terrorism training centers and border facilities. Though U.S. authorities regularly proclaim that they are not playing a "great game" and that their security engagement in the region is limited, the close relationships and infrastructure that the U.S. military has built are of particular concern to Russia and China, who remain skeptical about U.S. regional intentions, even after a formal drawdown in Afghanistan.

Unlike this security engagement, which has supported most U.S. operational needs, Washington's "soft power" over the decade has declined considerably. The erosion of U.S. credibility, as Chapter 6 showed, as an exporter of democratic values and human rights champion, with an accompanying loss of prestige, remains the greatest casualty of Washington's engagement with the Central Asian regimes. Perhaps more damagingly, U.S. officials have ceded the terms of the "values" debate by even allowing local elites to frame external engagement on security and democracy as antithetical. Given the overwhelming importance of the U.S. campaign in Afghanistan, concessions on these issues might be viewed as unfortunate, but necessary; in that case, U.S. policymakers should at least acknowledge that supporting Central Asia's authoritarian elites has been one of the Afghanistan campaign's many political and economic costs.

As U.S. foreign aid budgets increasingly get trimmed, money for activities such as civil society promotion, anti-corruption initiatives, and media freedom is also likely to dry up, especially as already limited funds are diverted to more high-priority areas, such as the Arab Spring countries. Nor does Washington's influence over institutions like the IMF and World Bank matter as much in an environment where Russia, China, and other country donors can more readily provide aid-like funds without the same conditional demands. Perhaps the most important mechanisms of U.S. soft power are educational programs and exchanges, but these, too, now find competition from other suitors such as China, Russia, India, and Europe. In the wake of the impending U.S. drawdown from Afghanistan, it is doubtful that this steady decline in overall U.S. regional influence will be reversed.

The Bear: Influence for the Sake of Influence?

Moscow's strategic successes are less clear-cut. As we have explored, the goal of maintaining a "privileged role" is difficult to measure, as Russia's own sense of status in Central Asia has tended to fluctuate as a function of its prevailing relations with the other great powers.

If we define "privileged role" in the "maximalist" position, or the view that Moscow seeks to monopolize Central Asian relations with the outside world, then Moscow has clearly failed. Notwithstanding some Western media commentators, however, there seem to be very few Russian policymakers who actually aspire to such a neo-imperial vision. The one exception might be in the area of energy policy, specifically Russia's ability to limit Central Asian gas suppliers from building and using non-Russian transit networks; but even in this particular sector, Russia's pipeline monopoly was broken in December 2009, not by a Transcaspian pipeline going west, against which it had long fought, but by the new Central Asia–China pipeline flowing east from Turkmenistan. Perhaps the renewed talk of a Eurasian Union, led by Russia, will raise Moscow's regional ambitions once more, but such a bloc will be difficult to control, let alone construct, given the diversity of foreign policy ties that all of the Central Asian states now enjoy.

But the levers of soft power that Moscow wields are broad and deep. As this study has shown, some of these are Soviet legacies (the pipeline network, the linguistic and technical heritage), but others are more recent developments, such as growing bilateral trade, more formalized security interactions, and, perhaps most important, the millions of Central Asian migrants who now earn their living and send valuable remittances back home. The collapse of the Bakiyev government in 2010 was spurred by Russian soft power and, more importantly, was broadly understood to have been orchestrated by Moscow. Russia's influence, both real and perceived, is still felt throughout the region.

Moreover, the impending drawdown of U.S. forces in Afghanistan does not leave many alternatives to Russia for playing an extended role as the region's security guarantor. As with the early Putin years, the Russian defense establishments will view the U.S. drawdown in Afghanistan and concerns about possible regional destabilization as a justification to deepen their military ties with the region. Indeed, the announcement in September 2011 that Tajikistan will renew the lease on the Russian base and will possibly allow Russian advisors and troops to return to the border suggests that Russian planners are already positioning themselves for a post-Afghanistan world. For all its posturing on the issue, Moscow is essentially correct that it would still be the only viable external power that could intervene militarily if the Central Asian states were to dramatically destabilize. The bigger question would be, as with the Kyrgyz crises of 2010, would Moscow be willing to discharge such an open-ended stability operation, especially in a politically uncertain environment?

The bottom line is that, although all of the Central Asians states have acted like Russian clients at some point, none of them wants to exclusively remain under Russian tutelage. If the Kremlin can accept such an elevated, but non-exclusive, regional role, then Russia's privileged status in the region can endure for another generation. However, if, as it seems of late, the Kremlin pushes ahead to increase integration via its preferred regional organizations, these plans may backfire. If Russia deepens regional organizations such as the CSTO or expands the Customs Union to include Kyrgyzstan and Tajikistan, these vehicles of influence may force the Central Asian states and their publics to confront the practical consequences of more formal Russian control, such as high customs duties. If, however, this prompts countries to opt out of these mechanisms, as Uzbekistan has with the Customs Union or the CSTO rapid response mechanism, then Russia's prestige may even be damaged. There is a paradox here: looser arrangements with the Central Asian countries in areas like security and the economy might well allow the Central Asian states the necessary room to acknowledge Russia's special status, without having either to align themselves completely with Moscow or reject Russian proposals publicly.

The Dragon: The Winner on Points

If we had to declare a winner in the new Central Asian contest, China is clearly the candidate ahead on points, especially when we consider its initial starting position. As recently as the mid-1990s, China still harbored border disputes with its Central Asian neighbors and had negligible trade relations and minimal regional contacts. By the end of the 2000s, Beijing had successfully established the Shanghai Cooperation Organization (SCO) and used it to conduct an effective regional crackdown on the activities of Uighur groups. China had also supplanted Moscow as the area's largest trading partner, constructed two new major energy pipelines that bypassed Russian territory, and was upgrading the area's infrastructure in a bid to reorient the region to interface with Xinjiang. The fact that Chinese officials do not openly talk of wanting to exert influence in Central Asia is consistent with Beijing's low-key approach, but it should not distract us from recognizing its transformative regional role.

Throughout this period, Beijing also proved the most geopolitically adept of the three powers, understanding early on the importance of pivoting along both axes of the strategic triangle. When the United States initially sought to partner with Russia in the War on Terror, ushering in a possible "grand bargain" about Central Asia, Chinese policymakers deftly forged ahead with the SCO agenda to draw Russia back into its regional security institution, even while it offered to support Washington in exchange for recognizing its own campaign in Xinjiang as part of this global effort; when U.S.-Russian relations deteriorated in 2003–2005, Beijing was well positioned to support Russian attempts to counter U.S. influence, without ever actually making any sacrifices in doing so. China's public acknowledgement that the region is Russia's "privileged" sphere and its commitments to maintaining a "strategic partnership" helped to keep Russian sights firmly fixed on the West. Not only has China faced few checks on its expansion of influence, but, as in the case of its pipeline construction, many of these projects were supported by Washington as part of its efforts to diversify Central Asia's economic partnerships.

At the same time, Chinese officials have been loath to grant Washington any major support for Afghanistan, meaning that as the country's largest foreign investor, China effectively continues to free-ride on the U.S. security umbrella. Beijing may push for a more elevated role for the SCO as the United States draws down in Afghanistan, but it is most likely to call for people-to-people training, reconstruction, and economic projects, without committing any kind of troop presence. Looking further ahead, with its economic and energy interests now secure, China may well be willing to maintain a low profile and free-ride on an expanded Russian regional security presence, just as it has done with the United States.

To be sure, China faces its own future challenges. For one, Russian policymakers are increasingly anxious about how to check and counter China's rise; Moscow is particularly hesitant to support any broad SCO economic initiatives, while the Central Asian states are also nervous that their economies will be overrun by Chinese plans for more trade, greater investment, and even the possible internationalization of the *renminbi*. If it fails to sufficiently demonstrate that it is acting for the broader good, and not just as a plunderer of the region's natural resources and energy, China also potentially faces the prospect of a mounting social backlash from disgruntled Central Asian publics or populist politicians, as it has in parts of Africa. Finally, it is still unclear what will happen if countries that have made commitments to China renege on the terms of their deals or fail to pay off their debts. How China manages its growing influence in Central Asia will be a good indicator of how Beijing views its changing role in world politics and global governance.

Different Players, Same Rules: The European Union and India

Though this study has concentrated on the great power strategic triangle, other world powers have also engaged with Central Asia and have even developed their own regional strategies. At some point, leaders from India, the European Union, Turkey, Iran, Pakistan, Japan, and even South Korea have viewed Central Asia as a natural arena in which to project their influence. But a brief view of the experience of the European Union countries and India suggests that these other players have confronted the same dilemmas as the "Big Three," while the Central Asian governments have pushed them to also play by local rules.

European Base Politics and the EU's Central Asia Policy

Like U.S. policymakers, the European countries that are members of the ISAF mission have had to cope with their own Central Asian "base politics" challenges. France and Spain, for example, both used Manas and were left scrambling for other options by the Kyrgyz government's 2009 announcement that it would close the base. While U.S. officials were busy renegotiating at a greater cost, French and Spanish officials refused to pay more in rent and fees and were excluded from using the renegotiated Manas Transit Center. According to one U.S. account, the Kyrgyz did offer the French a way back to Manas in the fall of 2009, but it was conditional on President Sarkozy granting President Bakiyev a public meeting in Paris and a broadening of the French-Kyrgyz economic relationship.[1] Paris has also been on the receiving end of informal quid pro quo demands from Tajikistan, which allows a small French contingent to use a limited area of Dushanbe airport for staging operations. Though Paris does not pay formal rent, Tajik authorities regularly attempt to leverage the relationship for their benefit; for example, Paris was asked to bear the cost of constructing a new terminal at the Dushanbe airport in time for Tajikistan's 20-year anniversary commemoration.[2]

However, such episodes are relatively minor compared to Germany's more vexing "base politics" experience in Uzbekistan. Germany is the only EU country to maintain a formal embassy in every Central Asian country, while its foreign ministry views Central Asia as an area of special interest and German leadership.[3] At the beginning of the Afghanistan campaign, Germany established an air base at Termez in southern Uzbekistan, near the Afghan border, making it the first overseas German military base since World War II. The facility hosts about 300 German troops, five Stallion CH-53 helicopters, and nine C-130 transport planes. Berlin also has maintained somewhat of a privileged status among Uzbekistan's Western security partners; in the wake of Andijan and the U.S. eviction from K2, Germany was the only NATO country allowed to retain its basing rights.

But, like their U.S. counterparts, German officials have had to provide important economic and political concessions to Uzbek authorities to maintain access to Termez. According to a German parliamentary report that was released in 2011 (but was soon reclassified at the request of the Uzbek government), Berlin has paid the government of Uzbekistan annually between 12.4 million euros (in 2005) and 15.2 million euros (in 2008) to lease the base.[4] The German government, according to a *Spiegel* report, also provides a number of additional indirect payments by overpaying for construction projects, service contracts, and hotel rooms in the city.[5] In addition, Germany has trained Uzbek officers and has provided military hardware to Uzbek security services, while the German state development agency GTZ remains one of the country's most active external donors, and German foundations are among the few foreign NGOs that survived the sweeping purge of 2005–2007.[6]

Not coincidentally, Germany has been the most vociferous advocate of maintaining Western engagement with Tashkent. Within the European Union, Berlin led the campaign to repeal the sanctions regime that was imposed by Brussels in the wake of Andijan. Even while the sanctions were in effect, Germany issued a waiver to allow Zokirjon Almatov, the Uzbek Minister of Internal Affairs who was involved in the planning of the Andijon crackdown, to receive medical treatment in Hanover. German officials also successfully spearheaded the 2008 easing of the EU's travel ban and the 2009 overturn of its weapons sales ban.

It is unclear what practical benefits this political support has brought to Germany. Though Berlin officials in public stress the importance of their security cooperation, in private they have expressed mounting frustration with Tashkent. According to a leaked U.S. cable, the German Ambassador to Uzbekistan in 2007 described the German-Uzbek counterterrorism relationship as "stagnant," with the Germans unable to independently assess the true Islamic or terrorist threat in the country; the ambassador continued that Uzbeks welcomed German "equipment and money," including for Termez, but not German values such as "respect for human rights."[7]

Germany also headed the effort to formulate the EU strategy toward Central Asia that was adopted during its EU presidency in 2007.[8] The strategy brought together a diverse set of goals; on the strategic side, the plan called for working on energy production, counterterrorism and border management, and regional cooperation, while the "values" side emphasized promoting rule of law initiatives and establishing regular human rights and civil society dialogues.[9] Yet, the strategy itself reads more like a checklist of wishes and does not attempt to describe how to reconcile these objectives when they are in tension.

Maintaining momentum on the values questions has proven particularly difficult for Brussels. European NGOs and Central Asian civil society leaders have observed that by bracketing human rights meetings in a dedicated forum, EU leaders do not have to stress the issue in their regular consultations with Central Asian leaders.[10] But, as revealed in decisions over opening energy dialogues with Turkmenistan or evaluating the sanctions regime in Uzbekistan, Brussels's "soft power" remains weak in areas of the world that do not aspire for membership and where EU conditionality mechanisms are not in play.[11] Perhaps what is most striking about EU–Central Asia relations is how, over the decade, rather than promoting change in the targeted Central Asian states, the EU's engagement with the region appears, instead, to have magnified intra-EU tensions and exposed the limits of the EU's nascent foreign policy mechanisms. Most notably, the acrimonious intra-EU debates about the Uzbekistan sanctions regime exposed lingering tensions among Brussels policymakers on whether the EU should be a normative or strategic actor.[12]

India and the Quest for a "Northern Strategy"

Like China or the United States, India has engaged with the Central Asian states primarily in the service of an adjacent strategic goal—to counter Pakistan's role in Central Asia and Afghanistan.[13] Since 1998, the year of India's nuclear tests, expanding influence in this "northern neighborhood" also has become an important marker of India's self-identification as a great power and its new elevated status in international affairs.[14]

Viewing India as a potential great power rival to Russia, China, and the United States, Indian analysts have written extensively within the "Great Game" framework, advocating that New Delhi match China's growing economic influence or check the geopolitical expansion of the United States and its Central Asian bases.[15] Yet, despite all this attention and frequent exaggeration of India's current and future role, few analysts pay much attention to understanding Central Asia's local rules. India may share some broad common goals with the Central Asian states, such as countering militant Islam and ensuring regional stability, but these have proven insufficient for Central Asian elites to elevate their relations with India to the level befitting a "regional power."

Economically, India faces commercial and geographic constraints that probably make it impossible for it to have an important impact in the near term. India's exports are unlikely to make large inroads in what are already saturated Central Asian markets from the flood of Chinese manufactured goods. For instance, in 2009 India's trade with the five Central Asian countries totaled a paltry $416 million ($196 m imports, $220 m exports), about two percent of Russian or Chinese volumes from the same year.[16] Nor has India developed the same level of aid and investment packages as Beijing to act as a regional public goods provider or an alternative to Western sources of development assistance and project financing. Regarding Central Asia's energy resources, Indian companies have been active in bidding for contracts in Kazakhstan and Uzbekistan. However, unlike China or Russia, India remains severely constrained by geography and cannot build a direct pipeline to its home territory without traversing some hostile spots in between. In this light, the proposed Turkmenistan-Afghanistan-Pakistan-India pipeline does promise a tangible benefit to New Delhi, but the inclusion of Pakistan in the project would seem to obviate its strategic impact as traditionally envisioned by Indian defense planners.

The large gap between India's aspirations and its local realities is best exemplified by its own embarrassing "base politics" episode with Tajikistan. India and Tajikistan had forged close security ties in the 1990s, when they jointly supported the Northern Alliance in Afghanistan and, until 2002, the Indian military hosted a small medical facility at the Farkhor base to treat Northern Alliance fighters. Soon after, in a bid to secure a foothold in the region, India appears to have offered Tajikistan a deal to refurbish the Ayni air base, just outside Dushanbe, in exchange for either joint or trilateral (India-Tajikistan-Russia) use of the facility.[17] Over the next 10 years, India would employ 50 members of its Border Roads Organization, also active in Afghanistan, sinking $60–70 million into extending Ayni's runway, building new hangars and a new air traffic control tower; the prospect of India's first foreign military base seemed to captivate the Indian defense establishment, bloggers and security commentators. According to diplomats in Tajikistan, the Indian mission made little effort to dampen speculation that it was, indeed, building a base for future use.[18]

But after the Indian workers completed their projects and handed back the facility, Tajik officials reneged on any promises for future access. In January 2011, Tajikistan's Foreign Minister publicly confirmed that India would not be permitted to deploy a combat squadron at Ayni, thus ending Delhi's nine-year bid to achieve Central Asian "base status" and dealing India's prestige an embarrassing public relations blow.[19] Though Russian pressure may well have influenced Dushanbe to terminate this ambiguous arrangement, Tajikistan also appears to have actively "played" Delhi into refurbishing the facility with promises of access that never materialized.

In sum, despite India's self-image as a regional "great power," its actual projection of influence has failed to match its ambitious aspirations. More importantly, as the Ayni base debacle revealed, India too often ignored local rules and the potential for the Central Asian governments to leverage Delhi's perceptions of geopolitical competition for their own gain, offering little in return. If India's role in Central Asia is an indicator of India's broader rise as a global power, Delhi still has some way to go before it develops the necessary strategy and instruments to more effectively compete with regional powers such as China and Russia.

The New Regional Contests of a Multipolar World: The United States, China, and Regional Powers

What broader lessons might the new great power contest for Central Asia—and Central Asian reactions to it—offer as we enter this emerging era of multipolar politics? Skeptics might reasonably point to Central Asia's particularities—its importance to U.S. planners for the unique Afghanistan campaign, its proximity to China and its historical importance to Russia—and argue that this trilateral convergence of interests hardly exists in other regional settings.

One possible direct analogy to Central Asia may be parts of Africa where local governments, especially the ones sitting on energy and mineral resources, now find themselves courted by multiple external patrons. Chief among them are the U.S. military, which has expanded its military engagement with region following 9/11 and has established the new U.S. African Command (AFRICOM), and China, which dramatically has increased its regional economic role as a trading partner, investor, and infrastructure builder.[20] Completing these strategic triangles across the continent are the individual European former colonial powers, which are doing their best to preserve their special post-colonial economic, security, and cultural ties, much like Russia in Central Asia.

Such triangular dynamics may soon characterize Angola, the country that in 2006 ditched negotiations with the IMF when China offered a loan in exchange for access to a stake in its considerable oil wealth. Since, Angola has emerged as China's most important African energy supplier; in April 2008, it overtook Saudi Arabia as China's largest crude oil supplier.[21] Angolan and Portuguese (the country's former colonial power) companies are increasingly collaborating on commercial and financial ventures, while U.S. defense officials and think tanks have been pressing to develop a strategic partnership with their Angolan counterparts, particularly on maritime and naval issues.[22] Similarly, Chinese aid and major infrastructure investments in Kenya and Ethiopia are ongoing at a time of intensifying military contacts between the U.S. security community and these countries, suggesting that, as in Central Asia, these expanding outside contacts are not mutually exclusive. However, the potential for a Sino-U.S. proxy confrontation in Africa is higher on the Sudanese border, as the United States is reportedly spending $100 million a year to forge a security partnership with the newly independent country of Southern Sudan, to the concern of its northern neighbor that, over the last decade, has enjoyed the often-criticized patronage of Beijing.[23]

The Evolution of U.S. Power: Increasing Hard Power, Diminished Influence?

Beyond mounting competition in Africa, we see several of the themes that we have observed in Central Asia cropping up in different corners of the world. First, we see an increasing gap between the United States' formidable military capabilities and the fading of its soft power and normative influence. The United States continues to maintain hundreds of facilities and hundreds of thousands of personnel in over 130 countries. As with Central Asia, these security arrangements are not always publicized, often at the requests of host governments, and much of this security assistance is controlled by the regional commands that increasingly are using their budgets to project soft power. Part of the confusion and initial skepticism shown to AFRICOM, both on the continent and within the U.S. government circles, is that it seeks to engage with African countries on a range of non-military issues such as development, infrastructure, and humanitarian projects.[24] The regional command responds that its view of security is more holistic and deals as much in threat prevention as combat, but the command's mission clearly overlaps with the traditional portfolios of the State Department and the U.S. foreign aid community in Africa.

Moreover, with the onset of budget crunches and austerity measures in the United States, the State Department will suffer deeper cuts, scaling down official USAID projects and other soft power tools even further; again, this will magnify the relative influence of the Department of Defense and the Central Intelligence Agency, effectively transferring to them an even greater proportion of diplomatic activities and functions. Thus, the often criticized "militarization" of U.S. foreign policy is, in fact, being accompanied by rising "civilianization" of the U.S. military—the increased diplomatic functions and roles played by security officials and military commanders around the world.[25]

The other major problem faced by U.S. defense planners is that countries hosting U.S. bases and security facilities are increasingly politicizing the U.S. presence and security partnership, either by directly courting alternative partners or by attempting to ransom Washington's security needs to demand concessions on seemingly unrelated domestic political matters. In Ecuador in 2008,

President Rafael Correa refused to renew the 10-year U.S. lease on the Manta base, officially used by U.S. SOUTHCOM to conduct anti-drug trafficking operations. Recalling the Manas bidding war, U.S. officials this time appear to have been outbid, as Correa reportedly offered a 30-year concession to run the airport and nearby port to Hutchison, a Hong-Kong based port operator in a $500 million deal, forcing the U.S. military to leave the facility in 2009.[26] The case of Bahrain shows great similarities to U.S. dilemmas in Uzbekistan, as U.S. officials, concerned with maintaining a naval base for the Fifth Fleet, have tempered their criticism of the regime's crackdown on anti-government protestors and human rights abuses.[27] And U.S.-Pakistani military relations have plummeted to an all-time low following the assassination of Osama Bin Laden by U.S. Special forces in Pakistan, reports that Pakistani intelligence services had aided insurgent attacks on U.S. forces in Afghanistan and an errant U.S. air strike on the Afghan border on November 26, 2011 that resulted in the deaths of 24 Pakistani soldiers. In response, Islamabad halted the transit of NATO supplies, evicted the United States from an air base used to launch Predator drone attacks, and has been eager to play up its relations with China as a possible alternative to U.S. security patronage. Throughout the world, as in Central Asia, the status of the U.S. military presence and security partnership seems to be increasingly wielded by host country governments to extract political and economic concessions from Washington.

China's Bottom-Up Leadership and Public Goods Provision

A second broader lesson is the rise of China, especially since the onset of the Western financial crisis, as a key provider of public goods across different regions. Most discussions of hegemony and world order start from the top down, examining how great powers such as Great Britain in the nineteenth century or the United States after World War II fashioned world orders.[28] A critical function of such global leaders has been to provide public goods to the international system and, in particular, to play a stabilizing role in times of economic crisis. From this perspective, China's rise in Central Asia and elsewhere threatens to erode U.S. leadership, not because Beijing has the appetite for a high-profile geopolitical battle, but because, at the ground level, China is providing short-term crisis lending, development assistance, and concessionary infrastructure financing.[29] Until very recently, Western actors exclusively discharged these public goods functions.

As with Beijing's engagement with Central Asia, these aid packages frequently have been bundled into bilateral energy deals. At the height of the financial crisis in 2008–2010, China provided about $77 billion in loans-for-energy packages to the Kazakhstan, Turkmenistan, Russia, Brazil, Ecuador, Venezuela, Angola, and Ghana.[30] Similarly, as with the SCO, China's enthusiastic backing of the BRICS group suggests that Beijing will continue to push much of its agenda through new non-Western organizations, thereby also avoiding outright confrontation with the United States within existing global organizations.

In turn, China's entry as a global investor and aid donor is likely to undercut Western donors and lending mechanisms. With alternative potential sources for aid, assistance, and investment, the Western political leverage that derived from controlling the purse strings of international financial institutions will continue to be diminished. Though IMF and the World Bank will continue to be important global actors, their monopoly over crisis financing and development lending is over. As shown in Africa and Central Asia, countries in need of external funding and assistance have other options and will exercise them with greater frequency.

Democratic Regression and New Regional Counterbalancers

Finally, as in Central Asia, the rise of multiple regional patrons is empowering targeted governments to buck external pressures for political reforms and greater democratization. For the fifth straight year, the NGO FreedomHouse's survey in 2011 found an overall global decline in democratic trends, noting backsliding across Eurasia, Latin America, and Africa.[31] Though the causal link between the rise of regional multipolarity and recent democratic retrenchment has yet to be systematically tested, at the very least, the overall trend suggests that the steady increase in democratization that coincided with the West's dominance during the immediate post–Cold War era has halted.[32]

Like Russia in Central Asia, an array of emerging powers now view themselves as leaders in the push-back against externally supported democracy promotion. In the Middle East, Saudi Arabia, a traditional U.S. ally, has aggressively supported regimes in the Gulf and North Africa in the face of anti-regime protests unleashed by the Arab Spring. Demonstrating similarities to the stabilizing mandate of the SCO, Saudi Arabia has used the Gulf Cooperation Council (GCC) to help crush pro-democracy movements and internal opposition in Bahrain and Yemen, with the purpose of countering Iranian influence. Saudi Arabia's own active new role was emphasized in March 2011, when hundreds of Saudi security troops poured over the King Fahd causeway to support Bahrain's embattled ruling family against mainly Shiite pro-democracy protestors. Riyadh also extended the offer of GCC membership to Morocco and Jordan, traditional U.S. security partners.[33] As if to emphasize their new role as local regime guarantors, Saudi officials insisted that, in return for their support of the NATO military campaign in Libya, Washington stop criticizing the Bahraini government for its crackdown.[34]

A common refrain to such observations about anti-democratic backlash is that while Western-sponsored democratic movements may be on the decline, the rise of indigenous civil society, political parties, and rights-promoting groups may actually be democratically empowering citizens with their own localized values.[35] Even Western organizations that promote universal rights are now looking to become more regional; for example, Human Rights Watch now plans to open regional chapters in Brazil, South Africa, Turkey, and Indonesia in a bid to translate its advocacy mission to a more tailored local set of concerns.[36] There is little doubt that the Western practice of uncritically promoting democratic agendas requires better tailoring to the needs and local challenges of different regions; but the Central Asian cases also suggest that arguments about "indigenous democracy," inappropriate democratic ideals, and cultural specificity can be cynically wielded by elites to deflect criticism of their own shortcomings.

The Post-Arab Spring Environment

These three trends—engagement with non-Western security partners, the entry of non-Western public goods providers, and a new regional environment that permits democratic backsliding—bode ill for Western attempts to spearhead and shape democratic transitions following the Arab Spring. Scarred by its inconsistent support for anti-regime protest movements in the Arab world and the tarnish of the military campaigns in Iraq and Afghanistan, U.S. status and credibility in the Middle East are vastly diminished, and Washington faces severe constraints in shaping the region's political transitions. In fact, the aftermath of the Arab Spring has been noteworthy for politicians tacking away from the West, under populist pressure from their publics, and emphasizing the importance of regional organizations and neighboring states in their new post-authoritarian efforts.

In terms of funding the transition, the diminished position and relative capacity of the West stand in great contrast to the years following the Communist collapse, when the IMF and Western advisors set Russia and Eastern Europe on a path of Western-oriented rapid reforms and the "end of history" was declared, with the West triumphant. A Tunisian minister in February 2011 referred to the EU's initial pledge to provide 258 million euros to help with the country's transition as "ridiculous."[37] In May 2011, the G8 did announce a plan to provide $40 billion in aid to Tunisia and Egypt, but non-Western donors were an increasingly large part of that pot. Just a few weeks later, the Egyptian finance minister announced that Egypt would no longer solicit loans from the IMF or the World Bank; reports that Cairo was negotiating new aid packages with the Gulf States of Qatar, Kuwait, and Saudi Arabia seemed to have emboldened its shunning of these traditional donors.[38] In response, U.S. State Department officials have lobbied Congress to relax political conditions on the disbursal of aid packages to Egypt and Tunisia, including provisions that these countries demonstrate that they hold fair and free elections and support civil societies.[39] Like China's loans to Central Asia and Africa, Gulf funding may well displace the West as a source of external funding, but without the democracy or good governance provisions of Western aid.

Principles for Statecraft in the New World of Influence

In the short or even medium term, the United States is not likely to be overtly challenged as a global leader by China or any other power. But if we focus too much on high-profile questions of global leadership, world order, and primacy, we risk missing the nuances of the political shifts currently underway in regions like Central Asia. More likely, the erosion of what has been referred to as the U.S.-led "liberal order" will take place region by region, regime by regime, deal by deal. As we have seen in Central Asia, and as is now the case in the Middle East and Africa, U.S. power, authority, and rule-making are being challenged on a regional level by a variety of actors. In some cases, local actors are forcing U.S. policy to adapt to a new regional context, while in others they are opposing it outright. The search for a magic formula to resurrect American primacy or the U.S.-led world order is likely to be fruitless;[40] however, the new Central Asian great game does offer some guidance to Western policymakers who are now confronting a series of new regional contests.

First, the Central Asian cases suggest that U.S. policymakers need to remain flexible about regional partnerships, while avoiding becoming locked into any overarching principle such as "anyone but Russia" or, in the global arena, what Bruce Jentleson has referred to as the "anyone but terrorists" test.[41] China's effective diplomacy in Central Asia has been rooted in its nimble ability to pivot back and forth along the legs of the strategic triangle, forging partnerships with both Washington and Moscow when it was expeditious to do so, while remaining closely focused on its security priorities. In the Central Asian arena, as in other areas of emerging interest, U.S. policymakers must similarly learn to "embrace the triangle." Multipolar dynamics are difficult enough to predict without self-inflicted constraints about who should and should not be part of any meaningful regional dialogue and partnership.

Second, with the decline in Western soft power and the rise of alternative norms, laws, and regional orders, Western policymakers must now be prepared to engage with, and sometimes challenge, these orders and practices that may be antithetical to Western institutions and rules. From this perspective, the operative question for the West in dealing with the Shanghai Cooperation Organization should not be whether or not to engage with the new regional body, but how to shape and sequence the engagement agenda so that policymakers both find areas of common interests and constructively push to amend certain organizational practices that may be in clear conflict with international norms and Western values (such as the SCO's consolidated blacklist of extremist organizations and individuals). Regional organizations and the values that they embody are not static—both ASEAN and the African Union have greatly evolved from their origins, when they were criticized as "clubs for dictators," into dynamic, multifaceted organizations that promote regional deliberation, problem solving, and broadly democratic values.[42]

Third, and finally, with so much attention paid to U.S. decline and diminished resources, policymakers should not forget that the essence of multipolar politics, for target states, is to pursue a variety of partnerships. The United States and the West will always be attractive partners, if not always for the ideals that they represent, but, in more calculating terms, to prevent governments from becoming locked into exclusive relationships with other regional patrons. Just as Uzbekistan tacked back to the West after its initial post-Andijan rupture, so too will other countries that face the prospect of being captured by a dominant regional power such as Russia. The real question confronting U.S. policymakers is whether they will, when approached by such countries, pare their demands and compromise on their values agenda, as they have in the Central Asian cases, or whether they will insist on pursuing engagement on a broad range of issues. From this perspective, what Washington and Brussels say and do domestically matters enormously for their ability to promote a diverse agenda of issues abroad. In this search to craft policies toward and to influence distant regions, how we act at home, now more than ever, reflects on both our global image and our credibility to lead in this changing world.

Appendix 1

Laws Passed after Color Revolutions That Introduced New Restrictions on NGOs and the Media[1]

Russia	
2006	**Law on Introducing Amendments to Certain Legislative Acts of the Russian Federation**
	Made it more difficult and costly to start and operate an NGO in Russia; gave the authorities broad powers to audit and shut down NGOs.
2006	**Law on Introducing Amendments to Articles 1 and 15 of the Federal Law on Countering Extremist Activity**
	Expanded the official definition of extremist activity to include publicly slandering a government official, justifying terrorism, and using or threatening violence against a government official or his or her family.
2006	**Law on Introducing Amendments to Certain Legislative Acts of the Russian Federation in Connection with Advancement of Public Administration in the Area of Countering Extremism**
	Included public debate of terrorism and extremism into list of prohibited extremist activities. Allowed government to suspend media outlets that do not comply with anti-extremism laws. Gave the government broader wiretapping powers.

(continued)

2003   **Regulation on the State Registration and Re-registration of Representative Offices, International Branches, and Foreign Nongovernmental Organizations in the Republic of Uzbekistan**

Required international organizations to re-register; required accreditation of employees of foreign NGOs; required foreign NGOs in Uzbekistan to submit additional documentation and pay additional fees for registration and accreditation.

Decree on Undertaking Additional Measures to Support the Activities of the Women's Committee of Uzbekistan

Required women's organizations, reportedly a majority of NGOs in Uzbekistan, to re-register with Ministry of Justice. Many chose to close instead of re-registering.

Amendments to Law on Nongovernmental Non-commercial Organizations

Introduced additional restrictions on banking by NGOs and on the transfer of grants.

2005   **Amendments to the Code of Administrative Penalties**

Increased fines for non-compliance with strict reporting requirements, leading to the closing of many organizations.

2006   **Amendments to Criminal Code and Code of Administrative Liability of the Republic of Uzbekistan**

Tightened system of laws that penalize public criticism of the president with up to five years in prison.

Decree on Confirming the Main Rules on Regulating the Professional Work of Foreign Correspondents

Forbade foreign correspondents from insulting Uzbek citizens or interfering in their lives; introduced restrictions on interaction between foreign correspondents and Uzbek citizens.

2007	**Law on the Guarantees of Activity of Nongovernmental and Non-commercial Organizations**
	Vague law, which, absent implementing regulations, appears to have had little impact.
2008	**On Measures Aimed at Enhancing Support for Nongovernmental Non-commercial Organizations and Other Civil Society Institutions**
	Modified law on non-commercial organizations to provide for state support of certain NGOs; made it more difficult for independent NGOs to get funding.
2009	**Law on Introducing Changes and Additions to the Tax Code of the Republic of Uzbekistan**
	Tax legislation tightened, making filing taxes more difficult and requiring the recalculation of taxes for past years; caused the closing of about 20% of NGOs.

Tajikistan

2004	**Amendments to Law on Television and Radio Broadcasting and to Law on Licensing of Individual Types of Activities**
	Introduced strict requirements for licensing of broadcast programs, which, according to some outlets, have been applied retroactively; resulted in low numbers of domestic broadcasters.
2007	**Law on Public Associations**
	Required all local and international NGOs to re-register by end of year and subjected NGOs that work with foreign organizations to additional scrutiny. Many NGOs were unable or chose not to re-register, reducing their ranks by 70%. The law also has been praised for tax benefits and other changes it introduced.
	Law on Changes and Amendments to the Criminal Code
	Extended criminal libel and defamation provisions to internet content. Possible fines can reach US$5,000 and up to two years in prison; instituted restrictions on the collection and distribution of private data.

(continued)

2009	**Law on State Registration of Legal Entities and Individual Entrepreneurs**
	Required NGOs not registered under the legal form public associations to re-register with local tax authorities.
2010	**Amendments to the Law on Public Associations**
	New amendments required branches and representative offices of local and international public associations to register with the Ministry of Justice, a more burdensome registration process.

Kazakhstan

2006	**Amendments to Law on National Security**
	Amended to require extensive and more burdensome reporting of expenses by NGOs to the tax authorities; prohibited the glorification of "extremism" by the media, although "extremism" is not defined.
2008	**Tax Code Modifications**
	Removed some tax exemptions that NGOs were previously able to claim, making it more difficult for them to operate.
2009	**Law on Introducing Amendments and Additions to Some Legislative Acts of the Republic of Kazakhstan Concerning Protection of the Rights of Citizens to Privacy**
	Mandated jail time for publishing information about individuals' private lives, raising concerns that investigative journalists could be targeted for prosecution.
2009	**Law on Introducing Amendments and Additions to Some Legislative Acts of the Republic of Kazakhstan Concerning Information-Communication Networks**
	Granted the authorities greater latitude in closing Internet sites, including under extremism statutes; extended criminal libel liability to all Internet content.

2006	**Law on Introducing Amendments and Additions to Some Legislative Acts of the Republic of Kazakhstan Concerning Mass Media**
	Imposed high registration fees for journalists and allowed authorities more leeway in denying registration; required outlets to submit names of editors with registration applications, mandating re-registration in case of change of editors.

Kyrgyzstan

2008	**Amendments to Law on Freedom of Conscience and Religious Organizations**
	Made registering religious organizations more challenging, requiring that they have at least 200 members.

2008	**Law on Mass Media and Radio Broadcasting**
	Allowed president to appoint executives to Kyrgyz National Television and Radio Corporation; enhanced regulators' ability to revoke broadcasting licenses without judicial oversight; and established new programming requirements that may be detrimental to some broadcasters.

Turkmenistan

2003	**Law on Public Associations**
	Required re-registration of NGOs and their grants; prohibited the operation of unregistered organizations, forcing many NGOs to discontinue their work.

1. Compiled by Matthew Schaff from USAID's NGO Sustainability Index (http://www.usaid. gov/locations/europe_eurasia/dem_gov/ngoindex/); the International Center for Not-for-Profit Law's NGO Law Monitor reports (http://www.icnl.org/knowledge/ngolawmonitor/index.htm); the U.S. State Department's annual Human Rights Reports (http://www.state.gov/g/drl/rls/ hrrpt/); news reports; a review of the relevant laws; and reports by human and civil rights groups, including Human Rights Watch (http://www.hrw.org), Freedom House (http://www.freedomhouse. org), Civicus (http://www.civicus.org), the Committee to Protect Journalists (http://www.cpj. org), Article 19 (http://www.article19.org/), the Open Net Initiative (http://www.opennet.net), and Reporters Without Borders (http://www.rsf.org).

Appendix 2

OSCE, SCO, and CIS Evaluations of Major Central Asian Elections, 2005–2008

	SCO	CIS	OSCE
Kazakhstan 2005 Presidential	"carried out in compliance with the Kazak constitution and relevant laws" "conducive to the country's further development as well as regional peace and stability"[1]	"The state electoral bodies that organized elections in the Republic of Kazakhstan ensured the realization and protection of the electoral rights of citizens in the presidential elections of Kazakhstan," "International observers from the CIS concluded that Kazakhstan's presidential elections of 4 December 2005 were held in accordance with the country's legislation. We assess them as free, open, and legitimate."[2]	"a number of significant shortcomings during the election campaign limited the possibility for a meaningful competition whereby all candidates could enjoy equal opportunities to convey their views to the electorate" "Overall, despite some improvement in the administration of this election in the pre-election period, the election did not meet a number of OSCE commitments and other international standards for democratic elections"[3]
2007 Parliamentary	"legitimate and free and open, and was in compliance with election laws of the Republic of Kazakhstan and international commitments" "some technical shortcomings revealed during the election could not significantly affect its final results"[4]	"in line with generally recognised democratic approaches to organising elections and with the election legislation of the country" "free and transparent and believe that they have reflected the stable social and economic development of Kazakhstan, were the continuation of political reforms in the country and an important factor for further democratisation of society's life" "some shortcomings and violations were exposed during the elections"[5]	"Despite some progress in the process during the pre-election period and in certain aspects of voting, the election did not meet a number of OSCE commitments, in particular with regard to elements of the legal framework and to the vote count and tabulation."[6]

(*continued*)

	SCO	CIS	OSCE
Kyrgyzstan 2005 Parliamentary	"complied with international standards" "conformed to the republic's constitution, laws, democratic norms and universal standards" "deepened democratic processes"[7]	"legitimate, free and transparent" "the defects and mistakes committed during the preparations and arrangement of the elections have had no substantial effect on the expression of the free will by the voters" "concern over illegal actions of some participants in the election campaign who had organized protests demanding a review of the voting results of the first round" "approved the Kyrgyz authorities who, at this turbulent period, 'demonstrated support, competence and willingness to do all it takes to provide franchise and freedom of citizens'"[8]	"while more competitive than previous elections, fell short of OSCE commitments and other international standards for democratic elections in a number of important areas." "The conduct of the second round of elections demonstrated some technical improvements over the first round, but significant shortcomings remained."[9]
2005 Presidential	"passed freely, open, transparently and legitimate"[10]	"proceeded in accordance with the law" "some individual violations in the election campaign had taken place, but that they had not affected the free will of the voters and the results of the voting" "unhappy about the procedure of 'marking' the voters"[11]	"marked tangible progress by the Kyrgyz Republic towards meeting OSCE commitments, as well as other international standards for democratic elections. This was the case in particular during the pre-election period and the conduct of voting, although the quality of the election day process deteriorated somewhat during the counting of votes." "Fundamental civil and political rights, such as freedom of expression and freedom of assembly, were generally respected throughout the election process."[12]

2007 Parliamentary	"recognized legitimacy of the parliamentary election in Kyrgyzstan and its concurrence with the national legislation and international standards" "absence of serious complaints from representatives of political parties and voters themselves enabled. . . observers to praise the atmosphere of the election as tranquil and transparent"[13]	"met the norms of the election legislation in effect in the country, as well as commonly accepted approaches to holding democratic elections" "free and transparent" "flaws exposed in the course of monitoring of the election process were not of system nature and did not affect the expression of will of the voters"[14]	"failed to meet a number of OSCE commitments. This was despite respect for some commitments that underscore existing pluralism. If the progress evident during the 2005 presidential election is to be underpinned, further efforts and political will are necessary."[15]
Russia 2007 Parliamentary	"slight technical mistakes that did not affect the election results were registered" "legitimate, free, transparent and met Russian legal requirements and international commitments"[16]	"elections were free, everybody had enough opportunities to express his opinion" "high level of organization of the elections and well-coordinated work"[17]	OSCE unable to monitor 2007 elections because of "delays and restrictions," especially related to entry visas[18]

(continued)

	SCO	CIS	OSCE
2008 Presidential	"calm, benevolent and well-organised environment, which ensured free expression of the voters' will" "legitimate, free, open and transparent, and basically conformed to requirements of the national legislation of the Russian Federation and generally accepted international electoral standards. No violations were found, which would question the outcome of the voting in the election of the President of the Russian Federation."[19]	"free, open and transparent" "the number of complaints on any violations during the elections is decreasing" "certain violations at different polling stations. But these are isolated cases, which are of technical nature and have no impact on Russian citizens' will expression and on the results of the voting.' The elections in Russia were held in compliance with legislation and the norms of democratic elections"[20]	OSCE boycotted 2008 elections because "They have imposed restrictions and limitations which do not allow us to deliver a professional job."[21]

| Tajikistan 2005 Parliamentary | Unavailable | "will help put an end once and for all to the civil confrontation in the country, strengthen peace and stability in Tajikistan" | "the shortcomings and flaws, recorded during the voting,' did not exert any substantial influence on the free expression of the electors' will"

"in accordance 'with the norms of the national electoral legislation' and were 'legitimate, free and transparent'"

"corresponds on the whole to the standards of the international law and includes all the electoral institutions and procedures that are required to hold democratic elections in the republic."[22] | "failed to meet many of the key OSCE commitments for democratic elections contained in the 1990 Copenhagen Document, and they were also not conducted fully in accordance with domestic law. Although some efforts were made to improve the legislative and administrative framework for democratic elections, a commensurate effort to ensure effective implementation was largely lacking. Therefore, despite some improvement over previous elections, large-scale irregularities were evident, particularly on election day."[23] |

(continued)

	SCO	CIS	OSCE
2006 Presidential	"free, open and complied with Tajik laws and its international obligations"[24]	"in line with the election law" "election free, open and transparent" "irregularities observed were technical and did not have a serious impact on the election results"[25]	"did not fully test democratic electoral practices as outlined in the 1990 OSCE Copenhagen Document, due to a lack of genuine choice and meaningful pluralism, and revealed substantial shortcomings." "Despite the presence of five candidates and some administrative improvements, the 6 November 2006 presidential election was characterized by a marked absence of competition. Parties that determined themselves as political opposition to the incumbent chose not to nominate candidates. As a result, voters were presented with a choice that was only nominal."[26]
Turkmenistan 2007 Presidential	SCO not invited	CIS not invited to 2007 Presidential elections[27]	Needs Assessment Mission Report only, no findings or conclusions; only present as unofficial observers: "absolutely not free and fair"[28]

Uzbekistan 2007 Presidential	"the elections were held in correspondence with universally accepted international election standards and democratic norms" "the observers did not reveal any violations of provisions of the Law 'On elections of President of Uzbekistan'" "legitimate, free and transparent and fully corresponded to the requirements of the national legislation and international election standards"[29]	"free, open and transparent"[30] "proceeded in line with the country's election legislation and universally recognized norms for holding democratic elections" "a major factor in further democratization of social life in Uzbekistan"[31]	Interim Report only, no conclusions To the press: "held in a strictly controlled political environment, leaving no room for real opposition, and the election generally failed to meet many OSCE commitments for democratic elections"[32]

Compiled with the assistance of Nadia Bulkin.

1. "Kazak President Pledges More Support for SCO"—Xinhua General News Service, December 6, 2005.

2. "Kazakhstan: Officials Declare Nazarbayev Winner of the Presidential Election"—RFE/RL, December 5, 2005.

(continued)

3. OSCE Final Report, February 21, 2006.

4. "Shanghai Group Observers Say Kazakh Election 'Legitimate'"—BBC Monitoring International Reports, August 19, 2007.

5. "CIS Observers Satisfied with Democratic Polls in Kazakhstan"—ITAR-TASS, August 19, 2007.

6. OSCE Final Report, October 30, 2007.

7. "SCO Observers Positive about Kyrgyz Elections"—Interfax News Agency, February 28, 2005.

8. "CIS Observers Find Kyrgyz Elections Legitimate"—RIA-Novosti, March 14, 2005.

9. OSCE Final Report, May 20, 2005.

10. "SCO Observers: Kyrgyz Presidential Elections Free, Open, Transparent and Legitimate"—AKIPress, July 12, 2005.

11. "Presidential Elections in Kyrgyzstan Legal—Observers"—RIA-Novosti, July 11, 2005.

12. OSCE Final Report, November 7, 2005.

13. "Kyrgyzstan: President Bakiyev's Ak Jol Is the Leader of the Parliamentary Race"—Ferghana.ru Info Agency, December 17, 2007.

14. "Kyrgyz Elections Not Fully Meet International Norms—EU"—ITAR-TASS, December 18, 2007.

15. OSCE Preliminary Report, April 24, 2008.

16. "SCO Observers Not Expose Violations at Duma Elections"—ITAR-TASS, December 3, 2007.

17. "CIS Observers Note Transparency of Russian Parliamentary Polls"—ITAR-TASS, December 4, 2007.

18. "ODIHR Unable to Observe Russian Duma Elections"—OSCE Press Release, November 16, 2007.

19. Main Events of SCO Secretariat in 2008, SCO web site.

20. "CIS Observers Recognise Elections in RF as Free, Open, Transparent"—ITAR-TASS, March 3, 2008.

21. "OSCE to Boycott Russian Election"—BBC, February 7, 2008.

22. "CIS Monitors Found Tajik Elections Legitimate and Free"—ITAR-TASS, February 28, 2005.

23. OSCE Final Report, May 31, 2005.

24. "CIS, SCO Observers Positive on Tajik Vote"—Xinhua General News Service, November 7, 2006.

25. "CIS, SCO Observers Positive on Tajik Vote"—Xinhua General News Service, November 7, 2006.

26. OSCE Final Report, November 6, 2006.

27. "CIS Not to Send Observers to Turkmenistan Presidential Elections"—ITAR-TASS, February 9, 2007.

28. "Turkmenistan: Presidential Election Deemed Neither Free Nor Fair"—RadioFreeEurope/RadioLiberty, February 12, 2007.

29. "SCO Mission: 'Elections Were Free & Transparent'"—Uzbek Consulate, December 25, 2007.

30. "CIS Mission: 'Elections Were Important for Further Democratization of Public Life in Uzbekistan'"—Jahon Information Agency, December 26, 2007.

31. "Uzbekistan's Elections Labeled 'Undemocratic'"—Christian Science Monitor, December 26, 2007.

32. "Uzbekistan's Elections Labeled 'Undemocratic'"—Christian Science Monitor, December 26, 2007.

NOTES

Chapter 1

1. For representative examples, see Philip Pan, "Russia Is Said to Have Fueled Unrest in Kyrgyzstan," *Washington Post*, April 12, 2010; Ariel Cohen, "Obama's Stake in the Second Kyrgyz Revolution," *Wall Street Journal*, April 12, 2010; Simon Tisdall, "Kyrgyzstan: A Russian Revolution?" *Guardian*, April 8, 2011.

2. For overviews that draw on nineteenth-century accounts and travelogues, see Peter Hopkirk, *The Great Game: The Struggle for Empire in Central Asia* (New York: Kodansha, 1990); Karl E. Meyer and Shareen Blair Brysac, *Tournament of Shadows: The Great Game and the Race for Empire in Central Asia*, revised edition (New York: Basic, 2006).

3. Though, a closer examination of the historical record also casts doubt on how many of these events and policies were actually set by British officials in London, as opposed to being local reactions to sudden crises. See Gordon Martel, "Documenting the Great Game: 'World Policy' and the 'Turbulent Frontier' in the 1890s," *The International History Review* 2, no. 2 (April 1980), 288–320. Also see the more skeptical treatment in Gerald Morgan, "Myth and Reality in the Great Game," *Asian Affairs* 4, no. 1 (1973), 55–65.

4. See Hopkirk's harrowing account of the massacre. Hopkirk, *The Great Game*, 243–269.

5. H. J. Mackinder, "The Geographical Pivot of History," *The Geographical Journal* 23, no. 4 (April 1904), 434–436.

6. Mackinder, "The Geographical Pivot of History," 436.

7. See Pascal Venier, "The Geopolitical Pivot of History and Early Twentieth Century Political Culture," *The Geographic Journal* 170, no. 2 (December 2004), 330–336; Gearóid Ó Tuathail, "Putting Mackinder in His Place: Material Transformations and Myth," *Political Geography* 11, no. 1 (January 1992), 100–118.

8. See Peter Golden, *Central Asia in World History* (New York: Oxford University Press, 2011). On the distinctly illiberal institutional legacies bequeathed by these competing external powers, see Stephen Kotkin, "Mongol Commonwealth: Exchange and Governance across the Post-Mongol Space," *Kritika: Explorations in Russian and Eurasian History* 8, no. 3 (Summer 2007).

9. For critical assessments of the analogy, see Nick Megoran, "Revisiting the 'Pivot': The Influence of Harold Mackinder on Analysis of Uzbekistan's Foreign Policy," *The Geographical Journal* 170, no. 4 (December 2004), 347–358; Matthew Edwards, "The New Great Game and the New Great Gamers: Disciples of Mackinder and Kipling," *Central Asian Survey* 22, no. 1 (March 2003), 83–102.

10. See, especially, Brzezinski's use of the "chessboard metaphor" in reference to Eurasia. Zbigniew Brzezinski, *The Grand Chessboard: American Primacy and Geostrategic Imperatives* (New York: Basic, 1997).

11. On the scramble for Caspian oil, see Lutz Kleveman, *The New Great Game: Blood and Oil in Central Asia* (New York: Grove Press, 2003). A more nuanced account is provided in Steve LeVine, *The Oil and the Glory: The Pursuit of Empire and Fortune on the Caspian Seas* (New York: Random House, 2007). China's interest in Central Asian energy is assessed in Stephen Blank, "Eurasia's Energy Triangle: China, Russia and the Central Asian States," *Brown Journal of World Affairs* 12, no. 2 (2006), 523–568. On post-9/11 regional geopolitics, see Richard Weitz, "Averting a New Great Game in Central Asia," *The Washington Quarterly* 29, no. 3 (Summer 2006), 155–167; Rajan Menon, "The New Great Game in Central Asia," *Survival* 45, no. 2 (Summer 2003). For a more skeptical view, see Kathleen A. Collins and William C. Wohlforth, "Central Asia: Defying 'Great Games' Expectations," in *Strategic Asia 2003–2004* (Seattle: National Bureau of Asian Research, 2003).

12. For accounts of the collapse of these Kyrgyz regimes, see Scott Radnitz, *Weapons of the Wealthy: Predatory Regimes and Elite-Led Protests in Central Asia.* (Ithaca, NY: Cornell University Press, 2010).

13. Edwards, "The New Great Game and the New Great Gamers," 89–90.

14. On the changing political systems of the region, see Kathleen Collins, *Clan Politics and Regime Transition in Central Asia* (New York: Cambridge University Press, 2006); Pauline Jones Luong, ed., *The Transformation of Central Asia: States and Societies from Soviet Rule to Independence* (Ithaca, NY: Cornell University Press, 2003); Gregory Gleason, *Markets and Politics in Central Asia: Structural Reform and Political Change* (New York: Routledge, 2003).

15. On the end of territorial conquest as an international practice, see Tanisha M. Fazal, *State Death: The Politics of and Geography of Conquest, Occupation, and Annexation* (Princeton: Princeton University Press, 2007). On how rulers of weak states strategically use their sovereignty, see Stephen Krasner, *Sovereignty: Organized Hypocrisy* (Princeton: Princeton University Press, 1999).

16. On the difficulties of Western engagement with the region, see David Lewis, *The Temptations of Tyranny in Central Asia* (New York: Columbia University Press, 2008); Martha Brill Olcott, *Central Asia's Second Chance* (Washington, DC: Carnegie Endowment for Peace, 2005). For an overview of the foreign policy interests of major external powers, see Emilian Kavalski, ed., *The New Central Asia: The Regional Impact of International Actors* (Singapore: World Scientific, 2010).

17. Realists argue that the anarchic system forces states to consider not only the gains from actions such as international cooperation, but how well they fare relative to their main systemic competitors. See Joseph Grieco, *Cooperation among Nations: Europe, America, and Non-Tariff Barriers to Trade* (Ithaca, NY: Cornell University Press, 1990).

18. For a measured analysis of the "strategic triangle," see Bobo Lo, *Axis of Convenience: Moscow, Beijing, and the New Geopolitics* (Washington DC: Brookings, 2008); Kotkin's review essay of the book: Stephen Kotkin, "The Unbalanced Triangle: What Chinese-Russian Relations Mean for the United States," *Foreign Affairs* 88, no. 5 (September/October 2009), 130–138. Also see Elizabeth Wishnick, *Russia, China and the United States in Central Asia: Prospects for Great Power Competition and Cooperation in Central Asia* (Carlisle, PA: U.S. Army War College, Strategic Studies Institute, 2009).

19. Marcel de Haas, "The Shanghai Cooperation Organisation and the OSCE: Two of a Kind?" *Helsinki Monitor* no. 3 (November 2007).

20. See David Lake, *Hierarchy in International Relations* (Ithaca, NY: Cornell University Press, 2010).

21. For applications of the "multiple-principals" framework to studies of the diminishing authority of colonial trading companies, NGOs, and international organizations, see, respectively, Julia Adams, "Principals and Agents, Colonialists and Company Men: The Decay of

Colonial Control in the Dutch East Indies," *American Sociological Review* 61, no. 1 (February 1996); Alexander Cooley and James Ron, "The NGO Scramble: Organizational Insecurity and the Political Economy of Transnational Action," *International Security* 27, no. 1 (Summer 2002); Darren Hawkins et. al., eds., *Delegation and Agency in International Organizations* (New York: Cambridge University Press, 2006).

22. On Kazakhstan's geopolitical balancing act, see Sally Cummings, *Kazakhstan: Power and the Elite* (New York: Palgrave Macmillan, 2005).

23. See David Lewis, "Reassessing the Role of OSCE Police Assistance Programming in Central Asia," New York: Central Eurasia Project Working Paper Series, no. 4, April 2011.

24. Amitav Acharya, "How Ideas Spread: Whose Norms Matter? Norm Localization and Institutional Change in ASEAN," *International Organization* 58, no. 2 (Spring 2004), 244.

25. See Edward Schatz, "Access by Accident: Legitimacy Claims and Democracy Promotion in Authoritarian Central Asia," *International Political Science Review* 27, no. 3 (2006), 263–284.

26. See Luca Anceschi, *Turkmenistan's Foreign Policy: Positive Neutrality and the Consolidation of the Turkmen Regime* (New York: Routledge, 2008).

27. See the critical account in John Heathershaw, *Post-Conflict Tajikistan: The Politics of Peace* (New York: Routledge, 2009).

28. On the Islamic Movement of Uzbekistan's rise and regional incursions, see Ahmed Rashid, *Jihad: The Rise of Militant Islam in Central Asia* (New Haven: Yale University Press, 2002).

29. See Cedric Jourde, "The International Relations of Small Neoauthoritarian States: Islamism, Warlordism and the Framing of Stability," *International Studies Quarterly* 51, no. 2 (June 2007).

30. Robert Keohane, "The Big Influence of Small Allies," *Foreign Policy*, no. 2 (April 1971); Keohane, "Lilliputians' Dilemmas: Small States in International Politics," *International Organization* 23, no. 2 (Spring 1969). On competitive clientalism in the Middle East during the Cold War, see Rashid Khalidi, *Sowing Crisis: the Cold War and American Dominance in the Middle East* (Boston: Beacon Press, 2009).

31. See Glenn Snyder, *Alliance Politics* (Ithaca, NY: Cornell University Press, 1997); Stephen Walt, *The Origins of Alliances* (Ithaca, NY: Cornell University Press, 1990).

32. See Thad Dunning, "Conditioning the Effects of Aid: Cold War Politics, Donor Credibility and Democracy in Africa," *International Organization* 54, no. 2 (Spring 2004), 409–423.

33. Fareed Zakaria, *The Post-American World* (New York: W. W. Norton, 2008).

34. Parag Khanna, *The Second World: Empires and Influence in the New Global Order* (New York: Random House, 2008).

35. See Robert Pape, "Soft-Balancing Against the United States," *International Security* 30, no. 1 (Summer 2005); Stephen Walt, *Taming American Power: The Global Response to U.S. Primacy* (New York: Norton, 2005). For a response, see Stephen Brooks and William C. Wohlforth, *World Out of Balance: International Relations and the Challenge of American Primacy* (Princeton: Princeton University Press, 2008).

36. Nazneen Bartha, Ely Ratner, and Stephen Weber, "A World Without the West," *National Interest* no. 90 (July/August 2007).

37. For representative examples, see Stefan A. Halper, *The Beijing Consensus: How China's Authoritarian Model Will Dominate the Twenty-first Century* (New York: Basic, 2010); Joshua Kurlantzick, *Charm Offensive: How China's Soft Power Is Transforming the World* (New Haven: Yale University Press, 2007); Bates Gill and Yanzhong Huang, "Sources and Limits of Chinese 'Soft Power'," *Survival* 48, no. 2 (Summer 2006), 17–36.

Chapter 2

1. For representative introductions, see Scott Radnitz, *Weapons of the Wealthy* (Ithaca, NY: Cornell University Press, 2010); Eric Sally Cummings, ed., *Power and Change in Central Asia* (New York: Routledge, 2002); Pauline Jones Luong, *Institutional Change and Political Continuity in Central Asia: Power, Perceptions and Pacts* (New York: Cambridge University Press, 2002).

2. On the political importance of clans, see Kathleen Collins, *Clan Politics and Regime Transition in Central Asia* (New York: Cambridge University Press, 2006); and Edward Schatz, *Modern Clan Politics: The Power of "Blood" in Kazakhstan and Beyond* (Seattle: University of Washington Press, 2004). For a critique, see Idil Tunçcr-Kilavuz, "Political and Social Networks in Tajikistan and Uzbekistan: 'Clan,' Region and Beyond," *Central Asian Survey* 28, no. 3 (September 2009), 323–334.

3. On Russian imperial rule in Central Asia, see Alexander Morrison, *Russian Rule in Samarkand 1868–1910: A Comparison with British India* (Oxford: Oxford University Press, 2008); Seymour Becker, *Russia's Protectorates in Central Asia: Bukhara and Khiva, 1865–1924* (Cambridge, MA: Harvard University Press, 1968). On Soviet rule, see Edward Allworth, *Central Asia: 130 years of Russian Dominance* (Durham, NC: Duke University Press, 1994).

4. For theoretically informed application of the post-colonial approach, see Mark Beissinger and Crawford Young, eds., *Beyond State Crisis? Postcolonial Africa and Post-Soviet Eurasia in Comparative Perspective* (Baltimore: Johns Hopkins University Press, 2002).

5. I expand on this argument in more detail in Alexander Cooley, *Logics of Hierarchy: The Organization of Empires, States and Military Occupations* (Ithaca, NY: Cornell University Press, 2005).

6. See Nazif Shahrani, "Muslim Central Asia: Soviet Developmental Legacies and Future Challenges," in Mohiaddin Mesbahi, ed., *Central Asia and the Caucasus after the Soviet Union* (Gainesville: University of Florida Press, 1993), 56–71. On imperial structure and administration, see Alexander Motyl, *Imperial Ends: The Decay, Collapse and Revival of Empires* (New York: Columbia University Press, 2001).

7. Francine Hirsch, *Empire of Nations: Ethnographic Knowledge and the Making of the Soviet Union* (Ithaca, NY: Cornell University Press, 2005), 160–165.

8. Oksana Dmitrieva, *Regional Development: The USSR and After* (London: UCL Press, 1996), ix.

9. The definitive account of the origins and practice of Soviet nationalities can be found in Terry Martin, *The Affirmative Action Empire: Nations and Nationalism in the Soviet Union, 1923–1939*, (Ithaca, NY: Cornell University Press, 2001). Also see Yuri Slezkine, "The USSR as a Communal Apartment, or How a Socialist State Promoted Ethnic Particularism," *Slavic Review* 53, no. 2 (Summer 1994), 414–452; Nancy Lubin, *Labour and Nationality in Soviet Central Asia: An Uneasy Compromise* (Princeton: Princeton University Press, 1984).

10. On Central Asian cadre development, see Steven L. Burg, "Muslim Cadres and Soviet Political Development," *World Politics* 37, no. 1 (October 1984), 24–47.

11. Luong, *Institutional Change and Political Continuity in Central Asia*.

12. See the now classic denouncement of these practices by Soviet anthropologist Sergei Poliakov, *Everyday Islam: Religion and Tradition in Rural Central Asia* (Armonk, NY: M. E. Sharpe, 1993).

13. On patrimonialism and the Brezhnev era, see Philip Roeder, *Red Sunset: The Failure of Soviet Politics* (Princeton: Princeton University Press, 1993); John Willerton, *Patronage and Politics in the USSR* (New York: Cambridge University Press, 1993).

14. Gregory Gleason, "Nationalism or Organized Crime? The Case of the 'Cotton Scandal' in the USSR," *Corruption and Reform* 5, no. 2 (1990), 87–108; James Critchlow, *Nationalism in Uzbekistan: A Soviet Republic's Road to Sovereignty* (Boulder, CO: Westview, 1991), 39–52.

15. See for example, Michael Rywkin, *Moscow's Muslim Challenge: Soviet Central Asia* (Armonk, NY: M. E. Sharpe, 1990).

16. The underlying conditions behind the Osh riots—lingering tensions over Uzbek representation in Kyrgyz administrative structures, a lack of central authority under the Perestroika political experiment in decentralization—would also be important enabling conditions when ethnic violence erupted again in Osh and Jalalabad 20 years later, in June 2010.

17. Eric McGlinchey. *Blood, Chaos and Dynasty: Islam and Patronage Politics in Central Asia* (Pittsburgh: University of Pittsburgh Press, 2011).

18. See Barnett Rubin, "Russian Hegemony and State Breakdown in the Periphery: Causes and Consequences of the Civil War in Tajikistan," in Barnett Rubin and Jack Snyder, eds., *Post-Soviet Political Order: Conflict and State-Building* (New York: Routledge, 1998).

19. On IMF relations with the Central Asian and post-Communist states, see André Broom, *The Currency of Power: The IMF and Monetary Reform in Central Asia* (New York: Palgrave Macmillan, 2010); Randall Stone, *Lending Credibility: The International Monetary Fund and the Post-Communist Transition* (Princeton: Princeton University Press, 2002).

20. See Richard Pomfret, *The Economies of Central Asia* (Princeton: Princeton University Press, 1995).

21. On the collapse of the ruble zone, see Rawi Abdelal, *National Purpose and the World Economy* (Ithaca, NY Cornell University Press, 2002), 45–59.

22. Fiona Adamson, "Global Liberalism Versus Political Islam: Competing Ideological Frameworks in International Politics, " *International Studies Review* 7, no. 4 (2005), 547–569.

23. For insightful overviews of U.S., Russian, and Chinese policy toward Kazakhstan and the Central Asian states in the 1990s, see Robert Legvold, ed. *Thinking Strategically: the Major Powers. Kazakhstan, and the Central Asian Nexus* (Cambridge, MA: American Academy of Arts & Sciences, 2003).

24. On Central Asia's energy politics in the 1990s, see Robert Ebel and Rajan Menon, eds., *Energy and Conflict in Central Asia and the Caucasus* (New York: Rowman & Littlefield, 2000).

25. On Central Asia's stagnation during the 1990s, see Martha Brill Olcott, *Central Asia's Second Chance* (Washington DC: Carnegie Endowment for Peace, 2005). For a critical reflection on the transition paradigm, see Thomas Carothers, "The End of the Transition Paradigm," *Journal of Democracy* 13, no. 1 (January 2002), 5–21.

26. On the theoretical underpinnings of survivorship politics, see Bruce Bueno de Mesquita, et al., *The Logic of Political Survival* (Cambridge, MA: MIT Press, 2003). For an application to the Central Asian states, see McGlinchey, *Blood, Chaos and Dynasty*. On foreign policy and survivalism, see Luca Anceschi, "Integrating Domestic Politics and Foreign Policy Making: The Cases of Turkmenistan and Uzbekistan," *Central Asian Survey* 29, no. 2 (June 2010), 143–158.

27. Erica Marat, *The Military and the State in Central Asia: From Red Army to Independence* (New York: Routledge, 2009).

28. See Martha Brill Olcott, *Kazakhstan: Unfulfilled Promise?* Washington, DC: Carnegie Endowment for Peace, 2010; Bhavna Dave, *Kazakhstan: Ethnicity, Language and Power* (New York: Routledge. 2007); Sally Cummings, *Kazakhstan: Power and the Elite* (New York: Palgrave Macmillan, 2005).

29. See Edward Schatz, "Transnational Image Making and Soft Authoritarian Kazakhstan," *Slavic Review* 67, no. 1 (Spring 2008), 50–62.

30. "Kazakh President in German Hospital: Report," *AFP,* July 19, 2011.

31. "Unrest in Kazakhstan: Thicker than Oil," *The Economist,* December 31, 2011.

32. On the dynamics of patronage politics and the collapse of Kyrgyz regimes, see McGlinchey, *Blood, Chaos and Dynasty*; Radnitz, *Weapons of the Wealthy*.

33. On Uzbekistan's independence, see Laura Adams, *The Spectacular State: Culture and National Identity in Uzbekistan* (Durham, NC: Duke University Press, 2010); Neil Melvin, *Uzbekistan: Transition to Authoritarianism on the Silk Route* (New York: Routledge, 2000).

34. See English-language summary at: http://humanrightshouse.org/Articles/16130.html.

35. U.S. Embassy Cable, 05TASHKENT2473, "Gulnora Karimova Looks to Improve Her Image." U.S. Embassy in Tashkent, September 5, 2005, http://wikileaks.org/cable/2005/09/05TASHKENT2473.html.

36. See International Crisis Group, "Cracks in the Marble: Turkmenistan's Failing Dictatorship," ICG Asia Report no. 44, January 17, 2003; and International Crisis Group, "Repression and Regression in Turkmenistan: A New International Strategy," ICG Asia Report no. 85, November 4, 2004.

37. See Barnett Rubin, "Russian Hegemony and State Breakdown in the Periphery: Causes and Consequences of the Civil War in Tajikistan," in Barnett R. Rubin and Jack Snyder, eds., *Post-Soviet Political Order: Conflict and State-Building* (New York: Routledge, 1998).

38. See John Heathershaw, *Post-Conflict Tajikistan: The Politics of Peacebuilding and the Emergence of Legitimate Political Order* (New York: Routledge, 2009); International Crisis Group, "Tajikistan: on the Road to Failure," ICG Asia Report no. 162. February 12, 2009; Lena Jonson, *Tajikistan in the New Central Asia: Geopolitics, Great Power Rivalry and Radical Islam* (London: I.B Taurus, 2006).

39. This case is forcefully made in Shahram Akbarzadeh, *Uzbekistan and the United States: Authoritarianism, Islamism and Washington's Security Agenda* (New York: ZED, 2005).

40. Alexander Cooley, "Principles in the Pipeline: Managing Transatlantic Values and Interests in Central Asia," *International Affairs* 84, no. 6 (November 2008), 1173–1188.

41. Robert Bates, *When Things Fell Apart: State Failure in Late-Century Africa* (New York: Cambridge University Press, 2008), 52.

42. The classic analysis of these informal Central Asian networks is found in Nancy Lubin, *Labour and Nationality in Soviet Central Asia: An Uneasy Compromise* (Princeton: Princeton University Press, 1984).

43. See Joseph E. Stiglitz, *Globalization and Its Discontents* (New York: W. W. Norton, 2002), 133–165; Michael McFaul, "State Power, Institutional Change, and the Politics of Privatization in Russia," *World Politics* 47, no. 2 (January 1995), 210–243. For an overview of post-Communist transitions reforms and debates, see Timothy Frye, *Building States and Markets after Communism: the Perils of Polarized Democracy* (New York: Cambridge, 2010).

44. See Kelly McMann, "Market Reform as a Stimulus to Particularistic Politics," *Comparative Political Studies* 42, no. 7 (July 2009), 971–994.

45. For details, see International Crisis Group, "Central Asia: Decay and Decline," ICG Asia Report no. 201. February 3, 2011, 11–13.

46. See Jason Sharman, "Offshore and the New International Political Economy," *Review of International Political Economy* 17, no. 1 (February 2010), 1–19.

47. On allegations against the company, see Megan Murphy, "Tajikistan Turns on Rusal after TALCO Deal," *Financial Times*, November 28, 2008.

48. See International Crisis Group, "Uzbekistan: Crisis and Uncertainty," ICG Asia Briefing no. 67. August 22, 2007, 5–6.

49. Deirdre Tynan, "Deconstructing Manas Fuel Suppliers' Corporate Structure," *Eurasianet*, April 19, 2010.

50. See Global Witness, "It's a Gas- Funny Business in the Turkmen-Ukraine Gas Trade." London and Washington DC, April 2006, http://www.globalwitness.org/sites/default/files/library/its_a_gas_april_2006_lowres.pdf.

51. See Daniel Nexon, *The Struggle for Power in Early Modern Europe: Religious Conflict, Dynastic Empires & International Change* (Princeton: Princeton University Press, 2009).

52. On multivocal signaling as a key component of successful state-building, see John F. Padgett and Christopher Ansell, "Robust Action and the Rise of the Medici," *The American Journal of Sociology* 98, no. 6 (May 1993), 1259–1319.

53. See Gregory Gleason, "Fealty and Loyalty: Informal Authority Structures in Soviet Asia," *Soviet Studies* 43, no. 1 (1991), 613–628.

54. World Bank, *Statistical Handbook: States of the Former USSR*, Washington DC: World Bank, 1992, 14–15.

55. See Alexander Cooley, "International Aid to the Former Soviet States: Agent of Change or Guardian of the Status Quo?" *Problems of Post-Communism*, 47, no. 4 (July/August 2000), 34–44.

56. "Audit Reveals Irregularities in Tajik Central Bank Deals," *Reuters*, April 19, 2009.

Chapter 3

1. See Thomas E. Ricks and Susan B. Glasser, "US Operated Secret Alliance with Uzbekistan," *Washington Post*, October 14, 2001.

2. Steve Coll, *Ghost Wars: The Secret History of the CIA, Afghanistan, and Bin Laden, from the Soviet Invasion to September 10, 2001* (New York: Penguin, 2004), 531.

3. See Ahmed Rashid, *Jihad: The Rise of Militant Islam in Central Asia* (New Haven: Yale University Press, 2002), 137–186.

4. "Draft Report of DEFSEC Meeting with President Karimov," October 5, 2001, http://www.rumsfeld.com/library/ (accessed February 14, 2011). Supporting documents for Donald Rumsfeld, *Known and Unknown: A Memoir* (New York: Sentinel, 2011).

5. "Draft Report of DEFSEC Meeting with President Karimov."

6. The possible other fields include Kokaidv, Jizak, and Shakhrisabz, though the use of additional facilities in Uzbekistan has not been publicly acknowledged by either Uzbek or U.S. officials. But these airfields are included in an inventory of Uzbek facilities used by the U.S. military, as part of the Uzbek government's bill to the United States. "Donald Rumsfeld to Jim MacDougall: Congressional Amendment on Uzbekistan," October 18, 2005, http://library.rumsfeld.com/doclib/sp/401/To%20Jim%20MacDougall%20re%20Congressional%20Amendment%20on%20Uzbekistan-%20Memo%20Attachment%2010-18-2005.pdf (accessed February 8, 2011).

7. See Olga Oliker and David A. Shlapak, *US Interests in Central Asia: Policy Priorities and Military Roles* (Santa Monica, CA: RAND Project Air Force, 2005), pp. 11–19. Despite some rumors that U.S. officials were interested in opening a base in Tajikistan, possibly at Kulob, such a facility did not emerge. U.S. forces did briefly use Dushanbe airport in 2001 and 2002. See Lena Jonson, *Tajikistan in the New Central Asia: Geopolitics Great Power Rivalry and Radical Islam* (New York: I. B. Taurus, 2006), 58–59.

8. Oliker and Shlapak, *US Interests in Central Asia*, 11–19.

9. See the apt warning in Pauline Jones Luong and Erika Weinthal, "New Friends, New Fears in Central Asia," *Foreign Affairs* 81, no. 2 (March/April 2002), 61–70.

10. Author's communication with U.S. defense official involved in initial negotiations with Uzbekistan.

11. Shahram Akbarzadeh, *Uzbekistan and the United States: Authoritarianism, Islamism & Washington's Security Agenda* (New York: ZED, 2005), 75 and 78.

12. Robert Kaiser, "Uzbek-US Declaration Kept Secret," *Washington Post*, July 1, 2002.

13. Zamira Eshanova, "Uzbekistan: UN Rapporteur Says Use of Torture Is 'Systemic,'" *Radio Free Europe/Radio Liberty* (RFE/RL), December 9, 2002.

14. The programs in question were the International Military Education and Training (IMET) and Foreign Military Financing (FMF). The State Department reportedly reprogrammed some of this aid so that only $8.5 million was actually withheld. See Jim Nichols, "Uzbekistan's Closure of the Airbase at Karshi-Khanabad: Context and Implications." Congressional Research Report for Congress, March 29, 2006.

15. Craig Murray, *Murder in Samarkand* (London: Mainstream Publishing, 2006).

16. Perhaps the most interesting item to appear was authored by influential conservative columnist Bill Kristol. See Stephen Schwartz and William Kristol, "Our Uzbek Problem," *Weekly Standard*, May 30, 2005.

17. See Martha Brill Olcott, *Central Asia's Second Chance* (Washington, DC: Carnegie Endowment for International Peace, 2005), 124–138.

18. Author's interviews with U.S. defense officials at Manas. January 2005.

19. Base briefing conducted at the Manas Transit Center, June 15, 2011.

20. Author's interviews with U.S. and Kyrgyz officials in Bishkek and Manas, Kyrgyzstan, January 2005.

21. Deborah Klepp, "The US Needs a Base *Where*? How the US Established an Air Base in the Kyrgyz Republic" (unpublished essay, National Defense University, National War College, 2004), 3–4.

22. Author's interviews with U.S. officials in Bishkek, Kyrgyzstan, January 2005.

23. For the investigation's final report, see *Mystery at Manas: Strategic Blind Spots in the Department of Defense's Fuel Contracts in Kyrgyzstan*, Report of the Majority Staff, Subcommittee on National Security and Foreign Affairs, Committee on Oversight and Government Reform, U.S House of Representatives, Washington D.C., December 2010.

24. In fact, as Mitchell has shown in his comprehensive account of Georgia's Rose Revolution, U.S. officials were nervous at the prospect of losing long-standing President Eduard Shevardnadze. See Lincoln Mitchell, *Uncertain Democracy: U.S. Foreign Policy and Georgia's Revolution* (Philadelphia: University of Pennsylvania Press, 2009).

25. Valerie Bunce and Sharon Wolchik, "International Diffusion and Postcommunist Revolutions," *Communist and Postcommunist Studies* 39, no. 3 (September 2006), 283–304.

26. On the importance of emulation or "modularity" in the diffusion of the Color Revolutions paradigm, see Mark Beissinger, "Structure and Example in Modular Political Phenomena: The Diffusion of the Bulldozer/Rose/Orange/Tulip Revolutions," *Perspectives on Politics* 5, no. 2 (June 2007), 259–275. For a critique of the diffusion thesis that stresses the structural similarities across these polities, see Lucan Way, "The Real Causes of the Colored Revolutions," *Journal of Democracy* 18, no. 2 (July 2008), 55–69.

27. See Radnitz, *Weapons of the Wealthy*.

28. See Craig Smith, "US Helped to Prepare the Way for Kyrgyzstan's Uprising," *International Herald Tribune*, March 30, 2005.

29. See S. Fredrick Starr, "A 'Greater Central Asia Partnership' for Central Asia and Its Neighbors," (Washington, DC: Johns Hopkins SAIS, Silk Route Paper. March 2005); and Starr, "A Partnership for Central Asia," *Foreign Affairs* 84, No. 4 (July–August 2005), 164–178.

30. The Department of Defense had moved the Central Asian states under CENTCOM jurisdiction in 1999.

31. See the comments made by Secretary Rice on "Transformational Diplomacy" at Georgetown University. January 18, 2006, http://www.state.gov/secretary/rm/2006/59306.htm (accessed October 1, 2008).

32. U.S. State Department, "The Bureau of South and Central Asian Affairs." Washington, DC, Office of the Spokesman, February 9, 2006.

33. At an Istanbul conference in June 2006 Assistant Secretary of State for South and Central Asian Affairs Richard Boucher commented, "Like the original Silk Road, good ideas don't need policy-makers to make them happen, but we can help things along by helping create the environment so that they can happen. That is what this conference is all about. At this conference we hope that the government participants will establish a framework to develop together a regional power-transmission corridor linking Central and South Asia." See Richard Boucher, "Electricity Beyond Borders: A Central Asia Power Sector Reform." Remarks by Assistant Secretary for South and Central Asian Affairs. Istanbul. June 13, 2006. Available at: http://islamabad.usembassy.gov/pakistan/h06061303.html (accessed February 10, 2011).

34. See Human Rights Watch, *Bullets Were Flying Like Rain: The Andjian Massacre* (New York: Human Rights Watch, June 2005).

35. Rumsfeld, *Known and Unknown*, 634.

36. For the text of the May 29, 2005, press conference, at http://uzbekistan.usembassy.gov/pr-052905.html.

37. For more details, see Scott G. Frickenstein, "Kicked Out of K2," *Airforce Magazine* 93, no. 9 (September 2010), 88–92; and Alexander Cooley, "Base Politics," *Foreign Affairs* 84, no. 6 (November/December 2005), 79–92.

38. Russian-Uzbekistani economic ties were also growing at the time. See Matteo Fumagalli, "Alignment and Realignment in Central Asia: The Rationale and Implications of Uzbekistan's Rapprochement with Russia," *International Political Science Review* 28, no. 3 (June 2007), 253–271; and Pavel Baev, "Russia's Counter Revolutionary Offensive in Central Asia." PONARS Policy Memo no. 399, December 2005.

39. Rumsfeld, *Known and Unknown*, 636.

40. Protocol between the Department of Defense of the United States of America and the Ministry of Defense of the Republic of Uzbekistan, November 14, 2006, at http://www.state.gov/documents/organization/85883.pdf.

41. Lora Lumpe, "US Military Aid to Central Asia, 1999–2009: Security Trumps Human Rights," Occasional Paper Series no. 1, Central Eurasia Project, October 2010, 25–32.

42. See also Dana Priest, *The Mission: Waging War and Keeping Peace with America's Military* (New York: W. W. Norton, 2004).

43. Lumpe, "US Military Aid to Central Asia, 1999–2009," 35. Also worth noting is that, even at the height of its concern about democratic rights violations and human rights abuses in 2005 and 2006, the U.S. government allowed and expanded U.S. arms industry sales to the Central Asian state, with total sales in FY 2008 having approached $400 million.

44. See Office of Inspector General, "Report of Inspection: U.S. Embassy in Bishkek, Kyrgyzstan." Report Number ISP-I-08-14A, February 2008.

45. Author's interviews in Bishkek, January 2008 and June 2009.

46. Base briefing conducted at the Manas Transit Center, June 15, 2011.

47. Deirdre Tynan, "US Intends to Construct US Military Training Center in Batken." *Eurasianet*, March 3, 2010.

48. "Y—Design/Build Construction services for the National Training Center located in Karatog, Tajikistan." Solicitation Number: W912ER-10-R-0065. Available at the Federal Business Opportunities web site at: www.fbo.gov/index?s=opportunity&;mode=form&id=4e b45f294cbb4bcfb076afaf4f2e63c2&tab=core&_cview=0 (accessed June 13, 2011). The solicitation description describes the facility accordingly: "The garrison compound includes administrative facilities, officer quarters and enlisted barracks, dining facility, and other supporting facilities to provide a secure, fully operational compound. The range facilities include weapons firing and qualification (rifle, pistol, crew-served weapons and explosive/unexploded ordinance), Military Operations in Urban Terrain (MOUT) facilities, vehicle operator training range, sniper/observer training and operations, repelling and fast rope towers, and support facilities (for example: control towers, outdoor classrooms, sanitary facilities)."

49. Deirdre Tynan, "Pentagon Looks to Plant New Facilities in Central Asia," *Eurasianet*, June 8, 2010.

50. The use of Mary 2 appears to have been granted in October 2006 by President Niyazov, who provided his oral agreement to allow "any flight" to land at the air base "at any time." The informal agreements over divert arrangements were extended by Niyazov's successor, President Berdymukhamedov. See U.S. Embassy Cable 06ASHGABAT1093, "President Niyazov Backs Away from Formal Divert." U.S. Embassy in Ashgabat, October 20, 2006, http://wikileaks.org/cable/2006/10/06ASHGABAT1093.html; and U.S. Embassy Cable 07ASHGABAT637, "Turkmenistan's President Tells CENTCOM Commander Mary Emergency Divert to Remain Verbal Agreement." U.S. Embassy in Ashgabat, June 29, 2007, http://wikileaks.org/cable/2007/06/07ASHGABAT637.html.

51. For an overview, see Catherine A. Fitzpatrick, "Is the U.S. Violating Turkmenistan's Neutrality with the NDN?" *Eurasianet*, August 1, 2010. Also see Victoria Panfilova, "American Airforce Lands in Turkmenistan," *Nezavisimaya Gazeta*, July 13, 2009.

52. "Surface Transportation Challenges in Pakistan/Afghanistan," (presentation made by APL Government Market). Available at: http://www.ndtahq.com/documents/SESSIONLennonSilkRoad.pdf (accessed January 10, 2011).

53. Craig Whitlock, "U.S. Turns to Other Routes to Supply Afghan War as Relations with Pakistan Fray," *Washington Post*, July 2, 2011.

54. Andrew Kuchins, Thomas M. Sanderson, and David A. Gordon, "The Northern Distribution Network and Afghanistan: Planning for the Future." (Washington, DC: Center for International and Strategic Studies, December 2009), 10.

55. Whitlock, "U.S. Turns to Other Routes to Supply Afghan War."

56. Joshua Kucera, "Washington to Expand Traffic on Northern Supply Route," *Eurasianet*, November 10, 2010.

57. Whitlock, "U.S. Turns to Other Routes to Supply Afghan War."

58. See Jonathan Stack, "Virtual Reality," *Defense Logistics Agency Loglines*, January–February 2010, 34–35.

59. There was also a related billing dispute when Ashgabat suspended the use of the blanket permission in response to the U.S. not paying $30,000 in charges for additional overflights in 2007 and 2008. See U.S. Embassy Cable 09ASHGABAT560, "Turkmenistan: Meredov Addresses Overflight and Other Key issues with DAS Krol." U.S. Embassy in Ashgabat, May 2, 2009, http://wikileaks.org/cable/2009/05/09ASHGABAT560.html; and U.S. Embassy Cable 09ASHGABAT992, "Turkmenistan: Scenesetter for the Visit of CENT-COM Commander General David Petraeus." U.S. Embassy in Ashgabat, August 5, 2009, http://wikileaks.org/cable/2009/08/09ASHGABAT992.html.

60. Deirdre Tynan, "Ashgabat Hosts US Refueling, Resupply Operations," *Eurasianet*, July 7, 2009.

61. U.S. fuel procurement through Turkmenistan has been documented by a number of professional and fuel publications. For example, see Cpt. John Foust, "Bulk Fuel Challenges in Afghanistan," *Quartermaster Professional Bulletin*, Spring 2007, 22–25. On the Central Asian activities of Red Star, the main fuel supply contractor, see Aram Roston, "Fueling the Afghan War," *The Nation*, May 10, 2010.

62. U.S. Embassy Cable 09ASHGABAT992, "Turkmenistan: Scenesetter for the Visit of CENTCOM Commander General David Petraeus."

63. Deirdre Tynan, "Karimov Gives Washington the Air Base It Needs for Afghan Operations," *Eurasianet*, May 10, 2009.

64. "A New Cargo Terminal Opens in Navoi," *Gazeta.uz*, August 10, 2010.

65. Tynan, "Karimov Gives Washington the Air Base It Needs for Afghan Operations."

66. See U.S. Embassy Cable 09TASHKENT669, "Uzbekistan: TRANSCOM Delegation Discusses Transit with GOU." U.S. Embassy in Tashkent, May 7, 2009, http://wikileaks.org/cable/2009/05/09TASHKENT669.html.

67. See U.S. Embassy Cable 09TASHKENT575, "Uzbekistan: Scenesetter for US TRANSCOM Commander General McNabb." Embassy in Tashkent, April 24, 2009, http://wikileaks.org/cable/2009/04/09TASHKENT575.html; and U.S. Embassy Cable 09TASHKENT1245, "Uzbekistan: USCENTCOM on the Eve of Construction." Embassy in Tashkent, July 7, 2009, http://wikileaks.org/cable/2009/07/09TASHKENT1245.html

68. See TAO Global Solutions, "Even Under Fire, Delivery Remains Priority for Hanjin Global Logistics," news release, July 11, 2009, http://www.free-press-release.com/news/200907/1247286771.html (accessed February 10, 2011).

69. Catherine Fitzpatrick, "Uzbekistan Triples Air Cargo Through Navoi," *Eurasianet*, November 18, 2010.

70. Andrew Kuchins, Thomas M. Sanderson and David A. Gordon, "Afghanistan: Building the Missing Link in the Modern Silk Road," *The Washington Quarterly* 33, no. 2 (April 2010), 33–47. Also see Kuchins, Sanderson, and Gordon, "The Northern Distribution Network and Afghanistan: Planning for the Future."

71. S. Fredrick Starr, "Afghanistan Beyond the Fog of Nation Building," *Silk Road Paper*, January 2011, 13.

72. ISAF, "Construction of Railway from Uzbekistan to Mazar-e-Sharif Begins," news release, May 28, 2010, http://www.isaf.nato.int/article/isaf-releases/construction-of-railway-from-uzbekistan-to-mazar-e-sharif-begins.html (accessed February 2, 2011).

73. "New 'Silk Road' Eyed for Afghanistan," *AFP*, September 21, 2011.

74. Office of the Undersecretary of Defense, Acquisition, Technology and Logistics. "Class Deviation to Implement Temporary Authority to Acquire Products and Services Produced in Countries along a Major Route of Supply to Afghanistan," Washington, DC, November 12, 2009.

75. Deirdre Tynan, "Documents Highlight Problems with Uzbek Corridor of Afghan Supply Route," *Eurasianet*, June 28, 2010.

76. As reported in Deirdre Tynan, "US Troop Surge Likely to Fuel Financial Bonanza for Central Asian States," *Eurasianet*, January 19, 2010.

77. Joshua Kucera, "NDN Operator: We Have No Connection to Gulnara Karimova," *Eurasianet*, December 7, 2010. For details on Karimova's business holdings and connections to

Zeromax, see International Crisis Group, "Uzbekistan: Stagnation and Uncertainty," ICG Asia Briefing no. 67, August 22, 2007, 5–6.

78. See U.S. Embassy in Tashkent, "10TASHKENT27, Uzbekistan: A to ZeroMax," January 1, 2010, http://www.wikileaks.org/cable/2010/01/10TASHKENT27.html.

79. Oliker and Shlapak, "U.S. Interests in Central Asia," 18.

80. Deirdre Tynan, "Pentagon Paid Airport Fees to Turkmenistan, But Can't Say How Much," *Eurasianet*, July 12, 2010.

81. Tynan, "US Troop Surge Likely to Fuel Financial Bonanza."

82. Quoted in Catherine Fitzpatrick, "Uzbekistan Weekly Roundup." *Eurasianet*, December 20, 2010.

83. Deirdre Tynan, "Did Karimov Tantrum Prompt NDN Transit Fee Hike?" *Eurasianet*, February 10, 2011. A TRANSCOM spokesperson, perhaps betraying an overtly nonchalant attitude, responded to the increase by stating, "Globally within the US Defense Transportation System, tariff adjustments are expected and part of the cost of doing business. . . .With this in mind, a hike in fees in Uzbekistan has little effect on the United States moving commercial-type cargo into Afghanistan."

84. Deirdre Tynan, "U.S. Senate Wants Pentagon to be More Transparent on NDN Contracts," *Eurasianet*, September 26, 2011.

Chapter 4

1. See, for instance, Edward Lucas, *The New Cold War: Putin's Russia and the Threat to the West* (New York: Palgrave, 2007).

2. On Russian fluctuating identity and foreign policy goals, see Andrei Tsygankov, *Russia's Foreign Policy: Change and Continuity in National Identity* (New York: Rowman & Littlefield, 2010, 2nd edition); Ted Hopf, *Social Construction of International Politics: Identities and Foreign Policies, Moscow, 1955 and 1999* (Ithaca, NY: Cornell University Press, 2002).

3. Following the 2008 Georgia War, Russian President Medvedev laid out five principles to guide Russia's foreign policy, including, most controversially, that Russia would maintain a region of privileged interests, a thinly veiled reference to institutionalizing Russian primacy in the post-Soviet space. See "New Russian World Order: The Five Principles," *BBC News*, September 1, 2008.

4. On the importance of status, see Alistair Ian Johnston, "Treating International Institutions as Social Environments," *International Studies Quarterly*, 45, no. (2001), 487–515.

5. See Andrei Tsygankov, "Preserving Influence in a Changing World: Russia's Grand Strategy," *Problems of Post-Communism* 58, no.1 (March/April 2011), 28–44; Celeste Wallander, "Russian Transimperialism and Its Implications," *The Washington Quarterly* 30, no. 2 (Spring 2007), 107–122.

6. On Russian cultural and soft power, especially policies toward ethnic Russians in Central Asia, see Marlène Laruelle, "Russia's Central Asia Policy and the Role of Russian Nationalism," *Silk Road Paper*. Washington, DC: Johns Hopkins University/Central Asia-Caucasus Institute, April 2008.

7. On these continuities, see Jeffery Mankoff, *Russian Foreign Policy: The Return of Great Power Politics* (New York: Rowan & Littlefield, 2009); Robert Legvold, ed., *Russian Foreign Policy in the Twenty-First Century and the Shadow of the Past* (New York: Columbia University Press, 2007).

8. See Bobo Lo, *Vladimir Putin and the Evolution of Russian Foreign Policy* (London: Royal Institute for International Affairs and Blackwell, 2003).

9. National Security Concept of the Russian Federation, 2000, http://www.russiaeurope.mid.ru/russiastrat2000.html.

10. Putin telegram to President Bush, September 11, 2001.

11. Statement by President Putin of Russia on the Terrorist Acts in the U.S., Moscow, September 12, 2001.

12. Mankoff, *Russian Foreign Policy*, 112–113. Reportedly, the Russian military even urged the Northern Alliance to defeat the Taliban before U.S. forces arrived to establish a presence in Afghanistan. Similarly, in early 2002, Putin supported the entry of 200 U.S. military troops into Georgia to help the embattled Georgian government clear the Pankisi Gorge of militants who were using the area as a safe haven from which to mount operations in Chechnya and the Russian North Caucasus.

13. Press Conference by President Bush and President Putin in Crawford, Texas, November 13, 2001. Putin further explained: "If we look at the relationship between the Russian Federation and the United States from the old standpoint—distrust and enmity—it's one thing. If we are looking through the prism of partnership and alliance, we have nothing to be afraid of." Transcript and audio available at: http://www.pbs.org/newshour/terrorism/international/bush-putin_11-13.html?print.

14. John O'Loughlin, Gearóid Ó Tuathail and Vladimir Kolossov, "A 'Risky Westward Turn'? Putin's 9-11 Script and Ordinary Russians," *Europe-Asia Studies* 56. No. 1 (January 2004), 3–34. 19

15. O'Loughlin, Ó Tuathail and Kolossov, "A 'Risky Westward Turn'?" 20. 48% of respondents believed that U.S. bases in Central Asia were intended to expand the U.S. zone of influence, 31% that they would secure oil and gas interests, and 37% thought that they would enable the U.S. to replace Russia as that country's primary partner.

16. Mankoff, *Russian Foreign Policy*, 119.

17. Tsygankov, *Russia's Foreign Policy*, Chapter 6.

18. See Lincoln Mitchell, *Uncertain Democracy: U.S. Foreign Policy and Georgia's Revolution* (Philadelphia: University of Pennsylvania Press, 2009).

19. See Michael McFaul, "Ukraine Imports Democracy: External Influences on the Color Revolutions," *International Security* 32, no. 2 (Fall 2007), 45–83

20. Jason Lyall, "Great Games: Russia and the Emerging Security Dilemma in Central Asia," Paper Delivered to the 100th Annual Meeting of the American Political Science Association, Washington, DC, September 2004.

21. Dmitri Trenin. "Russia and Central Asia: Interests, Policies, and Prospects," in Eugene Rumer, Dmitri Trenon, and Huasheng Zhao, eds., *Central Asia: Views from Washington, Moscow, and Beijing* (Armonk, NY: M. E. Sharpe, 2007), 124.

22. See Lena Jonson, *Vladimir Putin and Central Asia: The Shaping of Russian Foreign Policy.* (New York: I.B. Tauris, 2004), 63–78.

23. As quoted in Lena Jonson, *Vladimir Putin and Central Asia*, 69.

24. Mankoff, *Russian Foreign Policy*, 271.

25. On the CSTO's institutional design and guiding regionalism, see Yuliya Nikitina, *ODKB i ShoS: Modeli Regionalizma v Sfere Bezopasnosti* (Moscow: MGIMO and Navona, 2009).

26. See Alexander Nikitin, "Post-Soviet Military Integration: The Collective Treaty Organization and Its Relations with the EU and NATO,'" *China and Eurasia Forum Quarterly* 5, no. 1 (2007), 35–44.

27. Author's interviews with NATO officials. Brussels, October 2009.

28. "CIS Defence Body Questions NATO Expansion but Wants to Cooperate," *Interfax News Agency*, May 23, 2003.

29. As quoted in Lyall, "Great Games: Russia and the Emerging Security Dilemma in Central Asia," 23.

30. See the various speeches by Secretary General on the CSTO web site, http://www.odkb.gov.ru/start/index_engl_official_statements.htm.

31. A. l. Rekuta, "The Collective Treaty Security Organization: Averting Security Threats in Central Asia," *Military Thought: A Russian Journal of Military Theory and Strategy*, 15, no. 4 (2006), 1–9.

32. "CSTO Creates Russia-based Collective Rapid Reaction Force," *The Times of Central Asia*, February 11, 2009.

33. An editorial in *Nezavisimaya Gazeta* on February 9, 2011, firmly criticized Medvedev's NATO comparison in the following manner: "It appears that Russia's designers of military policy abroad are living in a virtual dream-world. Specialists can only smile at the wording produced by President Medvedev's speechwriters—about the CRRF being 'as good as NATO forces.' Comparing the CSTO to NATO sounds impressive, of course; but in reality, it's just a joke." Translated text provided by Eastview.

34. See Uzbekistan's official criticisms in "Tashkent Issues Critique of CSTO Rapid Reaction Force," *Eurasianet*, June 23, 2009.

35. See Alexander Cooley, "The Kyrgyz Crisis and the Political Logic of Central Asia's Weak Security Organizations." PONARS Eurasia Policy Memo no. 140. Moscow, March 2010.

36. See Lyudmila Alexandrova, "Collective Security Reform Is Coming," *ITAR-TASS*, September 9, 2011.

37. For detailed inventories and analyses of these Russian facilities, see Vladimir Paramonov and Oleg Stolpovski, "Russia and Central Asia: Bilateral Cooperation in the Defense Sector," Defence Academy of the United Kingdom, May 2008; "Vse Rossiyskie bazy," *Kommersant-vlast*, May 21, 2007.

38. The terms of the deal are laid out in detail in Lena Jonson, *Tajikistan in the New Central Asia: Geopolitics Great Power Rivalry and Radical Islam* (New York: I. B. Taurus, 2006), 77–81.

39. "Vse Rossiyskie bazy."

40. "CSTO to Tighten Rules on Foreign Bases in Member States," *RIA Novosti*, December 20, 2011.

41. On this point, also see Roy Allison, "Strategic Reassertion in Russia's Central Asia Foreign Policy," *International Affairs* 80, no. 2 (2004), 277–293.

42. On the importance of the CSTO as a vehicle for regime-preservation, see Roy Allison, "Virtual Regionalism, Regional Structures and Regime Security in Central Asia." *Central Asian Survey*, 27, no. 2 (June 2008), 185–202; Allison, "Regionalism, Regional Structures and Security Management in Central Asia," *International Affairs* 80, no. 3 (2004), 463–483.

43. See Gregory Gleason, "Financing Russia's Central Asian Expansion," *CACI Analyst*, March 11, 2004.

44. At the founding of the Customs Union Commission, Russia was awarded 40% of votes, Kazakhstan and Belarus 20% each, with Kyrgyzstan and Tajikistan 10% each.

45. Eurasian Economic Community Integration Committee Secretariat, "EurAsEC Today," Moscow, 2011, 3.

46. See Irina Filatova, "Putin Calls for New 'Eurasian Union' of Former Soviet Countries," *The Moscow Times*, October 5, 2011.

47. Keith Darden, *Economic Liberalism and Its Rivals: The Formation of International Institutions among the Post-Soviet States* (New York: Cambridge University Press, 2010).

48. Darden, *Economic Liberalism and its Rivals*, 82–83.

49. In 2007, the EU unveiled its Central Asia strategy. One year later, it announced plans to create the Eastern Partnership Initiative, differentiating and institutionalizing its relations with the six states of the Caucasus, Moldova, Belarus, and Ukraine.

50. Total trade volume fell to $12 billion in 2009, but recovered to $15 billion in 2010, http://www.gks.ru/bgd/regl/b10_13/IssWWW.exe/Stg/d6/25-07.htm.

51. Sergei Blagov, "Moscow Embraces New Initiative to Forge Post-Soviet Trade Bloc," *Eurasianet*, December 2, 2009.

52. Vladislav Inozemtsev, "Chem Prekrasen Nash Soyuz," *Ogonyok*, no. 13, April 4, 2011.

53. Irina Filatova and Olga Razumovskaya, "Medvedev Casts Customs Deal as Stepping Stone," *Moscow Times*, July 6, 2010.

54. Olzhas Auyazhov, "Russia Dominates Neighbors in Customs Union" *Reuters*, April 1, 2010.

55. See, for instance, the article on the Customs Union in the Kazakh magazine *Asian Center*. Excepts reprinted at http://www.regnum.ru/news/1388106.html (accessed April 17, 2011).

56. See Andrei Suzdaltsev, "Politics Ahead of the Economy," *Russia in Global Affairs*, April 9, 2010.

57. See Rawi Abdelal, "Interpreting Interdependence: National Security and the Energy Trade of Russia, Belarus and Ukraine." In Robert Legvold and Celeste Wallander, eds., *Swords and Sustenance: The Economics of Security in Belarus and Ukraine* (Cambridge, MA: American Academy of Sciences, 2004).

58. Bartlomiej Kaminski and Gaël Raballand, "Entrepot for Chinese for Chinese Consumer Goods in Central Asia: The Puzzle of Re-Exports Through Kyrgyz Bazaars," *Eurasian Geography and Economics* 50, no. 5 (2009), 581–590.

59. The author participated in a roundtable in New York with Kyrgyz President Otunbayeva in September 2011 that revealed interesting splits among the Kyrgyz delegation on the Customs Union issue. President Otunbayeva strongly supported Kyrgyzstan's entry, viewing Russia as a natural market for Kyrgyz textile sector. On the other hand, Edil Baisalov, the president's former chief of staff, opposed the proposal, commenting that the increase in tariffs would painfully hit middle classes and consumers, as had occurred in Kazakhstan.

60. Though some argue that Kyrgyzstan could adopt higher tariffs and offer alternative concessions to compensate affected members such as China, the WTO Secretariat may be reluctant to endorse the backtracking of one of its members on its most-favored national commitments.

61. According to the International Crisis Group, in 2004–2008, the number of Central Asians workers that left for Russia and Kazakhstan included 800,000 from Kyrgyzstan, 1,500,000 from Tajikistan, and 2,500,000 from Uzbekistan. See International Crisis Group, "Central Asian Migrants and the Economic Crisis," Asia Report no. 183, January 5, 2010, 1.

62. World Bank data in "Migration and Remittances" are based on officially logged data. The true volume, including unaccounted for transfers and informal networks, is likely significantly higher. Available at: http://econ.worldbank.org/WBSITE/EXTERNAL/EXT-DEC/EXTDECPROSPECTS/0,contentMDK:21121930~menuPK:3145470~pagePK:64165401~piPK:64165026~theSitePK:476883,00.html.

63. ILO figure quoted in Edward Lemon, "Central Asian Labor Migrants Facing an Uncertain Year," *Eurasianet*, January 5, 2011.

64. Human Rights Watch, "Are You Happy to Cheat Us? Exploitation of Migrant Construction Workers in Russia," (New York: Human Rights Watch, February 2009).

65. Kazuhiro Kumo, ed., "Sociology, Economics and the Politics of Central Asian Migrants in Moscow." Tokyo: Hitotsubashi University, Institute of Economic Reseearch 7–8, http://hermes-ir.lib.hit-u.ac.jp/rs/bitstream/10086/19068/1/DPb39.pdf.

66. Author's interviews with Tajik print journalists, Dushanbe, Tajikistan, May 2010.

67. Michael Schwartz, "With a Russian in a Tajik Jail, Moscow Aims its Reprisal at Migrant Workers," *New York Times*, November 16, 2011.

68. Fiona Hill, "Russia Discovers Soft Power," *Current History* 30, no. 2 (October 2006), 341–347.

69. See Kimberly Marten, "Russian Efforts to Control Central Asia Oil: The Kumkol Case," *Post-Soviet Affairs* 27, no. 1 (2007), 18–37.

70. On the history and politics of the BTC, see Steve LeVine, *The Oil and the Glory: the Pursuit of Empire and Fortune on the Caspian Sea* (New York: Random House, 2007).

71. Luong and Weinthal, *Oil Is Not a Curse*, 259–298.

72. For overviews, see Chow, Edward C. and Leigh E. Hendrik. "Central Asia's Pipelines: Field of Dreams and Reality," in Edward Chow et. al., *Pipeline Politics in Asia: The Intersection of Demand, Energy Markets, and Supply Routes*, Seattle: The National Bureau of Asian Research, Special Report no. 23, September 2010; Martha Brill Olcott, *Kazakhstan: Unfulfilled Promise?* (Washington DC: Carnegie Endowment for Peace, 2010, revised), 148–159.

73. For overviews of Gazprom strategy, see Rawi Abdelal, Sogomon Tarontsi, and Alexander Jorov, "Gazprom (A): Energy and Strategy in Russian History," Harvard Business School Case Study no. 9-709-008, July 7, 2009; Rawi Abdelal, Sogomon Tarontsi, and Alexander Jorov, "Gazprom (B): Energy and Strategy in a New Era," Harvard Business School Case Study no. 9-709-009, July 7, 2009; Jonathan Stern, *The Future of Russian Gas and Gazprom* (London: Oxford Institute for Energy Studies, 2005).

74. Anders Aslund, "Gazprom: Challenged Giant in Need of Reform," in Anders Aslund, Sergei Guriev, and Andrew Kuchins, eds., *Russia after the Global Economic Crisis* (Washington, DC: Peterson Institute, 2010), 154–155.

75. Boris Nemtsov and Vladimir Liov, "Putin i Gazprom: Nezavisimyy Ekspertnyy Doklad," Moscow, 2008, 8, http://www.milov.info/cp/wp-content/uploads/2008/09/putin-i-gazprom.pdf.

76. See Sergei Guriev and Aleh Tsyvinski, "Challenges Facing the Russian Economy after the Crisis," in Anders Aslund, Sergei Guriev and Andrew Kuchins, eds., *Russia after the Global Economic Crisis* (Washington, DC: Peterson Institute for International Economics, 2010), 9–38.

77. Author's interviews with Tajik journalists and think tank policy analysts, Dushanbe, May 2010. Also see Bruce Pannier, "Dushanbe Scraps Contract with Russia's RusAl," *RFE/RL* August 30, 2007.

78. Marat Gurt and Olzhas Auyezov, "Pipeline Blast Halts Turkmen Gas Exports to Russia," *Reuters*, April 9, 2009.

79. U.S. Embassy Cable 09ASHGABAT495, "Turkmen President Is Mightily Annoyed with Gazprom." U.S. Embassy in Ashgabat, April 20, 2009, http://wikileaks.org/cable/2009/04/09ASHGABAT495.html.

80. "Tajikistan Demands the Release of Freight Cars," *RIA Novosti*, March 24, 2010.

81. John C. K. Daly, "Russia Wades into Central Asian Water Dispute," *UPI*, January 30, 2009.

82. See Alexander Cooley, "Behind the Central Asian Curtain: The Limits of Russia's Resurgence," *Current History* 108, no. 720 (October 2009), 325–332.

83. On the logic of "divide and rule" politics in international hierarchies, see Daniel Neon and Thomas Wright, "What's at Stake in the American Empire Debate," *American Political Science Review* 101, no. 2 (May 2007), 253–271.

84. Tellingly, a report issued by INSOR, an influential think tank chaired by President Medvedev, observed that Uzbekistan's "special position" constituted a significant barrier to achieving consensus in CSTO decision-making. INSOR, "ODKB: Otvetstvennaya Bezopastnost," August 2011, 22–25, http://www.insor-russia.ru/files/ODKB-0709.pdf.

85. Lo, *Axis of Convenience*.

86. See Richard Weitz, "Why China Snubs Russia Arms," *The Diplomat*, April 5, 2010; Stephen Fidler, "Russian Weapons Sales to China Fall," *Financial Times*, March 30, 2008.

87. For a nuanced overview of CSTO and SCO relations, see Yulia Nikitina, "ODKB i ShOS: Konkurentsiya Formatov v Sfere Bezopasnosti na Postsovetskom Prostranstve," October 7, 2009, http://www.mgimo.ru/news/experts/document122805.phtml.

88. Ivan Safranchuk, "The Competition for Security Roles in Central Asia," *Russia in Global Affairs* 6, no. 1 (January–March 2008), 166.

89. Raffaello Pantucci and Alexandros Peterson, "Russia's Eastern Anxieties," *New York Times*, October 17, 2011.

90. Kotkin elaborates: "Beijing flatters Moscow with rhetoric about their 'strategic partnership' and coddles it by promoting the illusion of a multipolar world. In many ways, the Chinese-Russian relationship today resembles that which first emerged in the seventeenth century: a rivalry for influence in Central Asia alongside attempts to expand bilateral commercial ties, with China in the catbird seat." Stephen Kotkin, "The Unbalanced Triangle: What Chinese-Russian Relations Mean for the United States," *Foreign Affairs* 88, no. 5 (September/October 2009), 130–138.

91. "Russia Ready for Transparent Cooperation in Central Asia," *ITAR-TASS Daily*, April 13, 2011.

Chapter 5

1. There is some disagreement as to how planned this regional strategy was. See the contrasting views of David Kerr, "Strategic Regionalism: Central Asian and Russian Perspectives on China's Strategic Re-emergence," *International Affairs* 86, no. 1 (January 2010), 127–152; and Zhao's important observation that China's Central Asia policy has been ad hoc

and lacked overall strategic coherence. Huasheng Zhao, "Central Asia in China's Diplomacy," in Eugene Rumer, et al., *Central Asia: Views from Washington, Moscow and Beijing* (Armonk, NY: ME Sharpe, 2007).

2. Consistent with Bobo Lo's formulation, Sino-Russian relations in Central Asia have been a pragmatic "axis of convenience" rather than a fully blown strategic alliance against the West. Bobo Lo, *Axis of Convenience: Moscow, Beijing, and the New Geopolitics* (Washington, DC: Brookings, 2008).

3. On China as a new world power that undercuts Western norms and influence, see Stefan A. Halper, *The Beijing Consensus: How China's Authoritarian Model Will Dominate the Twenty-first Century* (New York: Basic, 2010); Joshua Kurlantzick, *How China's Soft Power Is Transforming the World* (New Haven: Yale University Press, 2007). For a response, see Edward S. Steinfeld, *Playing Our Game: Why China's Rise Doesn't Threaten the West* (New York: Oxford University Press, 2010).

4. See, for example, Xinhua News Agency, "Current Circumstance Underlines Need to Enhance the Shanghai Spirit." June 15, 2009.

5. See Michael Clarke, *Xinjiang and China's Rise in Central Asia—A History* (New York: Routledge, 2011); James Millward, *Eurasian Crossroads: A History of Xinjiang* (New York: Columbia University Press, 2009).

6. As quoted in Xinhua News Agency, "Full Text of 'White Paper' on Development and Progress in Xinjiang," September 21, 2009.

7. On Beijing's regional policies, administrative techniques, and local reactions see the essays in S. Frederick Starr, ed. *Xinjiang: China's Muslim Borderland* (Armonk, NY: M. E. Sharpe, 2004).

8. Information Office of the State Council of the People's Republic of China, "East Turkistan Forces Cannot Get Away with Impunity," January 21, 2002, http://news.xinhuanet.com/english/2002-01/21/content_247082.htm.

9. On the decline of Uighur violence after 1997, see James Milward, "Violent Separatism in Xinjiang: A Critical Assessment." East-West Center Washington, Policy Paper 6, 2004, http://www.eastwestcenter.org/fileadmin/stored/pdfs/PS006.pdf.

10. These included a May 1998 bus bombing in Osh, the March 2000 assassination of the leader of the Uighur émigré community in Kyrgyzstan, and a May 2000 attack on a Chinese delegation visiting Kyrgyzstan. See Milward, *Eurasian Crossroads*, 19–22.

11. Nicolas Bequelin, "Staged Development in Xinjiang," *The China Quarterly* 178 (July 2004), 358–378.

12. See Gaël Raballand and Agnès Andrésy, "Why Should Trade Between Central Asia and China Continue to Expand?" *Asia Europe Journal* 5, no. 2 (May 2007), 232–251.

13. Sean R. Roberts, "A 'Land of Borderlands': Implications of Xinjiang's Cross-Border Transactions," in Starr, ed. *Xinjiang: China's Muslim Borderland* (Armonk, NY: M. E. Sharpe, 2004), 220–225.

14. See Article 2 of the Charter of the Shanghai Cooperation Organization, http://www.sectsco.org/EN/show.asp?id=69.

15. See, for example, Thomas Ambrosio, "Catching the 'Shanghai Spirit': How the Shanghai Cooperation Organization Promotes Authoritarian Norms in Central Asia," *Europe-Asia Studies* 60, no. 8 (October 2008), 1321–1344.

16. In 2009, Belarus and Sri Lanka were awarded the title of "Special Dialogue Partners."

17. Alastair Iain Johnston, *Social States: China in International Institutions, 1980–2000* (Princeton: Princeton University Press, 2007).

18. See Nargis Kassenova makes a similar point in her survey of Chinese aid projects. See Nargis Kassenova, "China as an Emerging Donor in Tajikistan and Kyrgyzstan," Paris, IFRI Russia/NIS Center, January 2009, http://www.ifri.org/?page=contribution-detail&id=5257&id_provenance=97.

19. Author's interview at the SCO Secretariat, Beijing, China, October 2009.

20. See Stephen Aris, "The Shanghai Cooperation Organisation: 'Tackling the Three Evils,' *Europe-Asia Studies* 61, no. 3 (May 2009), 457–482; and Zhao Huasheng, "Security

Building in Central Asia and the Shanghai Cooperation Organization," presentation to Summer International Symposium, Hokkaido University, Japan (Summer 2003), http://src-h.slav.hokudai.ac.jp/coe21/publish/no2_ses/4-2_Zhao.pdf.

21. See Zhao, "Security Building in Central Asia and the Shanghai Cooperation Organization"; Pan Guang, "A Chinese Perspective on the Shanghai Cooperation Organisation," in Alyson Bailes et al., *The Shanghai Cooperation Organization*. Stockholm," SIPRI Policy Paper no. 17, (May 2007), 45–58.

22. See M. Taylor Fravel, *Strong Borders, Secure Nation: Cooperation and Conflict in China's Territorial Disputes* (Princeton: Princeton University Press, 2008), 160–166.

23. Author's interviews with Kyrgyz diplomatic officials and think tank analysts, Bishkek, Kyrgyzstan, June 2009.

24. See former Kyrgyz Ambassador to China Erlan Abdyldaev's analysis of the episode, "The Chinese Vector in the Foreign Policy of Kurmanbek Bakiyev," written for Institute of Public Policy, Bishkek, undated, http://www.ipp.kg/ru/analysis/235/.

25. George Gavrilis, *The Dynamics of Interstate Boundaries* (New York: Cambridge University Press, 2008), 123.

26. Indeed, prior to 9/11, the Chinese government did not even report on violent incidents in Xinjiang. See Huasheng Zhao, "Central Asia in China's Diplomacy," in Eugene Rumer et al. *Central Asia: Views from Washington, Moscow and Beijing* (Armonk, NY: M. E. Sharpe, 2007), 142–144.

27. See the statement by the Chinese Ministry of Foreign Affairs, Foreign Ministry Spokesman's Press Conference, November 11, 2001, http://www.fmprc.gov.cn/eng/xwfw/s2510/2511/t14731.htm. For an overview, see Chien-peng Chun, "China's 'War on Terror': September 11 and Uighur Separatism," *Foreign Affairs* 81, no. 4 (August 2002), 8–9. On concerns about the permanency of the U.S. military presence for Beijing, see Zhao Huasheng, "China, Russia, and the United States: Prospects for Cooperation in Central Asia," *China and Eurasia Forum Quarterly* (Winter 2005), 20–38.

28. "East Turkistan Forces Cannot Get Away with Impunity." January 21, 2002,

29. Andrew Small, "China's Caution on Afghanistan-Pakistan," *The Washington Quarterly* 33, no. 3 (July 2010), 83.

30. See Milward 2009, 322–325; and Michael Clarke, "Widening the Net: China's Anti-Terror Laws and Human Rights in the Uyghur Autonomous Region," *The International Journal of Human Rights* 14, no. 4 (July 2010), 542-558.

31. Author's interviews with Chinese analysts and officials. Beijing and Shanghai, China, October 2009.

32. On the New Security Concept, see Bates Gill, *Rising Star: China's New Security Diplomacy* (Washington, DC: Brookings, 2010, Revised); David Shambaugh, "China Engages Asia: Reshaping the International Order," *International Security* 29, no. 3 (Winter 2004–2005), 64–99.

33. See Rebecca Louise Nadin, "China and the Shanghai 5/Shanghai Cooperation Organisation: 1996–2006, A Decade on the New Diplomatic Frontier," PhD Diss., University of Sheffield, Department of East Asian Studies, July 2007, 187–188.

34. Nadin, "China and the Shanghai 5/Shanghai Cooperation Organisation," 190–193. Also see Guang, "A Chinese Perspective on the Shanghai Cooperation Organisation."

35. Author's interviews with Chinese Central Asia scholars and analysts. Beijing and Shanghai, October 2009.

36. See Titus C. Chen, "China's Reaction to the Color Revolutions," *Asian Perspective* 34, no. 2 (2010), 5–51.

37. Author's interview with a Chinese member of the Kyrgyz research team, Shanghai, October 2009.

38. See, for example, Adam Wolfe, "The 'Great Game' Heats Up in Central Asia," *Eurasianet*, August 3, 2005.

39. See Roger N. McDermott, "The Rising Dragon: SCO Peace Mission 2007." *Jamestown Foundation Occasional Paper*, October 2007.

40. Robert A. Pape, "Soft Balancing Against the United States," *International Security* 30, no. 1 (Summer 2005), 10. For a critical response, see Stephen Brooks and William Wohlforth, "Hard Times for Soft Balancing," *International Security* 30, no. 1 (Summer 2005), 72–108.

41. See Beissinger, "Structure and Example in Modular Political Phenomena."

42. Also see Lo, *Axis of Convenience*, 91–114.

43. For an extended analysis, see Elizabeth Wishnick, *Russia, China and the United States in Central Asia: Prospects for Great Power Competition and Cooperation in Central Asia* (Carlisle, PA: U.S. Army War College, Strategic Studies Institute, 2009).

44. Author's interview with a Russian newspaper correspondent who covered the Dushanbe summit, Moscow, September 2009.

45. At the same time, Chinese and Central Asian officials overwhelmingly express the view that Russia was justified in intervening in Georgia and that Tbilisi initiated the conflict. The legal question of recognition of the breakaway territories, however, is considered as a separate matter.

46. Author's interviews with Chinese analysts and SCO officials, Beijing, China, October 2009. On the declaration, see http://news.xinhuanet.com/english/2009-07/11/content_11693625.htm. Also see Alexander Cooley, "Cooperation Gets Shanghaied: China, Russia and the SCO," *Foreign Affairs*, December 14, 2009.

47. See the resulting report by Alexander Knyazev, ed., *Afghanistan, SCO, Security and the Geopolitics of Central Asia* (Bishkek: Alexander Knyazev Public Foundation, 2008).

48. Author's interviews with members of the SCO Secretariat, Beijing, China, October 2009.

49. Gavrilis, *The Dynamics of Interstate Boundaries*, 114–117; and Nancy Lubin, "Who's Watching the Watchdogs?" *Journal of International Affairs* 56, no. 2 (Spring 2003), 43–56.

50. Small, "China's Caution on Afghanistan-Pakistan."

51. Prior to 9/11, Beijing maintained regular contacts with Taliban, but these ties were subsequently downgraded. Author's e-mail communication with Andrew Small, September 28, 2011. In 2007, British officials raised the concern that the Taliban were obtaining Chinese weapons, but these appear to have been reexported via Iran. See Paul Danahar, "Taleban 'Getting Chinese Arms,'" *BBC News*, September 7, 2007.

52. Author's communications with Chinese Central Asia and Afghanistan experts at the 9th SCO Academic conference, Shanghai, China, July 2009.

53. Author's question and answer session following a presentation at the Shanghai Academy of Social Sciences, Shanghai, China, October 23, 2009.

54. Remarks made by Zhao Huasheng at the forum "10 Years of the Shanghai Cooperation Organization," Washington, DC, Center for International and Strategic Studies, May 4, 2011.

55. On the Central Asian cross-border shuttle trade, see *Cross-Border Trade Within the Central Asian Regional Cooperation* (World Bank, Washington, DC, 2007) http://www.carecinstitute.org/uploads/docs/Cross-Border-Trade-CAREC.pdf.

56. See Bartlomiej Kaminski and Gaël Raballand, "Entrepot for Chinese for Chinese Consumer Goods in Central Asia: The Puzzle of Re-Exports through Kyrgyz Bazaars," *Eurasian Geography and Economics* 50, no. 5 (2009), 581–590.

57. According to international development experts interviewed by the author in Tajikistan in May 2009, China is the largest single investor in Tajikistan's transportation and power-generating infrastructure.

58. Sebastien Peyrouse, "Economic Aspects of the Chinese-Central Asia Rapprochement," Silk Road Paper, Johns Hopkins University, Washington DC, September 2007, 13–15.

59. See "Go West, Young Chinaman: Chin and Central Asia," *The Economist*, January 6, 2007.

60. Ben Judah, "Dragon Meets Bear: Reshaping Central Asia," *Prospect*, February 3, 2011.

61. See Kassenova, "China as an Emerging Donor in Tajikistan and Kyrgyzstan," 15–16, and David Trilling, "A Chinese Road to the Future?" *Eurasianet*, July 31, 2007.

62. For representative examples, see Oksana Antonenko, "The EU Should Not Ignore the Shanghai Cooperation Organisation," Centre for European Reform Policy Brief, May

2007, http://www.cer.org.uk/pdf/policybrief_sco_web_11may07.pdf; Alyson JK Bailes, "The Shanghai Cooperation Organisation and Europe," *China and Eurasia Forum Quarterly* 5, no. 3 (2007): 13–18; Marcel de Haaas. "Central Asia's Waking Giant," *The Guardian*, January 5, 2009.

63. Author's interviews with representatives of international financial institutions, Bishkek, Kyrgyzstan, June 2009, and Dushanbe, Tajikistan, May 2010.

64. Jonathan Holslag, "China's Road to Influence," *Asian Survey* 50, no. 4 (July/August 2010), 641–662.

65. The alarming case is made in Halper, *The Beijing Consensus*. For a more positive assessment, see Deborah Brautigam, *The Dragon's Gift: The Real Story of China in Africa* (New York: Oxford University Press, 2009).

66. Author's personal communication with a senior U.S. government official, October 2010.

67. International Crisis Group, "Central Asia: Decay and Decline," *Crisis Group Asia Report* no. 201, Brussels, February 21, 2011, 13.

68. This section draws on International Crisis Group, "Central Asia: Decay and Decline," 17–18. Journalists interviewed by the author in Tajikistan confirmed this anecdote.

69. This episode was discussed at the 9th Annual SCO conference in Shanghai in July 2009 and confirmed by SCO officials to the author in meetings at the Secretariat in Beijing, China, October 2009.

70. Author's communications with Russian SCO observers at the 9th Annual SCO conference, Shanghai, China, July 2009.

71. Simon Hall, "China's Thirst for Oil at an All-Time High," *Wall Street Journal*. January 18, 2011.

72. This section draws on "Turkmenistan Natural Gas Outlook 2020: The Chinese Connection." Columbia University School of International and Public Affairs Capstone Report, New York, May 2011, http://www.sipa.columbia.edu/academics/workshops/documents/RANDTheFinalCopyIII.pdf.

73. For an inventory of major foreign oil ventures in Kazakhstan, see Martha Brill Olcott, *Kazakhstan: Unfulfilled Promise?* Washington, DC: Carnegie Endowment for Peace, 2010, Appendix 10, 312–318.

74. See Sebastien Peyrouse, "Chinese Economic Presence in Kazakhstan: China's Resolve and Central Asia's Apprehension," *China Perspectives* no. 3 (2008), 34–49.

75. Some international energy analysts estimate that total Chinese control of Kazakh oil production may be significantly higher, up to 40–50%, but information is suppressed for political reasons. The 26% figure is found in Yitzhak Shichor, "China's Central Asian Strategy and the Xinjiang Connection: Predicaments and Medicaments in a Contemporary Perspective," *China and Eurasia Forum Quarterly* 6, no. 2 (2008), 69.

76. Hal Foster, "China Will Be Involved in 50 Percent of Kazakhstan's 2010 Oil Output," *Central Asia Newswire*, August 20, 2010.

77. For an overview, see Sebastien Peyrouse, "The Hydrocarbon Sector in Central Asia and the Growing Role of China," *China and Eurasia Forum Quarterly* 56, no. 2 (2007), 131–148.

78. Author's interviews with representatives of international financial institutions in Tajikistan, Dushanbe, May 2010.

79. Data is from the General Customs Administration of the PRC, as reported separately in "China Dec Crude Oil and LNG Imports, Exports," *Reuters*, January 24, 2007; "Table of China December Oil, Oil Pdt and LNG Imports." *Dow Jones*, January 21, 2011. I am thankful to Erica Downs, Fellow and Chinese energy specialist at the Brookings Institution, for bringing these to my attention.

80. For details of the pipeline's construction and possible significance, see "Turkmenistan Natural Gas Outlook 2020: The Chinese Connection."

81. See Alexandros Peterson, "Did China Just Win the Caspian Gas War?" *Foreign Policy*, July 7, 2010.

82. See Naazneen Barma, Ely Ratner, and Steven Weber, "A World Without the West," *National Interest* 90 (July/August 2007), 23–30.

83. On differing modes of regional integration, see Alexander Cooley and Hendrik Spruyt, *Contracting States: Sovereign Transfers in International Relations* (Princeton: Princeton University Press, 2009).

Chapter 6

1. See Thomas Carothers, *Aiding Democracy Abroad: The Learning Curve* (Washington, DC: Carnegie Endowment for Peace, 1999).
2. See Vladimir D. Shkolnikov, "Missing the Big Picture? Retrospective on OSCE Strategic Thinking in Central Asia," *Security and Human Rights* no. 4 (2009), 294–306.
3. For a nuanced assessment of U.S. democracy assistance to Kyrgyzstan, see Thomas Wood, "Democracy Promotion in Central Asia: The Case of Kyrgyzstan." Paper presented to the Eleventh Annual Conference of the Central Asian Studies Society, East Lansing (October 2010). On the weaknesses of Eurasian civil society and its implications for U.S. assistance, see Thomas W. Simmons, *Eurasia's Frontiers: Young States, Old Societies, Uncertain Futures* (Ithaca, NY: Cornell University Press 2008). On the tension between promoting values and interests, see Alexander Cooley, "Principles in the Pipeline: Managing Transatlantic Values and Interests in Central Asia," *International Affairs* 84, No. 6 (November 2008), 1173–1188.
4. Kazakhstan, unlike its neighbors, did not ratify the treaties until 2005. The treaties are the International Covenant on Civil and Political Rights (ICCPR); International Covenant on Economic, Cultural and Social Right (ICESCR); Convention on Children's Rights; Convention on the Liquidation of all Forms of Racial Discrimination; Convention on the Elimination of all Forms of Discrimination Against Women; and the Convention Against Torture.
5. Eugheniy Zhovtis, "Democratisation and Human Rights in Central Asia: Problems, Prospects and the Role of the International Community," Centre for European Policy Studies Policy Briefs, No. 134 (July 2007).
6. International legal expert Beth Simmons attributes the ratification of these treaties to the Central Asian elites wanting to avoid being singled out by the international community, a practice she refers to as "social camouflage." See Beth Simmons, *Mobilizing for Human Rights* (New York: Cambridge University Press, 2009), 88–90.
7. David Lewis, *Temptations of Tyranny* (New York: Columbia University Press 2008); Irina Chernykh and Rustam Burnashev, "Conditions for Securitization of International Terrorism in Central Asia," *Connections: The Quarterly Journal* 4, no. 1 (Spring 2005), 131–142.
8. Kim Lane Sheppele, "Law in a Time of Emergency: States of Exception and the Temptations of 9/11," *University of Pennsylvania Journal of Constitutional Law* (May 2004), 1001–1083.
9. The units included a special Internal Affairs counterterrorism unit known as Bars, which had commanders that were trained in crisis-response in Louisiana in a State Department–sponsored program. See C. J. Chivers and Thom Shanker, "Uzbek Ministries Received U.S. Aid," *New York Times*, June 18, 2005.
10. Seth Jones, Olga Oliker, et al., *Securing Tyrants or Fostering Reform? U.S. Security Assistance to Repressive and Transitioning Regimes*, Washington DC; RAND, 2006. The authors concluded that "Uzbekistan clearly presents the challenges of undertaking a reform effort in a state where corruption and human rights violations are endemic and political reform is feared as a threat to the state,"10.
11. On coalitional dynamics and logrolling, see Jack Snyder, *Myths of Empire* (Ithaca, NY: Cornell University Press, 1995), 17–19.
12. U.S. and Chinese officials have also fallen out over other designations, most notably over returning 23 Uighurs detained at Guantanomo Bay as well as the status of the East Turkestan Liberation Organization, which Beijing considers to be a terrorist group.
13. Ministry of Foreign Affairs of the PRC, "China and Russia Issue a Joint Statement, Declaring the Trend of the Boundary Line Between the Two Countries Has Been Completely Determined," October 14, 2004, http://www.fmprc.gov.cn/eng/wjdt/2649/t165266.htm.

14. Andrei Soldatov and Irina Boragan, *The New Nobility: The Restoration of Russia's Security States and the Enduring Legacy of the KGB* (New York: PublicAffairs, 2010), 224.

15. See Gavin Sullivan and Ben Hayes. *Blacklisted: Targeted Sanctions, Preemptive Security, and Fundamental Rights* (Berlin: European Center for Constitutional and Human Rights, 2009).

16. For overviews of these UN regimes, see Rosemary Foot, "The United Nations, Counter Terrorism, and Human Rights: Institutional Adaptation and Embedded Ideas," *Human Rights Quarterly* 29, no. 2 (May 2007), 489–514.

17. See Eminent Jurist Panel, "Assessing Damage, Urging Action: Report of the Eminent Jurists Panel on Terrorism, Counter-Terrorism and Human Rights." Geneva: International Commission of Jurists, 2009, 114–118.

18. Sullivan and Hayes, *Blacklisted*, 26–39.

19. Kim Sheppele, "Other People's PATRIOT Acts: Europe's Response to September 11," *Loyola Law Review* 50 (2004), 89–148, 92.

20. Human Rights in China, "Counter-Terrorism and Human Rights: The Impact of the Shanghai Cooperation Organization" (New York: HRIC, March 2011), 85–86.

21. Martin Scheinin, "Promotion and Protection of All Human Rights, Civil, Political, Economic, and Cultural Rights, Including the Right to Development" (New York: United Nations, February 4, 2009), 10.

22. Human Rights Watch, "Eurasia: Uphold Human Rights in Combating Terrorism: Shanghai Cooperation Organization Must Not Punish Peaceful Dissent," New York: July 14, 2006.

23. Vladimir Bogdanov, "Bezopasnost Po Spisku," *Rossiskaya Gazeta*, March 5, 2011.

24. See Kenneth Roth, "The Law of War in the War on Terror," *Foreign Affairs* 83, no. 2 (March/April 2004), 2–8.

25. See: http://projects.washingtonpost.com/guantanamo/search/. Most of the Russian citizens appear to have been of Central Asian origin. Of these, all but one Tajik, one Russian, and five Chinese nationals were released; two Uzbeks were repatriated to Ireland, while six Chinese Uighurs were sent to the Pacific island of Palau, over the strong objections of the Chinese government.

26. See Center for Constitutional Rights, "Foreign Interrogators in Guantanamo Bay," available at: http://ccrjustice.org/files/Foreign%20Interrogators%20in%20Guantanamo%20 Bay_1.pdf (accessed April 11, 2011).

27. Center for Constitutional Rights, "Foreign Interrogators in Guantanamo Bay," 2.

28. See Asam's Combatant Status Review Tribunal Transcript, December 6, 2004. Available at: http://projects.nytimes.com/guantanamo/detainees/672-zakirjan-asam/documents/4 (accessed September 12, 2011).

29. Raffi Khatchadourian, "Terror at Jaslyk," *The Nation*, April 26, 2004.

30. This is one of the main arguments presented in Craig Murray, *Murder in Samarkand* (London: Mainstream Publishing, 2006). Murray has questioned whether the acceptance of such intelligence itself constituted a breach of the UK's commitment to the Convention Against Torture.

31. For the text, see: "The Shanghai Convention on Combating Terrorism, Extremism and Separatism," May 7, 2009. Available at: http://www.sectsco.org/EN/show.asp?id=68 (accessed April 2, 2011).

32. SCO Convention on Combating Terrorism," Articles VII and VIII.

33. "The Regional Anti-Terrorist Structure of the Shanghai Cooperation Organisation (RATS SCO," Agentura.ru. Available at: http://www.agentura.ru/english/dossier/ratssco/ (accessed April 10, 2011).

34. The HRIC notes, "Through the use of such blacklists, an SCO member state may bypass the step of independently determining according to law whether an individual has committed an act of terrorism; rather, another country's identification of the individual as a terrorist will suffice." HRIC, "Counter-Terrorism and Human Rights: The Impact of the Shanghai Cooperation Organization," 87.

35. See Jane Mayer, "Outsourcing Torture: the Secret History of America's 'Extraordinary Renditions' Program," *New Yorker*, February 14, 2005.

36. See Margaret L. Satterthwaite, "Rendered Meaningless: Extraordinary Rendition and the Rule of Law," *George Washington Law Review* 75, no. 5–6 (2006), 1333–1368.

37. Dick Marty, *Alleged Secret Detentions and Unlawful Inter-state Transfers of Detainees Involving Council of Europe Member States*, Report Prepared for the Council of Europe Parliamentary Assembly, June 12, 2006.

38. Mayer, "Outsourcing Torture."

39. Steve Coll, *Ghost Wars: The Secret History of the CIA, Afghanistan, and Bin Laden, from the Soviet Invasion to September 10, 2001* (New York: Penguin, 2004), 531.

40. Marty, *Alleged Secret Detentions and Unlawful Inter-state Transfers of Detainees Involving Council of Europe Member States*, 20.

41. See also Giovanni Claudio Fava, "On the Flights Operated by the CIA in Europe," European Parliament Temporary Committee on the Alleged Use of European Countries by the CIA for the Transport and Illegal Detention of Prisoners, Working Document 4, January 6, 2006.

42. Stephen Grey, *Ghost Plane: The True Story of the CIA Torture Program* (New York: St. Martin's, 2006), 181. Murray estimates that from 2003 to 2004, "CIA flights flew to Tashkent often, usually twice a week." See Don Von Natta, Jr. "US Recruits a Rough Ally to Be a Jailer," *New York Times*, May 1, 2005.

43. "President's Press Conference," The White House, March 16, 2005, http://www.whitehouse.gov/news/releases/2005/03/20050316-3.html.

44. "Intelligence Officer Claims That CIA Was Complicit in Torture in Uzbekistan," *The Scotland Herald*, September 13, 2008.

45. Jeremy Scahill, *Blackwater: The Rise of the World's Most Powerful Mercenary Army* (New York: Nation, 2008), 326–327.

46. Gabor Steingart, "Merchants of Death: Memos Reveal Details of Blackwater's Targeted Killings Program," *Spiegel*, August 24, 2009.

47. Deirdre Tynan, "Airlines with Ties to Blackwater Has Long Record of Service in the Region," *Eurasianet*, March 21, 2010.

48. Fava 2006, 6. Among the destinations reviewed from 32 monitored flight codes from 2001 to 2005 that were linked to the transportation of prisoners, 70 were to Azerbaijan, 52 to Turkmenistan and 46 to Uzbekistan.

49. "State Security Without Borders," [GB bez granits] *Novaya Gazeta*, August 21, 2008.

50. See HRIC, "Counter-Terrorism and Human Rights: The Impact of the Shanghai Cooperation Organization," 2011; Human Rights Watch, *"Saving its Secrets": Government Repression in Andijan* (New York: Human Rights Watch, May 2008); and Human Rights Watch, "Application No. 2947/06: Ismoilov and Others vs. Russia." July 24, 2007.

51. For a list of documented examples and a time line, see the Moscow-based Human Rights Organization, "Timeline of Illegal Expulsions of Refugees from Russia to their Countries of their Origin," August 2008, http://hro.org/files/Timeline_ENG.doc.

52. For details of individual cases, see HRIC, "Counter-Terrorism and Human Rights"; and Statement by Dolkun Isa, "Uighur Situation in Central Asian Countries." OSCE Human Dimension Implementation Meeting, Warsaw September 25, 2007. On the Celil case, see Madeline Earp, "Prisoner Profile: Huseyin Celil," Human Rights in China. Available at: http://hrichina.org/sites/default/files/oldsite/PDFs/CRF.4.2006/CRF-2006-4_Profile.pdf (accessed July 3, 2011).

53. Soldatov and Boragan, *The New Nobility*, 224.

54. See Memorial Human Rights Center, "Fabrication of 'Islamic Extremism' Criminal Cases in Russia: Campaign Continues," April 15, 2007.

55. For details, see Memorial Human Rights Center, "Alisher Usmanov, who was abducted from Kazan, was sentenced in Uzbekistan for 8 years," November 11, 2005.

56. "Cpyetssluzhby byvshyevo soyuza — na territorii Rossii," *Novaya Gazeta*, February 27, 2006.

57. For case facts and details, see European Court of Human Rights, "Case of Iskanadarov vs. Russia," Application no. 17185/05, available at: http://www.unhcr.org/refworld/pdfid/4ca1d1e52.pdf.
58. Borogan, "State Security Without Borders."
59. Soldatov and Boragan, *The New Nobility*, 218–219.
60. Irina Borogan, "With Friends Like These, Who Needs Enemies," *Ezhednevni Journal*, November 7, 2008.
61. *The New Nobility*, 225–226.
62. For case background and details, see: European Court of Human Rights, "Case of Ismoilov and Others vs. Russia," Application no. 2947/06. April 24, 2008; Vitaliy Ponomarev, "Refugees from Uzbekistan in the CIS (2005–2007)" (Moscow: Memorial Human Rights Center, September 2007).
63. See European Court of Human Rights, "Muminov vs. Russia." Application no. 42502/06. November 12, 2008.
64. Thomas Ambrosio, *Authoritarian Backlash: Russian Resistance to Democratization in the Former Soviet Union* (Burlington, VT: Ashgate, 2009).
65. See Michael McFaul, "Ukraine Imports Democracy: External Influences on the Color Revolutions," *International Security* 32, no. 2 (2007), 45–83; and Valerie Bunce and Sharon Wolchik, "International Diffusion and Postcommunist Electoral Revolutions," *Communist and Postcommunist Studies* 39, no. 3 (September 2006), 283–304.
66. This paragraph draws extensively on: International Helsinki Federation for Human Rights, "Central Asia: Human Rights Groups Facing Increasingly Restrictive Legislation." February 2006.
67. Figures from website (www.uzngo.info) as cited in U.S. Embassy Cable, 07TASHKENT1817, Embassy in Tashkent. October 22, 2007, http://www.wikileaks.org/cable/2007/10/07TASHKENT1817.html.
68. U.S. Embassy Cable, 05DUSHANBE72, Embassy in Dushanbe, October 20, 2005, http://www.wikileaks.org/cable/2005/10/05DUSHANBE1702.html.
69. See Shkolnikov, "Missing the Big Picture?" 298–301; Alexander Warkotsch, "The OSCE as an Agent of Socialization? International Norm Dynamics and Political Change in Central Asia," *Europe-Asia Studies* 55, no. 5 (July 2007), 829–846.
70. Author's copy of the memorandum.
71. Wood, "Democracy Promotion in Central Asia"; Edward Schatz, "The Soft Authoritarian Tool Kit: Agenda Setting Power in Kazakhstan and Kyrgyzstan," *Comparative Politics* 41, no. 2 (January 2009), 213.
72. Survey conducted on a 6-point scale, with 1 labeled the "most valuable" and 6 the least valuable. These figures combine category 1 and 2 responses. See Nancy Lubin and Arustan Joldastov, "Snapshots from Central Asia: Is America Losing in Public Opinion?" *Problems of Post-Communism* 57, no. 3 (May/June 2010), 53.
73. Vladislav Surkov, "Suverenitet—eto politicheski sinonim konkurentnosposobnosti," *Moscow News*, March 3, 2006.
74. Andrei Okara, "Sovereign Democracy: A New Russian Idea or PR Project?" *Russia in Global Affairs* 5, no. 3 (2007), 8–20.
75. Nursultan Nazarbaev, "Democracy Cannot Be Proclaimed, It Must Be Lived Through," *Geneva Diplomatic Magazine*, January 2003, http://www.akorda.kz/ru/speeches/articles/democracy_cannot_be_proclaimed_it_has_to_evolve_from.
76. Interview of the President of Kazakhstan, Nursultan Nazarbaev, with Interfax, Russian Newspaper, and the TV station Vesti, undated, http://www.akorda.kz/ru/speeches/interviews/interveyu_prezidenta_kazaxstana_nwrswltana_nazarbaeva.
77. See the founding Declaration of the Shanghai Cooperation Organization, June 15, 2001. For a critique of the "Shanghai Spirit," see Thomas Ambrosio, "Catching the 'Shanghai Spirit': How the Shanghai Cooperation Organization Promotes Authoritarian Norms," *Europe-Asia Studies* 60, no. 8 (September 2008), 1321–1344.
78. See, for example, the cable describing a 2008 meeting between Karimov and U.S. Assistant Secretary of State Richard Boucher. U.S. Embassy Cable, 08Tashkent624, "Karimov to

Boucher: Progress Possible, But Not Under Sanctions Embassy." Embassy in Tashkent, June 5, 2008, http://www.wikileaks.org/cable/2008/06/08TASHKENT624.html.

79. Edward Schatz and Renan Levine, "Framing, Public Diplomacy and Anti-Americanism in Central Asia," *International Studies Quarterly* 54, no. 3 (September 2010), 855–869.

80. Schatz and Levine, "Framing, Public Diplomacy and Anti-Americanism in Central Asia," 866.

81. Rick Fawn, "Battle over the Box: International Election Observation Missions, Political Competition, and Retrenchment in the post-Soviet space," *International Affairs* 82, no. 6 (November 2006), 1133–1153.

82. Declaration by the Nine Heads of State, "Appeal of the CIS Member States for the OSCE Partners, adopted in Astana," 526th Plenary Meeting of the PC, September 23, 2004, PC.Jour/562/Corr.1, available at: http://www.belarusembassy.org/news/digests/pr092004.html.

83. See "SCO Mission: 'Elections Were Free & Transparent'," Uzbek Consulate, December 25, 2007; and "CIS Mission: 'Elections Were Important For Further Democratization of Public Life In Uzbekistan,'" Jahon Information Agency, December 26, 2007.

84. OSCE, "OSCE/ODIHR Limited Election Observation Mission Final Report," April 23, 2008, http://www.osce.org/odihr/elections/uzbekistan/31600.

85. Judith Kelley, "The More the Merrier? The Effects of Having Multiple International Election Monitoring Organizations," *Perspectives on Politics* 7, no. 1 (2009), 59–63.

86. On the importance of this standard and the question of credibility, see Susan Hyde, *The Pseudo-Democrat's Dilemma: Why Election Observation Became and International Norm* (Ithaca, NY: Cornell University Press, 2011).

87. See the 2010 ODIHR Handbook, at: http://www.osce.org/files/documents/5/e/68439.pdf

Chapter 7

1. See David Lewis, *The Temptations of Tyranny in Central Asia* (New York: Columbia University Press, 2008).

2. See, for instance, Philip Pan, "Russia Is Said to Have Fueled Unrest in Kyrgyzstan," *Washington Post*, April 12, 2010; and Ariel Cohen, "Obama's Stake in the Second Kyrgyz Revolution," *Wall Street Journal*, April 12, 2010.

3. Samuel Huntington. *Political Order in Changing Societies* (New Haven: Yale University Press, 1968).

4. For a review, see Ken Hurwitz, "Contemporary Approaches to Political Stability," *Comparative Politics* 5, no. 3 (April 1973), 449–463.

5. Keith M. Dowding and Richard Kimber, "The Meaning and Use of 'Political Stability,'" *European Journal of Political Research* 1, no. 3 (September 1983), 229–243.

6. On the Kazakh case, see Edward Schatz, "Access by Accident: Legitimacy Claims and Democracy Promotion in Authoritarian Central Asia," *International Review of Political Science* 27, no. 3 (2006), 263–284. On Turkmenistan see Luca Anceschi, *Turkmenistan's Foreign Policy: Positive Neutrality and the Consolidation of the Turkmen Regime* (London: Routledge, 2008).

7. See Scott Radnitz, *Weapons of the Wealthy: Predatory Regimes and Elite-Led Protests in Central Asia* (Ithaca, NY: Cornell University Press).

8. On patronage and repression in Uzbekistan, see Eric McGlinchey, *Chaos, Violence, Dynasty: Politics and Islam in Central Asia* (Pittsburgh: University of Pittsburgh Press, 2011).

9. See Kiren Aziz Chaudhry, "The Price of Wealth: Business and State Labor Remittance and Oil Economies," *International Organization* 43, no. 1 (December 1989), 101–145.

10. See, respectively, Barnett Rubin's account of the breakdown of Soviet-era patronage networks and the onset of the Tajik Civil War and Eric McGlinchey's account of Kyrgyzstan's shift from foreign aid dependence, during the first decade of Akayev's tenure, to a more

narrow dependence on base-related revenues during Bakiyev's tenure. Barnett Rubin, "Russian Hegemony and State Breakdown in the Periphery: Causes and Consequences of the Civil War in Tajikistan," in Barnett R. Rubin and Jack Snyder, eds., *Post-Soviet Political Order: Conflict and State-Building* (London: Routledge, 1998); and McGlinchey, *Chaos, Violence, Dynasty*, 80-113.

11. This is a version of the "rentier state" thesis. For an overview, see Michael L. Ross, "Does Oil Hinder Democracy?" *World Politics* 53, no. 3 (April 2001), 325–361. For a critical application of the theory to the Eurasian cases, see Pauline Jones Luong and Erika Weinthal, *Oil Is Not a Curse: Ownership Structure and Institutions in Soviet Successor States* (New York: Cambridge University Press, 2010).

12. As Global Witness notes, revenues to Turkmenistan in the later 1990s were funneled into then President Niyazov's offshore bank account. Global Witness, "It's a Gas: Funny Business in the Turkmen-Ukraine Gas Trade," http://www.globalwitness.org/library/its-gas-funny-business-turkmen-ukraine-gas-trade.

13. See, for instance, Erica Weinthal, "Beyond the State: Transnational Actors, NGOs, and Environmental Protection in Central Asia," in Pauline Jones, ed., *The Transformation of Central Asia: States and Societies from Soviet Rule to Independence* (Ithaca, NY: Cornell University Press, 2003).

14. Jesse Driscoll Russell, "Exiting Anarchy: Militia Politics after the Post-Soviet Wars." PhD diss., Stanford University, 2009; John Heathershaw, *Post-Conflict Tajikistan: The Politics of Peacebuilding and the Emergence of Legitimate Order* (New York: Routledge, 2009).

15. The argument parallels some of Bates's recent observations about the breakdown of the post-colonial African state. See Robert Bates, *When Thing Fell Apart: State-Failure in Late Century Africa* (New York: Cambridge University Press, 2008).

16. "Chtoby podnyat' ekonomiku, nuzhna zheleznaya distsiplina," Interview with President Bakiyev of Kyrgyzstan. *Kommersant*, February 15, 2006.

17. "U.S. Military Base in Kyrgyzstan Comes into Play as Domestic Political Confrontation Brews," *Eurasianet*, April 26, 2006.

18. Personal communications with an official from Kyrgyzstan's Ministry of Foreign Affairs, March 2006 and May 2006. According to this Kyrgyz representative involved in the negotiations, U.S. officials claimed that they could secure access to "two bases" for the $200 million annual price tag.

19. Though, during the Cold War even NATO allies such as Greece and Turkey openly flouted this policy by openly calling for more rent during negotiations for basing rights. See Alexander Cooley, *Base Politics: Democratic Change and the U.S. Military Overseas* (Ithaca, NY: Cornell University Press, 2008).

20. Author's interviews with Kyrgyz National Security officials and base negotiators, Bishkek, Kyrgyzstan, January 2008.

21. For the text, see "Joint Statement the United States and the Kyrgyz Republic on Coalition Airbase," Embassy of the United States to the Kyrgyz Republic, July 14, 2006, http://kyrgyz.usembassy.gov/july_14_joint_statement_on_coalition_airbase.html.

22. Author's interviews with Kyrgyz National Security officials and base negotiators, Bishkek, Kyrgyzstan, January 2008.

23. See Bruce Pannier, "Bishkek Wants U.S. to Hand Over Airman," *Radio Free Europe/Radio Liberty*, March 21, 2007.

24. See, for instance, the U.S. Department of State's Inspector General's report from February 2008 that points to simmering Embassy-Base tensions. Available at: http://oig.state.gov/documents/organization/113921.pdf.

25. For details and analysis of Bakiyev-era state corruption, see Erica Marat, "The Criminalization of the State Before and After the Tulip Revolution," *China and Eurasia Forum Quarterly* 6, no.2 (2008), 15–22.

26. See Shairbek Juraev, "The Logic of Kyrgyzstan's Base Policy," PONARS Eurasia Policy Memo no. 72, September 2009, http://www.gwu.edu/~ieresgwu/assets/docs/pepm_072.pdf.

27. U.S. Embassy Cable 08BISHKEK1002, "U.S under 'Enormous Pressure' from Russia." U.S. Embassy in Bishkek. October 2, 2008, http://wikileaks.org/cable/2008/10/08BISHKEK1002.html.

28. U.S. Embassy Cable 09BISHKEK744, "Russia Offers Kyrgyzstan $2.5 billion to Shut Down Manas Airbase." U.S. Embassy in Bishkek. July 9, 2009, http://www.wikileaks.org/cable/2009/07/09BISHKEK744.html.

29. U.S. Embassy Cable 09MOSCOW1827, "The GOR's 'Secret' Visit to Kyrgyzstan." U.S. Embassy in Moscow, July 15, 2009, http://www.wikileaks.org/cable/2009/07/09MOSCOW1827.html.

30. U.S. Embassy Cable 09BISHKEK108, "What Does Bakiyev Really Want for the Base? Maybe 'Only' $450 Million." U.S. Embassy in Bishkek, February 5, 2009, http:// wikileaks.org/cable/2009/02/09BISHKEK108.html.

31. U.S. Embassy Cable 09BISHKEK131, "Manas, Moscow, and Money: A Proposal." U.S. Embassy in Bishkek, February 12, 2009, http://wikileaks.org/cable/2009/02/09BISHKEK131.html.

32. U.S. Embassy Cable 09BISHKEK131.

33. For details on the final negotiations, see U.S. Embassy Cable 09BISHKEK299, "Kyrgyzstan: Provisional Agreement Reached to Continue Operations at Manas." U.S. Embassy in Bishkek, April 4, 2009, http://wikileaks.org/cable/2009/04/09BISHKEK299.html.

34. Deirdre Tynan, "Corruption Crackdown Intensifies in Bishkek," *Eurasianet*, November 2, 2010.

35. U.S. Embassy Cable 09BISHKEK157, "(C) Kyrgyz President's Son Alleges Interests in the U.S.-Manas Deal." U.S. Embassy in Bishkek, February 23, 2009, http://wikileaks.org/cable/2009/02/09BISHKEK157.html.

36. U.S. Embassy Cable 09BISHKEK744, "Kyrgyzstan: Dinner at Maxim's." U.S. Embassy in Bishkek, July 9, 2009, http://www.wikileaks.org/cable/2009/07/09BISHKEK744.html.

37. U.S. Embassy Cable 09BISHKEK744.

38. U.S. Embassy Cable 09BISHKEK1065, "Lunch with Max: Soup to Nuts." U.S. Embassy in Bishkek, September 22, 2009, http://www.wikileaks.org/cable/2009/09/09BISHKEK1065.htm.

39. "Mystery at Manas: Strategic Blind Spots in the Department of Defense's Fuel Contracts in Kyrgyzstan," Report of the Majority Staff, Subcommittee on National Security and Foreign Affairs, Committee on Oversight and Government Report. (Washington, D.C.: December 2010), 30.

40. See "Uzbekistan Throws Temper Tantrum over New Russian Base in Kyrgyzstan," *Eurasianet*, August 3, 2009.

41. OSCE, "Kyrgyz Republic Presidential Election OSCE/ODIHR Election Observation Mission Final Report," July 23, 2009, http://www.osce.org/odihr/elections/kyrgyzstan/39923.

42. See Erica Marat, "Kyrgyzstan," *Nations in Transit 2009* (New York: FreedomHouse, 2009), 284–299.

43. On the Tulip Revolution and international actors, see David Lewis, "Dynamics of Regime Change: Domestic and International Factors in the 'Tulip Revolution,'" *Central Asian Survey* 27, no. 3–4 (September 2008), 265–277.

44. See U.S. Embassy Cable 09BISHKEK1201, "Kyrgyzstan Proposes Joint Counterterrorism Center in the South." U.S. Embassy in Bishkek, November 16, 2009, http://wikileaks.org/cable/2009/11/09BISHKEK1201.html.

45. Deirdre Tynan, "U.S. Intends to Construct Military Training Center at Batken," *Eurasianet*, March 3, 2010.

46. A helpful list has been compiled by Ryskelde Satke. "Russian Media Offensive, Pre and Post-Crisis Kyrgyzstan," http://agonist.org/20101129/russian_media_offensive_pre_post_crisis_kyrgyzstan

47. "Otets i Syn," *Nezavisimaya Gazeta*, November 2, 2009.

48. See "Mystery at Manas," 46; and David Trilling and Chinghiz Umetov, "Is Putin Punishing Bakiyev?" *Eurasianet*, April 5, 2010.

49. See Eugene Huskey, "If You Want to Understand Kyrgyzstan, Read This," *Salon*, April 9, 2010.

50. Author's interviews with Kyrgyz Interim Government officials, Bishkek, May 2010.

51. Steve Crabtree, "U.S. Approval Gains Intact in Most CIS Countries," *Gallup*, March 9, 2011, http://www.gallup.com/poll/146528/Approval-Gains-Intact-CIS-Countries.aspx.

52. Author's interviews with Kyrgyz Interim Government officials, Bishkek, Kyrgyzstan, May 2010.

53. Detailed accounts of the historical origins and proximate causes of the violence are given in: Kyrgyzstan Inquiry Commission, "Report of the Independent International Commission of Inquiry into the Events in Southern Kyrgyzstan in June 2010," http://www.kic.org/images/stories/kic_report_english_final.pdf; Neil Melvin, "Promoting a Stable and Multiethnic Kyrgyzstan: Overcoming the Causes and Legacies of Violence," Central Eurasia Working Paper Series, No. 3. March 2011; and International Crisis Group, "The Pogroms in Kyrgyzstan," ICG Asia Report no. 193, August 23, 2010.

54. Kyrgyzstan Inquiry Commission, "Report of the Independent International Commission of Inquiry into the Events in Southern Kyrgyzstan in June 2010."

55. Eric McGlinchey, "Exploring Regime Instability and Ethnic Violence in Kyrgyzstan," *Asia Policy* no. 12 (July 2011), 79–98.

Chapter 8

1. See Keith Darden, "The Integrity of Corrupt States: Graft as an Informal Institution," *Politics & Society* 36, no. 1 (March 2008), 35–60.

2. For an overview of the so-called resource curse arguments and literature, see Michael L. Ross, "The Political Economy of the Resource Curse," *World Politics* 51, no. 2 (1999), 297–322. For an examination of the issue in Central Asia, see Svetlana Tsalik, ed., *Caspian Oil Windfalls: Who Will Benefit?* (New York: Open Society Institute, 2003). On the institutionalization of international aid, corruption, and patrimonialism in Africa, see Nicolas van de Walle, *African Economies and the Politics of Permanent Crisis, 1979–1999* (New York: Cambridge University Press, 2001).

3. See Edward C. Chow and Leigh E. Hendrik, "Central Asia's Pipelines: Field of Dreams and Reality," in Ed Chow et al., *Pipeline Politics in Asia: The Intersection of Demand, Energy Markets, and Supply Routes* (Seattle: The National Bureau of Asian Research, September 2010).

4. See "Kazakhstan Ends Tax Break after China Cut from Project," *Platt's Oilgram News*, May 19, 2003.

5. See Kimberly Marten, "Russian Efforts to Control Kazakhstan's Oil: The Kumkol Case," *Post-Soviet Affairs* 27, no. 1 (2007), 18–37.

6. As quoted in "Gazprom, CNPC Circle Kazakhstan's Oil Fields 'Like Vultures,' Leak Shows," *Bloomberg*, December 1, 2010.

7. David Chaikin and J. C. Sharman, *Corruption and Money Laundering: A Symbiotic Convergence* (London: Palgrave Macmillan, 2009), 1.

8. On the contours and politics of the offshore realm, see Ronen Palan, Richard Murphy, and Christian Chavagneux, *Tax Havens: How Globalization Really Works* (Ithaca, NY: Cornell University Press, 2010); Jason Sharman, "Offshore and the New International Political Economy," *Review of International Political Economy* 17, no. 1 (January 2010), 1–19.

9. John Heathershaw, "Tajikistan Amidst Globalization: State Failure or State Transformation?" *Central Asian Survey* 30, no. 1 (March 2011), 147–168.

10. Megan Murphy, Tajikistan Turns on Rusal after TALCO Deal," *Financial Times*, November 28, 2008.

11. Data from National Bank of the Republic of Kazakhstan, as of June 22, 2011, accessed at http://www.nationalbank.kz/?docid=680.

12. See Jason C. Sharman, "Chinese Capital Flows and Offshore Centers," *Pacific Review*, (forth-coming 2013); William Vlsek, "Byways and Highways of Direct Investment: China and the Offshore World," *Journal of Chinese Current Affairs* 39, no. 4 (2010), 112–114.

13. See Global Witness, "It's a Gas: Funny Business in the Turkmen-Ukraine Gas Trade," London and Washington, DC, April 2006. According to a leaked U.S. Embassy cable, Itera also allegedly gifted Turkmenistan's new president a 60 million euro luxury yacht. See "U.S. Embassy Cables: President of Turkmenistan Wanted 'Abramovich-style' Yacht," *The Guardian*, December 2, 2010.

14. The most detailed investigative analysis of Giffen's role can be found in Steve LeVine, *The Oil and the Glory: the Pursuit of Empire and Fortune on the Caspian Sea* (New York: Random House, 2007).

15. Seymour Hersh, "The Price of Oil: What was Mobil up to in Kazakhstan and Russia?" *The New Yorker*, July 9, 2001, 51. Giffen was also the model for the shady middleman played by Tim Blake Nelson in the popular movie *Syriana* (2005).

16. Hersh, "The Price of Oil," 51; and LeVine, *Oil and the Glory*, 288–289.

17. For a fascinating account of this investigative trail, see Levine, *Oil and the Glory*, 374–377; and Steve Levine and Bill Powell, "Following the Monday; Behind the Case That Won't Go Away. New Clues on the Trial of Oil and Cash," *Newsweek*, July 24, 2000.

18. *United States of America v. James H. Giffen*, United States District Court, Southern District of New York, 473 F.3d. April 2, 2003. All case material accessed at: http://www.justice.gov/criminal/fraud/fcpa/cases/giffen-etal.html. LeVine notes that the cash payments were greater as they included bonuses paid by European companies, but these were not illegal at the time according to European bribery laws. LeVine *Oil and the Glory*, 375.

19. *United States of America v. James H. Giffen*, at paragraph 32.

20. *United States of America v. James H. Giffen*, at paragraphs 15–17.

21. Kenneth Gilpin, "Former Mobil Executive Pleads Guilty to Tax Evasion," *New York Times*, June 13, 2003.

22. Jeff Gerth, "U.S. Businessman Is Accused of Oil Bribes to Kazakhstan," *New York Times*, April 1, 2003.

23. Ron Stodghill, "Oil, Cash and Corruption," *New York Times*, November 5, 2006; and "Nursultan Nazarbayev in 'Kazakhgate' Cover-up," *Kommersant*, September 26, 2006.

24. See U.S. Embassy Cable, 07ASTANA1430, "Kazakhstan Economic and Energy Update, April 29–May 12, 2007." U.S. Embassy in Astana, May 28, 2007, http://wikileaks.org/cable/2007/05/07ASTANA1430.html.

25. See "Bribery Case Hinges on National Security," *Washington Times*, December 17, 2005; and Stodghill, "Oil, Cash and Corruption."

26. See Elizabeth Spahn, "Discovering Secrets: Act of State Defenses to Bribery Cases," *Hofstra Law Review* 38, no. 1 (2009) 163–210.

27. U.S. Department of Justice, "New York Merchant Bank Pleads Guilty to FCPA Violation; Bank Chairman Pleads Guilty to Failing to Disclose Control of Foreign Bank Account," August 6, 2010, http://www.justice.gov/opa/pr/2010/August/10-crm-909.html.

28. David Glovin, "Cold War Patriot Defense Helps Oil Man Beat U.S. Bribe Charge," *Bloomberg*, December 16, 2010.

29. See Guy Chazan, "Kazakh Spat Casts Light on China Deals: Exiled Banker Alleges Chinese Oil Firm Routed $166 Million to Associate of Top Oil Executive, as Part of 2003 State Sell," *Wall Street Journal*, March 26, 2010. Also see Steve LeVine's blog commentary on the case after a personal review of these documents. Steve LeVine, "China, $165 Million and Kazakhstan's Second Son-in-Law," *Oil and Glory* (weblog), March 27, 2010, http://stevelevine.info/2010/03/china-165-million-and-kazakhstans-second-son-in-law-2.

30. Mukhamedhzan Adil, "Baksheesh Dlya Zyatya?" *Respublika*, January 22, 2010, http://www.respublika-kaz.biz/news/polit_process/3626/

31. "CNPC Pays $140-mil for Control of Caspian Unit," *Platts Oilgram News*, October 13, 2005.

32. Chazan, "Kazakh Spat Casts Light on China Deals"; Levine, "China, $165 Million and Kazakhstan's Second Son-in-Law." Also see Ablyazov's open letter to Chinese officials, "Naydite i Nakazhite Vzyatkodatele!" *Respublika*, February 1, 2010, http://respublika-kz.info/news/politics/7371.

33. See "Kazakh Newspapers Seized for Alleging Corruption by President's Son-In-Law," *RFE/RL*, February 2, 2010.

34. As laid out in Ablyazov's Letter to the Chair of the UK Parliamentary Committee on Foreign Affairs. "HR 217: Letter to the Chair from Mukhtar Ablyazov," March 9, 2010, at http://www.publications.parliament.uk/pa/cm200910/cmselect/cmfaff/memo/human/m21702.htm.

35. "CNPC Says It Complied with Laws in 2003 Kazakh Deal," *Reuters*, March 12, 2010.

36. I am thankful to Steve Levine for his insights on this point.

37. See Alexander Cooley "Manas Hysteria: Why the United States Can't Keep Buying Off Kyrgyz Leaders to Keep its Vital Base Open," *Foreign Policy*, April 12, 2010.

38. Author's briefing with base officials at the Manas Transit Center, Kyrgyzstan, June 15, 2011.

39. "Mystery at Manas: Strategic Blind Spots in the Department of Defense's Fuel Contracts in Kyrgyzstan." Washington D.C.: Report of the Majority Staff, Subcommittee on National Security and Foreign Affairs, Committee on Oversight and Government, December 2010, ii.

40. "Mystery at Manas," 11–12.

41. David Cloud, "Pentagon's Fuel Deal Is Lesson in Risks of Graft-Prone Regions," *New York Times*, November 15, 2005.

42. Aram Roston, "A Crooked Alliance in the War on Terror?" *NBC News*, October 30, 2006. According to reports by their U.S. banks, "Manas and Aalam are tied to transactions with arms traffickers, Politically Exposed Persons (PEPs) and a myriad of suspicious U.S. shell companies associated with the Akaev Organization."

43. "Mystery at Manas," 26–28. Under Bakiyev, units of Manas International Services were renamed Aircraft Petrol Management (APM) and then Aero Fuels Service (AFS), both managed by a new company, Kyrgyz Aviation Services (KAS). In 2007, Red Star broke the duopoly of the suppliers by setting up, through KAS, a direct supply off-loading header around the perimeter of the base. Soon after Aalam and MIS were phased out and the supply subcontract was managed by a new company, Manas Aerofuels, which was 50% owned by an employee of Mina and Red Star, and 50% owned by a subsidiary of the Russian giant Gazprom (apparently unbeknown to DLA-Energy). In 2008, Mina apparently advanced money to Manas Aerofuels to purchase the storage facilities surrounding the base, while it also formed two additional supply companies.

44. See Deirdre Tynan, "Deconstructing Manas Fuel Suppliers' Corporate Structures," *Eurasianet*, May 3, 2010. Interestingly, these offices shared the same address as *Iraq Today*, a newspaper that briefly circulated after the U.S. invasion of Iraq in 2003.

45. In 2007 Mina's "net current assets" were valued at just 8,390 UK pounds, while in 2009 the total number of Mina shares was 20,002 shares, which were valued at 20,002 pounds. See Tynan, "Deconstructing Manas Fuel Suppliers' Corporate Structures."

46. "Mystery at Manas," 12–13.

47. Author's personal communications with Ronald Uscher, lawyer to IOTC. Also see Aram Roston, "Fueling the Afghan War," *The Nation*, April 21, 2010.

48. Department of the Army, "Memorandum of Understanding Between Red Star Enterprises Limited, Joint Logistics Command, and Task Force Cincinnatus, Bagram Airfield, Afghanistan," unspecified date. Agreement signed and dated by [redacted parties] September 19, October 3 and October 23, 2007.

49. The author testified on April 22, 2010, at the Subcommittee on Security and Foreign Relations, Committee of Oversight's first hearing. Testimony at http://democrats.oversight.house.gov/images/stories/subcommittees/NS_Subcommittee/4.22.2010_Crisis_in_Kyrgyzstan/Cooley_Testimony.pdf.

50. John Tierney, Letter Presenting Final Report, in "Mystery at Manas," ii.
51. "Mystery at Manas," 2–3.
52. "Mystery at Manas," 3.
53. Chuck Squires described the fuel certification scheme that flouted Russian law in the following manner: "We got one over on 'em. I am an old 'Cold Warrior,' I'm proud of it, we beat the Russians, and we did it for four or five years. Obviously it was not without their knowledge. If they looked at the volumes, they had to know where this was all going. But they were making money and they were all happy," "Mystery at Manas," 45.
54. This contrast between officially contested "high politics" and behind the scenes smuggling networks parallels Andreas's observations of the dynamics of the siege of Sarajevo. See Peter Andreas, *Blue Helmets and Black Markets: The Business of Survival in the Siege of Sarajevo* (Ithaca, NY: Cornell University Press, 2008).
55. Andrew E. Kramer, "Kyrgyzstan Opens an Inquiry into Fuel Sales to a U.S. Base," *New York Times*, May 4, 2010.
56. Roston, "Fueling the Afghan War."
57. "Otunbayeva Pledges to End Corrupt Fuel Deliveries to Transit Center," *Interfax*, January 24, 2011.
58. Scott Horton, "Base Politics and Fuel Contracts: The United States-Kyrgyzstan Relationship in Flux." Prepared remarks for the conference "How Central Is Central Asia?" Third Annual Russia/Eurasia Davis Center-Harriman Institute Forum, Columbia University, New York, October 25, 2010.
59. See Andrew Higgins, "Kyrgyz Contracts Fly under the Radar," *Washington Post*, November 1, 2010; Richard Orange, "Kyrgyz President Accuses U.S. Fuel Supplier of Trying to Corrupt Her Son," *The Telegraph*, January 24, 2011.
60. Glenn Kessler and Andrew Higgins, "U.S. Will Give a Share of the Fuel Contract to Kyrgyzstan, Clinton Says," *Washington Post*, December 3, 2010.
61. Deirdre Tynan, "Is Manas Fuel Supplier Pulling Out?" *Eurasianet*, June 23, 2011.
62. See Centralasia.ru, "Korruptsionnye skhemy pri postavkakh aviatopliva na aviabazu Manas v Kirgizii," February 8, 2011.
63. $1,268 represents the author's best calculations for final purchase price per metric ton. According to the Manas Transit Center web site, DLA paid Mina $3.73 per gallon for fuel. The weight of aviation fuel varies by quality and temperature. According to ExxonMobil, Russian TS-1 jet fuel has a density of 0.70 kg/liter, "World Jet Fuel Specifications," at http://www.exxonmobil.com/AviationGlobal/Files/WorldJetFuelSpecifications2005.pdf, 21.
64. Centralasia.ru, "Korruptsionnye skhemy pri postavkakh aviatopliva." In 2010, TKZ purchased a total of 23,000 tons of fuel, with only 7,000 tons purchased directly from the Russian supplier GazpromAero, while 16,000 were purchased from Mega Oil.

Chapter 9

1. On "strategic regionalism," see David Kerr, "Strategic Regionalism: Central Asian and Russian Perspectives on China's Strategic Re-emergence," *International Affairs* 86, no. 1 (January 2010), 127–152.
2. Roy Allison, "Virtual Regionalism, Regional Structures and Regime Security in Central Asia" *Central Asian Survey* 27, no. 2 (June 2008), 185–202. On the social construction of regions and their boundaries more broadly, see Rick Fawn, ed., *Globalising the Regional: Regionalising the Global* (New York: Cambridge University Press, 2009); Peter J. Katzenstein, *A World of Regions: Europe and Asia in the American Imperium* (Ithaca. NY: Cornell University Press, 2005).
3. On types of sovereignty, see Stephen Krasner, *Sovereignty: Organized Hypocrisy* (Princeton: Princeton University Press, 1999).
4. On so-called juridical sovereignty and African states, see Peter Jackson, *Quasi-States: Sovereignty, International Relations and the Third World* (New York: Cambridge University Press, 1993).

5. Author's interviews with members of the Kyrgyz interim government, Bishkek, May 2010.

6. For overviews, see Alexander Cooley, *Logics of Hierarchy: The Organization of Empires, States and Military Occupations* (Ithaca, NY Cornell University Press, 2005); Oksana Dmitrieva, *Regional Development: The USSR and After* (London: UCL Press, 1996); Boris Rumer, *Central Asia: 'A Tragic Experiment'* (Boston: Unwin Hyman, 1990).

7. Gregory Gleason, "Russia and the Politics of the Central Asian Electricity Grid," *Problems of Post-Communism* 50, no. 3 (May/June 2003), 42–52.

8. For an overview of the water issue, see Samuel Chan, "Pyrrhic Victory in the 'Tournament of Shadows': Central Asia's Quest for Water Security," *Asian Security* 6, no. 2 (2010), 121–145. On the social and political problems of the cotton sector, see Deniz Kandiyoti, ed., *The Cotton Sector in Central Asia: Economic Policy and Developmental Changes*. London: Proceedings of a conference held at the School of African and Oriental Studies, 2008. On related regional environmental challenges, see Erica Weinthal, *State Making and Environmental Cooperation: Linking Domestic and International Politics in Central Asia* (Cambridge, MA: MIT Press, 2002).

9. Indeed, as Weinthal (2002) argues, even in supposedly more successful cases of regional cooperation, such as designing a response to the catastrophic disappearance of the Aral Sea, Central Asian officials crafted a set of ad hoc regional arrangements, funded by the international community, that required the redistribution of international assistance to local elites, along traditional patronage lines, to buy their participation. The end result was politically efficient, but environmentally inefficient.

10. See Crisis Group, "Central Asia: Decay and Decline," *Crisis Group Asia Report* no. 201, Brussels, February 21, 2011.

11. U.S. Embassy Cable 09TASHKENT1577, "Uzbek Rail: Red Hot Wheels to Afghanistan." U.S. Embassy in Tashkent, November 12, 2009, http://wikileaks.org/cable/2009/11/09TASHKENT1577.html.

12. See Stephen Blank, "Infrastructural Policy and National Strategies in Central Asia: The Russian Example," *Central Asian Survey* 23, 3–4 (2004), 225–248.

13. Luke Harding, "U.S. Opens Route to Afghanistan Through Russia's Backyard," *The Guardian*, March 29, 2009.

14. See "The New Silk Road," *Newsweek*, May 10, 2010.

15. For overviews on state-centered approaches to regional integration, see Alexander Cooley and Hendrik Spruyt, *Contracting States: Sovereign Transfers in International Relations* (Princeton: Princeton University Press, 2009); Walter Mattli, *The Logic of Regional Integration: Europe and Beyond* (New York: Cambridge University Press, 1999); Andrew Moravcsik, *The Choice for Europe: State Power and Social Purpose from Messina to Maastricht* (Ithaca, NY: Cornell University Press, 1998).

16. For further elaboration, see Kathleen Collins, "Economic and Security Regionalism among Patrimonial Authoritarian Regimes: The Case of Central Asia," *Europe-Asia Studies* 61, no. 2 (March 2009), 249–281.

17. Asian Development Bank, *Central Asia: Increasing Gains from Trade Through Cooperation in Regional Trade Policy, Transport and Customs Transit*. Manila, 2006. Figures 3.2 and 3.3, 29–30.

18. United States Chamber of Commerce, "Survey of Investment Climate, Transport & Trade Facilitation." Prepared for the Eurasian Business Platform, February 2008, http://www.uschamber.com/sites/default/files/international/files/amchamsurvey.pdf.

19. Other Eurasian countries in the sample were Armenia, Azerbaijan, Georgia, Turkey, and Ukraine. No other Central Asian countries were included.

20. Malika Rakhmanova, "Complex Customs and Transportation Procedures Breeding Ground for Corruption, Says Expert," *ASIA-Plus*, June 17, 2008. Unofficial payments to the region's customs services varied somewhat, with Uzbek customs officers demanding on average $248, Kyrgyz customs officers $179, Kazakh customs officers and Tajik customs officers $59.

21. IMF and Central Asian figures from IMF, *Direction of Trade Statistics Yearbook, 2006.* Washington, DC, 2006. Chinese figures from People's Republic of China, Ministry of Commerce, http://english.mofcom.gov.cn/aarticle/statistic/lanmubb/chinaeuropeancountry/200702/20070204345877.html.

22. Richard Orange, "Russia Worries That Customs Union Outpost Is Smugglers' Paradise" *Eurasianet,* February 7, 2011.

23. Stanislav Zhukov and Oksana Reznikova, *Tsentralnaya Aziya i Kitay: Ekonomicheskoe Vzaimodeystvie v Usloviyakh Globalizatsii* [Central Asia and China: Economic Interactions Under Globalization] (Moscow: MGIMO, 2009), 54.

24. See World Bank, *Cross-Border Trade Within the Central Asia Regional Cooperation.* Report prepared for the Asian Development Bank's CAREC, August 2007, http://www.carecinstitute.org/uploads/docs/Cross-Border-Trade-CAREC.pdf.

25. World Bank 2007; and "Torgovyy Koridor Mezhdu Kazakhstanom i Kitaem Otkryt," *Kazinform,* March 28, 2006. Day traders are permitted to purchase up to $1,000 worth of goods not exceeding 50 kilograms.

26. Tellingly, the Kazakh administration of the new center was reassigned to Kazakh national railways two months before its opening, after the Kazakh Chief of Customs was implicated in a $130 million smuggling network. "Khorgos Border Trade Center to Open Friday," *Central Asian Economic Newswire,* November 29, 2011.

27. Nick Megoran, Gaël Raballand, and Jerome Bouyjou, "Performance, Representation and the Economics of Border Control in Uzbekistan," *Geopolitics* 10, no. 4 (2005), 712–740.

28. Megoran, Raballand, and Bouyjou, "Performance, Representation and the Economics of Border Control in Uzbekistan," 719–721.

29. Gavrilis, *Dynamics of Interstate Boundaries,* 147.

30. Gavrilis, *Dynamics of Interstate Boundaries,* 147–148.

31. Daur Dosybiev, "Smugglers' Paradise on Kazak-Uzbek Border," *Institute for War & Peace Reporting,* September 7, 2010, http://iwpr.net/report-news/smugglers-paradise-kazak-uzbek-border.

32. See United Nations Office on Drugs and Crime, "Illicit Drug Trends in Central Asia." Tashkent: UNODC, April 2008, 8. According to the UNODC, China is also increasingly becoming a destination for opiate trafficking.

33. Quoted in Nancy Lubin, "Who's Watching the Watchdogs?" *Journal of International Affairs* 56, no. 2 (Spring 2003), 47.

34. Gavrilis, *Dynamics of Interstate Boundaries,* 116.

35. See Erica Marat, "The State-Crime Nexus in Central Asia: State Weakness, Organized Crime and Corruption in Kyrgyzstan and Tajikistan," Washington, DC: Central Asia-Caucasus Institute and Silk Road Studies Program, October 2006, http://www.silkroadstudies.org/new/docs/Silkroadpapers/0610EMarat.pdf.

36. See UNODC, "Illicit Drug Trends in Central Asia," 6.

37. U.S. Embassy Cable 07DUSHANBE1420, "Tajik President Fires Senior Anti-Narcotics Officer to Protect a Relative." U.S. Embassy in Dushanbe, October 4, 2007, http://www.wikileaks.ch/cable/2007/10/07DUSHANBE1420.html.

38. George Gavrilis, "Beyond the Border Management Program for Central Asia (BOMCA)": *EUCAM EU-Central Asia Monitoring Report,* Brussels: No. 9 (November 2009); and George Camm, "Tajikistan Soldiers: What Have They Done with America's Dogs?" *Eurasianet,* August 25, 2011.

39. Nancy Lubin, Alex Klaits, and Igor Barsegian, "Narcotics Interdiction in Afghanistan and Central Asia: Challenge for US Assistance." New York: Report Prepared for the Open Society Institute, 2002, 13.

40. See Nicole J. Jackson, "The Trafficking of Narcotics, Arms and Humans in Post-Soviet Central Asia," *Central Asian Survey* 24, no. 1 (March 2005), 39–52.

41. See Peter Andreas and Kelly Greenhill, eds., *Sex, Drugs and Body Counts: The Politics of Numbers in Global Crime and Conflict.* Ithaca, NY: Cornell University Press, 2010.

42. See Nargis Hamroboyeva, "UNODC Renovates Border Post in Tajikistan with Funds Supplied by the US Government," *Asia-Plus, Tajikistan News,* May 17, 2005; and Victoria Panfilova, "Pogranichnyy Kambek," *Nezavisimaya Gazeta,* December 13, 2010.

43. See the descriptions in U.S. Embassy Cable 09ASHGABAT992, "Turkmenistan, Scenesetter for the Visit of CENTCOM Commander General David Petraeus." U.S. Embassy in Ashgabat, August 5, 2009, at http://wikileaks.org/cable/2009/08/09ASHGABAT992.html.

44. See U.S. Embassy Cable 10MOSCOW226, "Scenesetter for February 4 U.S.-Bilateral Presidential Drug-Trafficking Working Group Meeting." U.S. Embassy in Moscow, January 29, 2009, at http://wikileaks.org/cable/2010/01/10MOSCOW226.html.

45. See Alexander Cooley, "The Kyrgyz Crisis and the Political Logic of Central Asia's Weak Security Mechanisms," PONARS Eurasia Policy Memo 140, May 2011, http://www.gwu.edu/~ieresgwu/assets/docs/ponars/pepm_140.pdf.

Chapter 10

1. U.S. Embassy Cable 09BISHKEK1147, "Door to Manas May be Opening for the French." U.S. Embassy in Bishkek, October 23, 2010, http://wikileaks.org/cable/2009/10/09BISHKEK1147.html.

2. Author's interviews with French diplomatic officials, Dushanbe, May 2010. Also see David Trilling, "French Air Detachment in Dushanbe Quietly Carries Out Afghan Mission," *Eurasianet,* May 18, 2009.

3. Author's communications with German Foreign Ministry officials, Berlin, March 2010.

4. Deirdre Tynan, "Veil Is Lifted on German Payments for Termez Base," *Eurasianet,* March 24, 2011.

5. Christian Neef, "Germany's Favorite Despot," SpiegelOnline, August 2, 2006, http://www.spiegel.de/international/28 spiegel/0,1518,429712,00.html.

6. Alexander Cooley "Principles in the Pipeline," *International Affairs,* 84, no. 6 (November–December 2008), 1178–1180.

7. U.S. Embassy Cable 07TASHKENT093, "Germans Discuss Stagnant CT Relationship with Uzbeks." U.S. Embassy in Tashkent, May 8, 2007, http://wikileaks.org/cable/2007/05/07TASHKENT913.html.

8. Council of the European Union, "European Union and Central Asia: Strategy for a New Partnership," Brussels: October 2010, http://www.consilium.europa.eu/uedocs/cmsUpload/EU_CtrlAsia_EN-RU.pdf.

9. For overviews, see Neil Melvin, Bhavna Dave. and Michael Denison, eds. *Engaging Central Asia: The European Union's New Strategy in the Heart of Eurasia* (Washington. DC: Brookings, 2008). For an initial evaluation, see Neil Melvin and Jos Boonstra, "The EU Strategy for Central Asia @ Year One," *EUCAM Monitoring Report,* no. 1 (October 2008), http://www.fride.org/publication/512/the-eu-strategy-for-central-asia:-year-one.

10. Author's personal communications with NGO leaders in Brussels.

11. On the flaws in the EU's sanctions regime against Uzbekistan, see Andrea Schmitz, "Whose Conditionality? The Failure of EU Sanctions Against Uzbekistan." *CACI Analyst,* November 11, 2009, http://www.cacianalyst.org/?q=node/5216.

12. I am thankful to Jacqui Hale for her insights on this point.

13. See Scott Moore, "Peril and Promise: A Survey of India's Strategic Relationship with Central Asia," *Central Asian Survey* 26, no. 2 (September 2007), 279–291.

14. See especially Emilian Kavalski, *India and Central Asia: Mythmaking and International Relations of a Rising Power* (London: I. B. Tauris, 2010).

15. See, for instance, Nirmala Joshi, ed., "Reconnecting India and Central Asia," *CACI Paper,* 2010, http://www.silkroadstudies.org/new/inside/publications/Joshi.html; Sreeram Caulia, "India's Central Asian Struggle," *The International Indian* (June 2008), 22–23.

16. International Monetary Fund, *Direction of Trade Statistics 2010,* Washington, DC, 2010.

17. See, for instance, optimistic press reports like Rahul Bedi, "IAF to Station MiG-29s in Tajikistan," *The Tribune,* April 22, 2006, http://www.tribuneindia.com/2006/20060422/main6.htm.

18. Author's interviews with Western diplomats and defense officials, Dushanbe, May 2010. As one US cable from New Delhi aptly framed this base speculation, "India has compelling national security concerns in Central Asia, but its lack of capacity—unlike the Chinese and Russians—likely compels it to leak aspirational fiction about plans for airbases in order to keep rivals guessing." U.S. Embassy Cable 07NEWDELHI3521, "Indian Views of Central Asia: Airbase Hopes and Fears of Chinese Influence and Islamic Extremism." U.S. Embassy in New Delhi, August 3, 2007, http://wikileaks.org/cable/2007/08/07NEWDELHI3521.html. Also see the US cable that describes the Indian Ambassador's coy description about Indian motives at Ayni. U.S. Embassy Cable 06DUSHANBE 776, "India Looks to Revive Silk Road Heritage, Not Great Game." U.S. Embassy in Dushanbe, April 26, 2006, http://wikileaks.org/cable/2006/04/06DUSHANBE776.html.

19. See Archis Mohan, "Tajik Cold Water on Base Space," *The Calcutta Telegraph*, January 2, 2011. For analysis, see Roman Muzalevsky, "India Fails to Gain a Military Foothold in Tajikistan," *CACI Analyst*, February 2, 2011.

20. For the new command's mission statement, objectives and activities, see http://www.africom.mil/AboutAFRICOM.asp. The most comprehesive account of China's rise in Africa is found in Deborah Brautigam, *The Dragon's Gift: The Real Story of China in Africa* (New York: Oxford University Press, 2009).

21. "Angola Overtakes Saudi Arabia as Biggest Oil Supplier to China," *Bloomberg*, April 21, 2008.

22. See, for instance, Council on Foreign Relations, "Toward an Angola Strategy: Prioritizing US-Angola Relations." May 2007, http://www.cfr.org/energy-security/toward-angola-strategy/p13155.

23. See Maggie Fick, "US Millions Fund Sudan Army: Worry over Abuses," *Associate Press*, July 2, 2011.

24. On local negative reactions to AFRICOM, see A. Carl LeVan, "The Political Economy of African Responses to the U.S. Africa Command," *Africa Today* 57, no. 1 (Fall 2010), 3–23.

25. See Andrew Bacevich, *The New American Militarism: How Americans Are Seduced by War.* (New York: Oxford University Press, 2005).

26. A few months following the February 2008 announcement, Hutchison withdrew from the deal, citing the Ecuadorian government's changing of contractual terms. Following China's 2009 energy deal with Ecuador, reports resurfaced that Quito was courting Chinese investment to develop the facility as a commercial airport. See Eduardo Garcia, "Oil-Hungry China Moves to Strengthen Ecuador Ties," *Reuters*, July 13, 2009.

27. See Alexander Cooley and Daniel Nexon, "Bahrain's Base Politics: The Arab Spring and America's Military Bases," *Foreign Affairs.com*, April 5, 2011.

28. See Charles Kindleberger, *The World in Depression, 1929–1939* (Berkeley: University of California Press, 1976).

29. This point is sometimes overlooked in discussions of leadership and world orders, as in Ikenberry's otherwise comprehensive assessment of the state of the U.S.-led order. See G. John Ikenberry, *Liberal Leviathan: The Origins, Crisis, and Transformation of the American World Order* (Princeton: Princeton University Press, 2011).

30. Julie Jiang and Jonathan Sinton, "Overseas Investments by Chinese Oil Companies: Assessing the Drivers and Impacts," *International Energy Agency Information Paper.* (February 2011), 41, http://www.iea.org/papers/2011/overseas_china.pdf.

31. FreedomHouse, "Freedom in the World 2011," http://www.freedomhouse.org/images/File/fiw/FIW_2011_Booklet.pdf.

32. Though, see Levitsy and Way's important account of the post–Cold War rise of "competitive authoritarian" regimes; Steven A. Levitsky and Lucan Way, *Competitive Authoritarianism: Hybrid Regimes after the Cold War* (New York: Cambridge University Press, 2010), 16–20.

33. Randa Habib, "Jordan, Morocco Could Boost GCC 'Monarchy Club'," *AFP*, May 11, 2011.

34. Jim Lobe, "U.S. Keeps Quiet over Repression [Bahrain]" *IPS*, April 13, 2011.

35. Acharya refers to this regional adaptation of Western political norms as "constitutive local-ization." See Amitav Acharya, *Whose Ideas Matter? Agency and Power in Asian Regionalism* (Ithaca, NY: Cornell University Press, 2009).

36. Comments by Kenneth Roth, Executive Director of Human Rights Watch. New York: Columbia University forum on "Religion and Human Rights Pragmatism," September 24, 2011.

37. "Tunisian Minister Ridicules EU Aid Effort," *Euractiv.com*, February 18, 2011.

38. See "Egypt Drops Plans for IMF Loan among Popular Distrust," *BBC News*, June 25, 2011; and Ty McCormick, "Egypt Looks to Gulf Monarchies to Finance Budget Deficit," *Foreign Policy*, June 29, 2011.

39. Following a meeting with the foreign minister of Egypt on September 28, 2011, U.S. Secre-tary of State Hillary Rodham Clinton criticized the proposed conditioning of the aid package in the following terms, "We will be working very hard with the Congress to con-vince the Congress that that is not the best approach to take. We believe that the longstand-ing relationship between the United States and Egypt is of paramount importance to both of us. We support the democratic transition, and we don't want to do anything that in any way draws into question our relationship or our support." See Emily Cadei, "State Dept. Pushes Back Against Senate Aid to Arab Spring Countries," *Congressional Quarterly Online News*, September 30, 2011.

40. Though certain sound partial recommendations are now being made. See, for example, Bruce W. Jentleson and Steven Weber, *The End of Arrogance: America in the Global Compe-tition of Ideas* (Cambridge, MA: Harvard University Press, 2010).

41. Bruce W. Jentleson, "Beware the Duck Test," The Washington Quarterly, 34, no. 3 (Summer 2011), 137–149.

42. Acharya, *Whose Ideas Matter?*

BIBLIOGRAPHY

Abdelal, Rawi. "Interpreting Interdependence: National Security and the Energy Trade of Russia, Belarus and Ukraine," in Robert Legvold and Celeste Wallander, eds., *Swords and Sustenance: The Economics of Security in Belarus and Ukraine*. Cambridge, MA: American Academy of Sciences, 2004.

Abdelal, Rawi. *National Purpose in the World Economy: Post-Soviet States in Comparative Perspective*. Ithaca, NY: Cornell University Press, 2002.

Abdelal, Rawi, Sogomon Tarontsi and Alexander Jorov. "Gazprom (A): Energy and Strategy in Russian History," Harvard Business School Case Study no. 9-709-008, July 7, 2009.

Abdelal, Rawi, Sogomon Tarontsi and Alexander Jorov. "Gazprom (B): Energy and Strategy in a New Era," Harvard Business School Case Study no. 9-709-009, July 7, 2009.

Acharya, Amitav. *Whose Ideas Matter? Agency and Power in Asian Regionalism*. Ithaca, NY: Cornell University Press, 2009.

Acharya, Amitav. "How Ideas Spread: Whose Norms Matter? Norm Localization and Institutional Change in ASEAN," *International Organization* 58, no. 2 (Spring 2004).

Adams, Julia. "Principals and Agents, Colonialists and Company Men: The Decay of Colonial Control in the Dutch East Indies," *American Sociological Review* 61, no. 1 (February 1996).

Adams, Laura. *The Spectacular State: Culture and National Identity in Uzbekistan*. Durham, NC: Duke University Press, 2010.

Adamson, Fiona. "Global Liberalism Versus Political Islam: Competing Ideological Frameworks in International Politics," *International Studies Review* 7, no. 4 (December 2005).

Akbarzadeh, Shahram. *Uzbekistan and the United States: Authoritarianism, Islamism & Washington's Security Agenda*. London: ZED, 2005.

Allison, Roy. "Virtual Regionalism, Regional Structures and Regime Security in Central Asia." *Central Asian Survey* 27, no. 2 (June 2008).

Allison, Roy. "Regionalism, Regional Structures and Security Management in Central Asia," *International Affairs* 80, no. 3 (2004).

Allison, Roy. "Strategic Reassertion in Russia's Central Asia Foreign Policy," *International Affairs* 80, no. 2 (2004).

Allworth, Edward. *Central Asia: 130 years of Russian Dominance*. Durham, NC: Duke University Press, 1994.

Ambrosio, Thomas. *Authoritarian Backlash: Russian Resistance to Democratization in the Former Soviet Union*. Burlington, VT: Ashgate, 2009.

Ambrosio, Thomas. "Catching the 'Shanghai Spirit': How the Shanghai Cooperation Organization Promotes Authoritarian Norms in Central Asia," *Europe-Asia Studies* 60, no. 8 (October 2008).

Anceschi, Luca. "Integrating Domestic Politics and Foreign Policy Making: The Cases of Turkmenistan and Uzbekistan," *Central Asian Survey* 29, no. 2 (June 2010).

Anceschi, Luca. *Turkmenistan's Foreign Policy: Positive Neutrality and the Consolidation of the Turkmen Regime*. London: Routledge, 2008.

Andreas, Peter. *Blue Helmets and Black Markets: The Business of Survival in the Siege of Sarajevo*. Ithaca, NY: Cornell University Press, 2008.

Andreas, Peter, and Kelly Greenhill, eds. *Sex, Drugs and Body Counts: The Politics of Numbers in Global Crime and Conflict*. Ithaca, NY: Cornell University Press, 2010.

Aris, Stephen. "The Shanghai Cooperation Organisation: 'Tackling the Three Evils,'" *Europe-Asia Studies* 61, no. 3 (May 2009).

Asian Development Bank. *Central Asia: Increasing Gains from Trade through Cooperation in Regional Trade Policy, Transport and Customs Transit*. Manila: ADB, 2006.

Aslund, Anders. "Gazprom: Challenged Giant in Need of Reform," in Anders Aslund, Sergei Guriev, and Andrew Kuchins, eds., *Russia after the Global Economic Crisis*. Washington, DC: Peterson Institute, 2010.

Bacevich, Andrew. *The New American Militarism: How Americans Are Seduced by War*. New York: Oxford University Press, 2005.

Bailes, Alyson J. K. "The Shanghai Cooperation Organisation and Europe," *China and Eurasia Forum Quarterly* 5, no. 3 (2007).

Barma, Naazneen, Ely Ratner, and Steven Weber. "A World Without the West," *National Interest* no. 90 (2007).

Bates, Robert. *When Things Fell Apart: State Failure in Late-Century Africa*. New York: Cambridge University Press, 2008.

Becker, Seymour. *Russia's Protectorates in Central Asia: Bukhara and Khiva, 1865–1924*. Cambridge, MA: Harvard University Press, 1968.

Beissinger, Mark. "Structure and Example in Modular Political Phenomena: The Diffusion of the Bulldozer/Rose/Orange/Tulip Revolutions," *Perspectives on Politics* 5, no. 2 (June 2007).

Beissinger, Mark, and Crawford Young, eds. *Beyond State Crisis? Postcolonial Africa and Post-Soviet Eurasia in Comparative Perspective*. Baltimore: Johns Hopkins University Press, 2002.

Bequelin, Nicolas. "Staged Development in Xinjiang," *The China Quarterly* 178 (July 2004).

Blank, Stephen. "Eurasia's Energy Triangle: China, Russia and the Central Asian States," *Brown Journal of World Affairs* 12, no. 2 (2006).

Blank, Stephen. "Infrastructural Policy and National Strategies in Central Asia: The Russian Example," *Central Asian Survey* 23, 3–4 (2004).

Bueno de Mesquita, Bruce, Alistair Smith, Randolph M. Siverson, and James D. Murrow. *The Logic of Political Survival*. Cambridge, MA: MIT Press, 2003.

Brautigam, Deborah. *The Dragon's Gift: The Real Story of China in Africa*. New York: Oxford University Press, 2009.

Brooks, Stephen, and William Wohlforth. "Hard Times for Soft Balancing," *International Security* 30, no. 1 (Summer 2005).

Brooks, Stephen, and William C. Wohlforth. *World Out of Balance: International Relations and the Challenge of American Primacy*. Princeton: Princeton University Press, 2008.

Broom, André. *The Currency of Power: The IMF and Monetary Reform in Central Asia*. New York: Palgrave Macmillan, 2010.

Brzezinski, Zbigniew. *The Grand Chessboard: American Primacy and Geostrategic Imperatives*. New York: Basic, 1997.

Bunce, Valerie, and Sharon Wolchik. "International Diffusion and Postcommunist Electoral Revolutions," *Communist and Postcommunist Studies* 39, no. 3 (September 2006).

Burg, Steven L. "Muslim Cadres and Soviet Political Development," *World Politics* 37, no. 1 (October 1984).

Carothers, Thomas. "The End of the Transition Paradigm," *Journal of Democracy* 13, no. 1 (January 2002).

Chaikin, David, and J. C. Sharman. *Corruption and Money Laundering: A Symbiotic Convergence*. London: Palgrave Macmillan, 2009.

Chan, Samuel. "Pyrrhic Victory in the 'Tournament of Shadows': Central Asia's Quest for Water Security," *Asian Security* 6, no. 2 (2010).

Chaudhry, Kiren Aziz. "The Price of Wealth: Business and State Labor Remittance and Oil Econo-mies," *International Organization* 43, no. 1 (Winter 1989).

Chen, Titus C. "China's Reaction to the Color Revolutions," *Asian Perspective* 34, no. 2 (2010).

Chernykh, Irina, and Rustam Burnashev, "Conditions for Securitization of International Terrorism in Central Asia," *Connections: The Quarterly Journal* 4, no. 1 (Spring 2005).

Chow, Edward C., and Leigh E. Hendrik. "Central Asia's Pipelines: Field of Dreams and Reality," in Edward Chow, et al., *Pipeline Politics in Asia: The Intersection of Demand, Energy Markets, and Supply Routes.* Seattle: The National Bureau of Asian Research, Special Report no. 23, September 2010.

Chun, Chien-peng. "China's 'War on Terror': September 11 and Uighur Separatism," *Foreign Affairs* 81, no. 4 (July/August 2002).

Clarke, Michael. *Xinjiang and China's Rise in Central Asia: A History.* New York: Routledge, 2011.

Clarke, Michael. "Widening the Net: China's Anti-Terror Laws and Human Rights in the Uyghur Autonomous Region," *The International Journal of Human Rights* 14, no. 4 (July 2010).

Coll, Steve. *Ghost Wars: The Secret History of the CIA, Afghanistan, and Bin Laden, from the Soviet Invasion to September 10, 2001.* New York: Penguin, 2004.

Collins, Kathleen. "Economic and Security Regionalism among Patrimonial Authoritarian Regimes: The Case of Central Asia," *Europe-Asia Studies* 61, no. 2 (March 2009).

Collins, Kathleen. *Clan Politics and Regime Transition in Central Asia.* New York: Cambridge University Press, 2006.

Collins, Kathleen, and William C. Wohlforth. "Central Asia: Defying 'Great Games' Expectations," in *Strategic Asia 2003–2004*, Richard J. Ellings, Aaron L. Friedberg, and Michael Wills, eds., Seattle: National Bureau of Asian Research, 2003.

Cooley, Alexander. "Behind the Central Asian Curtain: The Limit's of Russia's Resurgence," *Current History* 108, no. 720 (October 2009).

Cooley, Alexander. *Base Politics: Democratic Change and the U.S. Military Overseas.* Ithaca, NY: Cornell University Press, 2008.

Cooley, Alexander. "Principles in the Pipeline: Managing Transatlantic Values and Interests in Central Asia," *International Affairs* 84, no. 6 (2008).

Cooley, Alexander. "Base Politics," *Foreign Affairs* 84, no. 6 (November/December 2005).

Cooley, Alexander. *Logics of Hierarchy: The Organization of Empires, States and Military Occupa-tions.* Ithaca, NY: Cornell University Press, 2005.

Cooley, Alexander. "International Aid to the Former Soviet States: Agent of Change or Guardian of the Status Quo?" *Problems of Post-Communism* 47, no. 4 (July/August 2000).

Cooley, Alexander, and James Ron. "The NGO Scramble: Organizational Insecurity and the Political Economy of Transnational Action." *International Security* 27, no. 1 (Summer 2002).

Cooley, Alexander, and Hendrik Spruyt. *Contracting States: Sovereign Transfers in International Relations.* Princeton: Princeton University Press, 2009.

Critchlow, James. *Nationalism in Uzbekistan: A Soviet Republic's Road to Sovereignty.* Boulder, Colo.: Westview, 1991.

Cummings, Sally. *Kazakhstan: Power and the Elite.* New York: Palgrave Macmillan, 2005.

Cummings, Sally, ed. *Power and Change in Central Asia.* New York: Routledge, 2002.

Darden, Keith. *Economic Liberalism and Its Rivals: The Formation of International Institutions among the Post-Soviet States.* New York: Cambridge University Press, 2010.

Darden, Keith. "The Integrity of Corrupt States: Graft as an Informal Institution," *Politics & Society* 36, no. 1 (March 2008).

Dave, Bhavna. *Kazakhstan: Ethnicity, Language and Power.* New York: Routledge. 2007.

Dmitrieva, Oksana Olga. *Regional Development: The USSR and After.* London: UCL Press, 1996.

Dowding, Keith M., and Richard Kimber. "The Meaning and Use of 'Political Stability,'" *European Journal of Political Research* 1, no. 3 (September 1983).

Driscoll, Jesse Russell. "Exiting Anarchy: Militia Politics after the Post-Soviet Wars." PhD diss., Stanford University, 2009.

Dunning, Thad. "Conditioning the Effects of Aid: Cold War Politics, Donor Credibility and Democracy in Africa," *International Organization* 54, no. 2 (Spring 2004).

Ebel, Robert, and Rajan Menon, eds. *Energy and Conflict in Central Asia and the Caucasus*. New York: Rowman & Littlefield, 2000.

Edwards, Matthew. "The New Great Game and the New Great Gamers: Disciples of Mackinder and Kipling," *Central Asian Survey* 22, no. 1 (March 2003).

Fawn, Rick, ed. *Globalising the Regional: Regionalising the Global*. New York: Cambridge University Press, 2009.

Fawn, Rick. "Battle over the Box: International Election Observation Missions, Political Competition, and Retrenchment in the post-Soviet Space," *International Affairs* 82, no. 6 (2006).

Fazal, Tanisha M. *State Death: The Politics of and Geography of Conquest, Occupation, and Annexation*. Princeton: Princeton University Press, 2007.

Foot, Rosemary. "The United Nations, Counter Terrorism, and Human Rights: Institutional Adaptation and Embedded Ideas," *Human Rights Quarterly* 29, no. 2 (May 2007).

Fravel, M. Taylor. *Strong Borders, Secure Nation: Cooperation and Conflict in China's Territorial Disputes*. Princeton: Princeton University Press, 2008.

Frye, Timothy. *Building States and Markets after Communism: The Perils of Polarized Democracy*. New York: Cambridge, 2010.

Fumagalli, Matteo. "Alignment and Realignment in Central Asia: The Rationale and Implications of Uzbekistan's Rapprochement with Russia," *International Political Science Review* 28, no. 3 (June 2007).

Gavrilis, George. *The Dynamics of Interstate Boundaries*. New York: Cambridge University Press, 2008.

Gill, Bates. *Rising Star: China's New Security Diplomacy*. Washington, DC: Brookings, 2010, revised.

Gill, Bates, and Yanzhong Huang, "Sources and Limits of Chinese 'Soft Power,'" *Survival* 48, no. 2 (Summer 2006).

Grey, Stephen. *Ghost Plane: The True Story of the CIA Torture Program*. New York: St. Martin's, 2006.

Guang, Pan. "A Chinese Perspective on the Shanghai Cooperation Organisation," in Alyson Bailes, et al., *The Shanghai Cooperation Organization*. Stockholm: SIPRI Policy Paper no. 17, (May 2007).

Gleason, Gregory. *Markets and Politics in Central Asia: Structural Reform and Political Change*. New York: Routledge, 2003.

Gleason, Gregory. "Russia and the Politics of the Central Asian Electricity Grid," *Problems of Post-Communism* 50, no. 3 (May/June 2003).

Gleason, Gregory. "Fealty and Loyalty: Informal Authority Structures in Soviet Asia," *Soviet Studies* 43, no. 1 (1991).

Gleason, Gregory. "Nationalism or Organized Crime? The Case of the 'Cotton Scandal' in the USSR," *Corruption and Reform* 5, no. 2 (1990).

Golden, Peter. *Central Asia in World History*. New York: Oxford University Press, 2011.

Grieco, Joseph. *Cooperation among Nations: Europe, America, and Non-Tariff Barriers to Trade*. Ithaca, NY: Cornell University Press, 1990.

Guriev, Sergei, and Aleh Tsyvinski. "Challenges Facing the Russian Economy after the Crisis," in Anders Aslund, Sergei Guriev and Andrew Kuchins, eds. *Russia after the Global Economic Crisis*. Washington, DC: Peterson Institute, 2010.

Halper, Stefan A. *The Beijing Consensus: How China's Authoritarian Model Will Dominate the Twenty-First Century*. New York: Basic, 2010.

Hawkins, Darren, David A. Lake, Daniel L. Nelson, and Michael J. Tierney, eds. *Delegation and Agency in International Organizations*. New York: Cambridge University Press, 2006.

Heathershaw, John. "Tajikistan Amidst Globalization: State Failure or State Transformation?" *Central Asian Survey* 30, no. 1 (March 2011).

Heathershaw, John. *Post-Conflict Tajikistan: The Politics of Peacebuilding and the Emergence of Legitimate Political Order*. New York: Routledge, 2009.

Hirsch, Francine. *Empire of Nations: Ethnographic Knowledge and the Making of the Soviet Union.* Ithaca, NY: Cornell University Press, 2005.

Hill, Fiona. "Russia Discovers Soft Power," *Current History* 30, no. 2 (October 2006).

Holslag, Jonathan. "China's Road to Influence," *Asian Survey* 50, no. 4 (July/August 2010).

Hopf, Ted. *Social Construction of International Politics: Identities and Foreign Policies, Moscow, 1955 and 1999.* Ithaca, NY: Cornell University Press, 2002.

Hopkirk, Peter. *The Great Game: The Struggle for Empire in Central Asia.* New York: Kodansha, 1990.

Human Rights Watch. *Are You Happy to Cheat Us? Exploitation of Migrant Construction Workers in Russia.* New York: Human Rights Watch, February 2009.

Human Rights Watch. *"Saving its Secrets": Government Repression in Andijan.* New York: Human Rights Watch, May 2008.

Human Rights Watch. *Bullets Were Flying Like Rain: The Andjian Massacre.* New York: Human Rights Watch, June 2005.

Huntington, Samuel. *Political Order in Changing Societies.* New Haven: Yale University Press, 1968.

Hurwitz, Ken. "Contemporary Approaches to Political Stability," *Comparative Politics.* 5, no. 3 (April 1973).

Hyde, Susan. *The Pseudo-Democrat's Dilemma: Why Election Observation Became and International Norm.* Ithaca, NY: Cornell University Press, 2011.

Ikenberry, John G. *Liberal Leviathan: The Origins, Crisis, and Transformation of the American World Order.* Princeton: Princeton University Press, 2011.

International Crisis Group. "Central Asia: Decay and Decline," *Asia Report no. 201.* February 3, 2011.

International Crisis Group. "Central Asian Migrants and the Economic Crisis," *Asia Report no. 183,* January 5, 2010.

International Crisis Group. "The Pogroms in Kyrgyzstan," *Asia Report no. 193,* August 23, 2010.

International Crisis Group. "Tajikistan: On the Road to Failure," *ICG Asia Report no. 162,* February 12, 2009.

International Crisis Group. "Repression and Regression in Turkmenistan: A New International Strategy," *Asia Report no. 85,* November 4, 2004.

International Crisis Group. "Cracks in the Marble: Turkmenistan's Failing Dictatorship," *Asia Report no. 44,* January 17, 2003.

Jackson, Nicole J. "The Trafficking of Narcotics, Arms and Humans in Post-Soviet Central Asia: (Mis)perceptions, Policies and Realities," *Central Asian Survey* 24, no. 1 (March 2005).

Jackson, Peter. *Quasi-States: Sovereignty, International Relations and the Third World.* New York: Cambridge University Press, 1993.

Jentleson, Bruce W. "Beware the Duck Test," *The Washington Quarterly* 34, no. 3 (Summer 2011).

Jentleson, Bruce W., and Steven Weber, *The End of Arrogance: America in the Global Competition of Ideas* (Cambridge, MA: Harvard University Press, 2010).

Johnston, Alastair Iain. *Social States: China in International Institutions, 1980–2000.* Princeton: Princeton University Press, 2007.

Johnston, Alastair Iain. "Treating International Institutions as Social Environments." *International Studies Quarterly* 45, no. 4 (2001).

Jones, Seth, et al. *Securing Tyrants or Fostering Reform? U.S. Security Assistance to Repressive and Transitioning Regimes.* Washington, DC: RAND, 2006.

Jones Luong, Pauline, ed. *The Transformation of Central Asia: States and Societies from Soviet Rule to Independence.* Ithaca, NY: Cornell University Press, 2003.

Jones Luong, Pauline, ed. *Institutional Change and Political Continuity in Central Asia: Power, Perceptions and Pacts.* New York: Cambridge University Press, 2002.

Jones Luong, Pauline, and Erika Weinthal. *Oil Is Not a Curse: Ownership Structure and Institutions in Soviet Successor States.* New York: Cambridge University Press, 2010.

Jones Luong, Pauline, and Erika Weinthal. "New Friends, New Fears in Central Asia," *Foreign Affairs* 81, no. 2 (March-April 2002).

Jonson, Lena. *Tajikistan in the New Central Asia: Geopolitics Great Power Rivalry and Radical Islam.* New York: I. B. Taurus, 2006.

Jonson, Lena. *Vladimir Putin and Central Asia: The Shaping of Russian Foreign Policy.* New York: I. B. Tauris, 2004.

Jourde, Cedric. "The International Relations of Small Neoauthoritarian States: Islamism, Warlordism and the Framing of Stability," *International Studies Quarterly* 51, no. 2 (June 2007).

Kaminski, Bartlomiej, and Gael Raballand. "Entrepôt for Chinese for Chinese Consumer Goods in Central Asia: The Puzzle of Re-Exports through Kyrgyz Bazaars," *Eurasian Geography and Economics* 50, no. 5 (2009).

Kaniyoti, Deniz, ed. *The Cotton Sector in Central Asia: Economic Policy and Developmental Changes.* London: Proceedings of a conference held at the School of African and Oriental Studies, 2008.

Katzenstein, Peter J. *A World of Regions: Europe and Asia in the American Imperium.* Ithaca, NY: Cornell University Press, 2005.

Kavalski, Emilian. *India and Central Asia: Mythmaking and International Relations of a Rising Power.* London: I.B. Tauris, 2010.

Kavalski, Emilian. *The New Central Asia: The Regional Impact of International Actors.* Singapore: World Scientific, 2010.

Kelley, Judith. "The More the Merrier? The Effects of Having Multiple International Election Monitoring Organizations," *Perspectives on Politics* 7, no. 1 (2009).

Kerr, David. "Strategic Regionalism: Central Asian and Russian Perspectives on China's Strategic Re-emergence," *International Affairs* 86, no. 1 (January 2010).

Keohane, Robert. "The Big Influence of Small Allies," *Foreign Policy*, no. 2 (April 1971).

Keohane, Robert. "Lilliputians' Dilemmas: Small States in International Politics," *International Organization* 23, no. 2 (Spring 1969).

Kindleberger, Charles. *The World in Depression, 1929–1939,* 2nd edition. Berkeley: University of California Press, 1986.

Kleveman, Lutz. *The New Great Game: Blood and Oil in Central Asia.* New York: Grove Press, 2003.

Knyazev, Alexander, ed. *Afghanistan, SCO, Security and the Geopolitics of Central Asia.* Bishkek: Alexander Knyazev Public Foundation, 2008.

Kotkin, Stephen. "Mongol Commonwealth: Exchange and Governance across the Post-Mongol Space," *Kritika: Explorations in Russian and Eurasian History* 8, no. 3 (Summer 2007).

Kotkin, Stephen. "The Unbalanced Triangle: What Chinese-Russian Relations Mean for the United States," *Foreign Affairs* 88, no. 5 (September/October 2009).

Krasner, Stephen. *Sovereignty: Organized Hypocrisy.* Princeton: Princeton University Press, 1999.

Kuchins, Andrew, Thomas M. Sanderson, and David A. Gordon. "Afghanistan: Building the Missing Link in the Modern Silk Road." *The Washington Quarterly* 33, no. 2 (April 2010).

Kuchins, Andrew, Thomas M. Sanderson, and David A. Gordon, *The Northern Distribution Network and Afghanistan: Planning for the Future.* Washington, DC: Center for International and Strategic Studies, December 2009.

Kurlantzick, Joshua. *Charm Offensive: How China's Soft Power Is Transforming the World.* New Haven: Yale University Press, 2007.

Lake, David. *Hierarchy in International Relations.* Ithaca, NY: Cornell University Press, 2010).

Lane Sheppele, Kim. "Law in a Time of Emergency: States of Exception and the Temptations of 9/11," *University of Pennsylvania Journal of Constitutional Law* (May 2004).

Laruelle, Marlène. *Russia's Central Asia Policy and the Role of Russian Nationalism.* Washington, DC: Central Asia-Caucasus Institute and Silk Road Studies Program, April 2008.

Legvold, Robert, ed. *Russian Foreign Policy in the Twenty-First Century and the Shadow of the Past.* New York: Columbia University Press, 2007).

Legvold, Robert, ed. *Thinking Strategically: The Major Powers. Kazakhstan, and the Central Asian Nexus.* Cambridge, MA: American Academy of Arts & Sciences, 2003.

LeVan, A. "The Political Economy of African Responses to the U.S. Africa Command," *Africa Today* 57, no. 1 (Fall 2010).

LeVine, Steve. *The Oil and the Glory: the Pursuit of Empire and Fortune on the Caspian Sea*. New York: Random House, 2007.

Levitsky, Steven A., and Lucan Way. *Competitive Authoritarianism: Hybrid Regimes after the Cold War*. New York: Cambridge University Press, 2010.

Lewis, David. "Reassessing the Role of OSCE Police Assistance Programming in Central Asia." *OSI Central Eurasia Working Paper Series*, no. 4. April 2011.

Lewis, David. "Dynamics of Regime Change: Domestic and International Factors in the 'Tulip Revolution,'" *Central Asian Survey* 27, no. 3–4 (September 2008).

Lewis, David. *The Temptations of Tyranny in Central Asia*. New York: Columbia University Press, 2008.

Lo, Bobo. *Axis of Convenience: Moscow, Beijing, and the New Geopolitics*. Washington D.C.: Brookings, 2008.

Lo, Bobo. *Vladimir Putin and the Evolution of Russian Foreign Policy*. London: Royal Institute for International Affairs and Blackwell, 2003.

Lubin, Nancy. "Who's Watching the Watchdogs?" *Journal of International Affairs* 56, no. 2 (Spring 2003).

Lubin, Nancy. *Labour and Nationality in Soviet Central Asia: An Uneasy Compromise*. Princeton: Princeton University Press, 1984.

Lubin, Nancy, and Arustan Joldastov. "Snapshots from Central Asia: Is America Losing in Public Opinion?" *Problems of Post-Communism* 57, no. 3 (May/June 2010).

Lucas, Edward. *The New Cold War: Putin's Russia and the Threat to the West*. New York: Palgrave, 2007.

Lumpe, Lora. "US Military Aid to Central Asia, 1999–2009: Security Trumps Human Rights." OSI Central Eurasia Working Paper Series, no. 1, October 2010.

Mackinder, H. J. "The Geographical Pivot of History," *The Geographical Journal* 23, no. 4 (April 1904).

Mankoff, Jeffery. *Russian Foreign Policy: The Return of Great Power Politics*. New York: Rowan & Littlefield, 2009.

Marat, Erica. *The Military and the State in Central Asia: From Red Army to Independence*. New York: Routledge, 2009.

Marat, Erica. "The Criminalization of the State Before and After the Tulip Revolution," *China and Eurasia Forum Quarterly* 6, no.2 (2008).

Marat, Erica. *The State-Crime Nexus in Central Asia: State Weakness, Organized Crime and Corruption in Kyrgyzstan and Tajikistan*. Washington, DC: Central Asia-Caucasus Institute and Silk Road Studies Program, October 2006.

Martel, Gordon. "Documenting the Great Game: 'World Policy' and the 'Turbulent Frontier' in the 1890s," *The International History Review* 2, no. 2 (April 1980).

Marten, Kimberly. "Russian Efforts to Control Kazakhstan's Oil: The Kumkol Case," *Post-Soviet Affairs* 27, no. 1 (2007).

Martin, Terry. *The Affirmative Action Empire: Nations and Nationalism in the Soviet Union, 1923–1939*. Ithaca, NY: Cornell University Press, 2001.

Mattli, Walter, *The Logic of Regional integration: Europe and Beyond*. New York: Cambridge University Press, 1999.

McFaul, Michael. "Ukraine Imports Democracy: External Influences on the Color Revolutions," *International Security* 32, no. 2 (Fall 2007).

McFaul, Michael. "State Power, Institutional Change, and the Politics of Privatization in Russia," *World Politics* 47, no. 2 (January 1995).

McGlinchey, Eric. *Chaos, Violence, Dynasty: Politics and Islam in Central Asia*. Pittsburgh: University of Pittsburgh Press, 2011.

McGlinchey, Eric. "Exploring Regime Instability and Ethnic Violence in Kyrgyzstan," *Asia Policy* no. 12 (July 2011).

McMann, Kelly. "Market Reform as a Stimulus to Particularistic Politics," *Comparative Political Studies* 42, no. 7 (July 2009).

Megoran, Nick. "Revisiting the 'Pivot': The Influence of Harold Mackinder on Analysis of Uzbekistan's Foreign Policy," *The Geographical Journal* 170, no. 4 (December 2004).

Megoran, Nick, Gaël Raballand, and Jerome Bouyjou. "Performance, Representation and the Economics of Border Control in Uzbekistan," *Geopolitics* 10, no. 4 (2005).

Melvin, Neil. "Promoting a Stable and Multiethnic Kyrgyzstan: Overcoming the Causes and Legacies of Violence," *Open Society Foundations Central Eurasia Working Paper Series*, no. 3, March 2011.

Melvin, Neil. *Uzbekistan: Transition to Authoritarianism on the Silk Route*. London: Routledge, 2000.

Melvin, Neil Bhavna Dave, and Michael Denison, eds. *Engaging Central Asia: The European Union's New Strategy in the Heart of Eurasia*. Washington, DC: Brookings, 2008.

Menon, Rajan. "The New Great Game in Central Asia," *Survival* 45, no. 2 (Summer 2003).

Meyer, Karl E., and Shareen Blair Brysac. *Tournament of Shadows: The Great Game and the Race for Empire in Central Asia*. Revised edition. New York: Basic, 2006.

Millward, James A. *Eurasian Crossroads: A History of Xinjiang*. New York: Columbia University Press, 2009.

Moore, Scott. "Peril and Promise: A Survey of India's Strategic Relationship with Central Asia," *Central Asian Survey* 26, no. 2 (September 2007).

Mitchell, Lincoln. *Uncertain Democracy: U.S. Foreign Policy and Georgia's Revolution*. Philadelphia: University of Pennsylvania Press, 2009.

Moravcsik, Andrew. *The Choice for Europe: State Power and Social Purpose from Messina to Maastricht*. Ithaca, NY: Cornell University Press, 1998.

Morgan, Gerald. "Myth and Reality in the Great Game," *Asian Affairs* 4, no. 1 (1973).

Morrison, Alexander. *Russian Rule in Samarkand, 1868–1910: A Comparison with British India*. New York: Oxford University Press, 2008.

Motyl, Alexander. *Imperial Ends: The Decay, Collapse and Revival of Empires*. New York: Columbia University Press, 2001.

Murray, Craig. *Murder in Samarkand*. London: Mainstream Publishing, 2006.

Nadin, Rebecca Louise. "China and the Shanghai 5/Shanghai Cooperation Organisation: 1996–2006, A Decade on the New Diplomatic Frontier." PhD diss., University of Sheffield, 2007.

Nexon, Daniel. *The Struggle for Power in Early Modern Europe: Religious Conflict, Dynastic Empires and International Change*. Princeton: Princeton University Press, 2009.

Neon, Daniel, and Thomas Wright. "What's at Stake in the American Empire Debate?" *American Political Science Review* 101, no. 2 (May 2007).

Nikitin, Alexander. "Post-Soviet Military Integration: The Collective Treaty Organization and Its Relations with the EU and NATO,'" *China and Eurasia Forum Quarterly* 5, no. 1 (2007).

Nikitina, Yuliya. *ODKB i ShoS: Modeli Regionalizma v Sfere Bezopasnosti* [CSTO and SCO: Models of Regionalism in the Security Sphere]. Moscow: MGIMO and Navona, 2009.

Okara, Andrei. "Sovereign Democracy: A New Russian Idea or PR Project?" *Russia in Global Affairs* 5, no. 3 (2007).

Olcott, Martha Brill. *Kazakhstan: Unfulfilled Promise?* 2nd edition. Washington, DC: Carnegie Endowment for Peace, 2010.

Olcott, Martha Brill. *Central Asia's Second Chance*. Washington, DC: Carnegie Endowment for Peace, 2005.

Oliker, Olga, and David A. Shlapak. *US Interests in Central Asia: Policy Priorities and Military Roles*. Santa Monica, CA: RAND Project Air Force, 2005.

O'Loughlin, John, Gearóid Ó Tuathail and Vladimir Kolossov. "A 'Risky Westward Turn'? Putin's 9–11 Script and Ordinary Russians," *Europe-Asia Studies* 56, no. 1 (January 2004).

Ó Tuathail, Gearóid. "Putting Mackinder in His Place: Material Transformations and Myth," *Political Geography* 11, no. 1 (January 1992).

Padgett, John F., and Christopher Ansell. "Robust Action and the Rise of the Medici," *American Journal of Sociology* 98, no. 6 (May 1993).

Palan, Ronen, Richard Murphy, and Christian Chavagneux. *Tax Havens: How Globalization Really Works*. Ithaca, NY: Cornell University Press, 2010.

Pape, Robert A. "Soft Balancing Against the United States," *International Security* 30, no. 1 (Summer 2005).

Peyrouse, Sebastien. "Chinese Economic Presence in Kazakhstan: China's Resolve and Central Asia's Apprehension," *China Perspectives* no. 3 (2008).

Peyrouse, Sebastien. *Economic Aspects of the Chinese-Central Asia Rapprochement.* Washington, DC: Central Asia-Caucasus Institute and Silk Road Studies Program, September 2007.

Peyrouse, Sebastien. "The Hydrocarbon Sector in Central Asia and the Growing Role of China," *China and Eurasia Forum Quarterly* 56, no. 2 (2007).

Poliakov, Sergei. *Everyday Islam: Religion and Tradition in Rural Central Asia.* Armonk, NY: M. E. Sharpe, 1993.

Pomfret, Richard. *The Economies of Central Asia.* Princeton: Princeton University Press, 1995.

Priest, Dana. *The Mission: Waging War and Keeping Peace with America's Military.* New York: W. W. Norton, 2004.

Raballand, Gaël and Agnès Andrésy. "Why Should Trade Between Central Asia and China Continue to Expand?" *Asia Europe Journal* 5, no. 2 (May 2007).

Radnitz, Scott. *Weapons of the Wealthy: Predatory Regimes and Elite-led Protests in Central Asia.* Ithaca, NY: Cornell University Press, 2010.

Rashid, Ahmed. *Jihad: The Rise of Militant Islam in Central Asia.* New Haven: Yale University Press, 2002.

Rekuta, A. L., "The Collective Treaty Security Organization: Averting Security Threats in Central Asia," *Military Thought: A Russian Journal of Military Theory and Strategy* 15, no. 4 (2006).

Roberts, Sean R. "A 'Land of Borderlands': Implications of Xinjiang's Cross-Border Transactions," in S. Frederick Starr, ed. *Xinjiang: China's Muslim Borderland.* Armonk, NY: M. E. Sharpe, 2004.

Roeder, Philip. *Red Sunset: The Failure of Soviet Politics.* Princeton: Princeton University Press, 1993.

Roth, Kenneth. "The Law of War in the War on Terror," *Foreign Affairs* 83, no. 2 (March/April 2004).

Ross, Michael L. "Does Oil Hinder Democracy?" *World Politics* 53, no. 3 (April 2001).

Ross, Michael L. "The Political Economy of the Resource Curse," *World Politics* 51, no. 2 (January 1999).

Rubin, Barnett. "Russian Hegemony and State Breakdown in the Periphery: Causes and Consequences of the Civil War in Tajikistan," in Barnett R. Rubin and Jack Snyder, eds., *Post-Soviet Political Order: Conflict and State-Building.* London: Routledge, 1998.

Rumer, Boris. *Central Asia: "A Tragic Experiment."* Boston: Unwin Hyman, 1990.

Rywkin, Michael. *Moscow's Muslim Challenge: Soviet Central Asia.* Armonk, NY: M. E. Sharpe, 1990.

Safranchuk, Ivan. "The Competition for Security Roles in Central Asia," *Russia in Global Affairs* 6, no. 1 (January–March 2008).

Satterthwaite, Margaret L. "Rendered Meaningless: Extraordinary Rendition and the Rule of Law," *George Washington Law Review* 75, no. 5–6 (2006).

Scahill, Jeremy. *Blackwater: The Rise of the World's Most Powerful Mercenary Army.* New York: Nation, 2008.

Schatz, Edward. "The Soft Authoritarian Tool Kit: Agenda Setting Power in Kazakhstan and Kyrgyzstan," *Comparative Politics* 41, no. 2 (January 2009).

Schatz, Edward. "Transnational Image Making and Soft Authoritarian Kazakhstan," *Slavic Review* 67, no. 1 (Spring 2008).

Schatz, Edward. "Access by Accident: Legitimacy Claims and Democracy Promotion in Authoritarian Central Asia," *International Political Science Review* 27, no. 3 (July 2006).

Schatz, Edward. *Modern Clan Politics: The Power of "Blood" in Kazakhstan and Beyond.* Seattle: University of Washington Press, 2004.

Schatz, Edward, and Renan Levine. "Framing, Public Diplomacy and Anti-Americanism in Central Asia," *International Studies Quarterly* 54, no. 3 (September 2010).

Shambaugh, David. "China Engages Asia: Reshaping the International Order," *International Security* 29, no. 3 (Winter 2004/05).

Sharman, Jason C. "Offshore and the New International Political Economy," *Review of International Political Economy* 17, no. 1 (February 2010).

Sharman, Jason C. "Chinese Capital Flows and Offshore Centers," *Pacific Review*, forthcoming (2013).

Sheppele, Kim. "Other People's PATRIOT Acts: Europe's Response to September 11," *Loyola Law Review* 50 (2004).

Shichor, Yitzhak. "China's Central Asian Strategy and the Xinjiang Connection: Predicaments and Medicaments in a Contemporary Perspective," *China and Eurasia Forum Quarterly* 6, no. 2, 2008.

Shahrani, Nazif. "Muslim Central Asia: Soviet Developmental Legacies and Future Challenges," in Mohiaddin Mesbahi, ed. *Central Asia and the Caucasus after the Soviet Union*. Gainesville: University of Florida Press, 1993.

Shkolnikov, Vladimir D. "Missing the Big Picture? Retrospective on OSCE Strategic Thinking in Central Asia," *Security and Human Rights* no. 4 (2009).

Simmons, Beth. *Mobilizing for Human Rights*. New York: Cambridge University Press, 2009.

Simmons, Thomas W. *Eurasia's Frontiers: Young States, Old Societies, Uncertain Futures*. Ithaca, NY: Cornell University Press, 2008.

Slezkine, Yuri. "The USSR as a Communal Apartment, or How a Socialist State Promoted Ethnic Particularism," *Slavic Review* 53, no. 2 (Summer 1994).

Small, Andrew. "China's Caution on Afghanistan-Pakistan," *The Washington Quarterly* 33, no. 3 (July 2010).

Snyder, Glenn. *Alliance Politics*. Ithaca, NY: Cornell University Press, 1997.

Snyder, Jack. *Myths of Empire*. Ithaca, NY: Cornell University Press, 1995.

Soldatov, Andrei, and Irina Boragan. *The New Nobility: The Restoration of Russia's Security States and the Enduring Legacy of the KGB*. New York: PublicAffairs, 2010.

Spahn, Elizabeth. "Discovering Secrets: Act of State Defenses to Bribery Cases," *Hofstra Law Review* 38, no. 1 (2009).

Spruyt, Hendrik. *Ending Empire*. Ithaca, NY: Cornell University Press, 2005.

Starr, S. Fredrick. *Afghanistan Beyond the Fog of Nation Building*. Washington, DC: Central Asia-Caucasus Institute and Silk Road Studies Program, January 2011.

Starr, S. Fredrick. *A 'Greater Central Asia Partnership' for Central Asia and its Neighbors*. Washington, DC: Central Asia-Caucasus Institute and Silk Road Studies Program, March 2005.

Starr, S. Fredrick. "A Partnership for Central Asia," *Foreign Affairs* 84, no. 4 (July-August 2005).

Starr, S. Fredrick, ed. *Xinjiang: China's Muslim Borderland*. Armonk, NY: M. E. Sharpe, 2004.

Steinfeld, Edward S. *Playing Our Game: Why China's Rise Doesn't Threaten the West*. New York: Oxford University Press, 2010.

Stern, Jonathan. *The Future of Russian Gas and Gazprom*. London: Oxford Institute for Energy Studies, 2005.

Stiglitz, Joseph E. *Globalization and Its Discontents*. New York: W. W. Norton, 2002.

Stone, Randall. *Lending Credibility: The International Monetary Fund and the Post-Communist Transition*. Princeton: Princeton University Press, 2002.

Sullivan, Gavin, and Ben Hayes. *Blacklisted: Targeted Sanctions, Preemptive Security, and Fundamental Rights*. Berlin: European Center for Constitutional and Human Rights, 2009.

Trenin, Dmitri. "Russia and Central Asia: Interests, Policies, and Prospects," in Eugene Rumer, Dmitri Trenin, and Huasheng Zhao, eds., *Central Asia: Views from Washington, Moscow, and Beijing* (Armonk, NY: M. E. Sharpe, 2007)

Tsalik, Svetlana. *Caspian Oil Windfalls: Who Will Benefit?* New York: Open Society Institute, 2003.

Tsygankov, Andrei. "Preserving Influence in a Changing World: Russia's Grand Strategy," *Problems of Post-Communism* 58, no.1 (March/April 2011).

Tsygankov, Andrei. *Russia's Foreign Policy: Change and Continuity in National Identity*, 2nd edition. New York: Rowman & Littlefield, 2010.

Tunçcr-Kilavuz, Idil. "Political and Social Networks in Tajikistan and Uzbekistan: 'Clan,' Region and Beyond," *Central Asian Survey* 28, no. 3 (September 2009).

Van de Walle, Nicolas. *African Economies and the Politics of Permanent Crisis, 1979–1999*. New York: Cambridge University Press, 2001.

Venier, Pascal. "The Geopolitical Pivot of History and Early Twentieth Century Political Culture," *The Geographic Journal* 170, no. 2 (December 2004).

Vlsek, William. "Byways and Highways of Direct Investment: China and the Offshore World," *Journal of Chinese Current Affairs* 39, no. 4 (2010).

Walt, Stephen. *Taming American Power: The Global Response to U.S. Primacy*. New York: Norton, 2005.

Warkotsch, Alexander. "The OSCE as an Agent of Socialization? International Norm Dynamics and Political Change in Central Asia," *Europe-Asia Studies* 55, no. 5 (July 2007).

Way, Lucan. "The Real Causes of the Colored Revolutions," *Journal of Democracy* 18, no. 2 (July 2008).

Weinthal, Erica. "Beyond the State: Transnational Actors, NGOs, and Environmental Protection in Central Asia," in Pauline Jones Luong, ed., *The Transformation of Central Asia: States and Societies from Soviet Rule to Independence*. Ithaca, NY: Cornell University Press, 2003.

Weinthal, Erica. *State Making and Environmental Cooperation: Linking Domestic and International Politics in Central Asia*. Cambridge, MA: MIT Press, 2002.

Weitz, Richard. "Averting a New Great Game in Central Asia," *The Washington Quarterly* 29, no. 3 (Summer 2006).

Willerton, John. *Patronage and Politics in the USSR*. New York: Cambridge University Press, 1993.

Wishnick, Elizabeth. *Russia, China and the United States in Central Asia: Prospects for Great Power Competition and Cooperation in Central Asia*. Carlisle, PA: U.S. Army War College, Strategic Studies Institute, 2009.

World Bank. *Cross-Border Trade Within the Central Asian Regional Cooperation*. Washington, DC: World Bank, 2007.

World Bank. *Statistical Handbook: States of the Former USSR*, Washington, DC: World Bank, 1992.

Zakaria, Fareed. *The Post-American World*. New York: W. W. Norton, 2008.

Zhao, Huasheng. "Central Asia in China's Diplomacy," in Eugene Rumer, Dmitri Trenin, and Huasheng Zhao, eds., *Central Asia: Views from Washington, Moscow and Beijing*. Armonk, NY: M. E. Sharpe, 2007.

Zhao, Huasheng. "China, Russia, and the United States: Prospects for Cooperation in Central Asia," *China and Eurasia Forum Quarterly* (Winter 2005).

Zhukov, Stanislav, and Reznikova, Oksana. *Tsentral'naya Aziya i Kitay: Ekonomicheskoe Vzaimodeystvie v Usloviyakh Globalizatsii* [Central Asia and China: Economic Interactions Under Globalization]. Moscow: MGIMO, 2009.

INDEX

Note: Page numbers in *italics* indicate figures; those with a *t* indicate tables.